How to Raise a Child
with a High EQ

How to Raise a Child with a High EQ

A Parents' Guide to Emotional Intelligence

Lawrence E. Shapiro, Ph.D.

HarperPerennial

A Division of HarperCollins*Publishers*

A hardcover edition of this book was published in 1997 by HarperCollins Publishers.

HarperCollins books may be purchased for educational, business, or sales promotional use. For information please write: Special Markets Department, HarperCollins Publishers, Inc., 10 East 53rd Street, New York, NY 10022.

First HarperPerennial edition published 1998.

Designed by Nancy Singer
Cartoon illustrations by Stuart Goldman
All other illustrations by Christopher Laughlin

The Library of Congress has catalogued the hardcover edition as follows:

Shapiro, Lawrence E.
    How to raise a child with a high EQ : a parents' guide to
emotional intelligence / by Lawrence E. Shapiro. — 1st ed.
        p. cm.
    Includes bibliographical references and index.
    ISBN 0-06-018733-6
    1. Emotions. 2. Emotions and cognition. 3. Emotions—Social
aspects. I. Title.
BF561.S52 1997
649'.64—dc21   97-5533

ISBN 0-06-092891-3 (pbk.)

00 01 02 ❖/RRD 10 9 8 7 6

To my mother, Frances Shapiro, a limitless source of emotional support

▪ C O N T E N T S ▪

Little Things Make a Difference

In a Detroit suburb, two boys who might normally be pummeling each other on the playground are sitting at a table in the back of their classroom agreeing to have their problems resolved by a peer mediator, another classmate. All three children are seven years old. In a Florida hospital, a ten-year-old laughs hysterically while waiting for her chemotherapy, having just been caught in the middle of a water-gun battle between her nurse and an intern dressed up like an alien clown. In Los Angeles, a father plays a cooperative game of tag with his three children, a game prescribed by their school counselor. In the two weeks that they have been playing cooperative games, family squabbles have virtually been eliminated.

These children are benefiting from what some are calling a revolution in child psychology: training in emotional and social skills. Peer-mediation training is being used in hundreds of schools throughout the country, and it is measurably reducing calls to parents, suspensions, and even school violence. Clowns are regularly seen in hospital wards handing out whoopee cushions and rubber chickens, because we know that humor not only helps children cope with the stress of a hospital stay, but may actually stimulate their immune system and speed their recovery. Cooperative games, where everybody wins or everybody loses, have been shown to build family cohesiveness and significantly decrease anger and aggression between children.

This book is about teaching your children similar activities and games to improve their emotional and social skills—what psychologists are now calling emotional intelligence or EQ. Although the term emotional intelligence is relatively new, I and other child therapists around the country have been prescribing these activities to help children solve their problems for more than twenty years. Now we are beginning to see that all children can benefit by learning the skills of emotional intelligence, not just the children referred for specific problems. We have come to believe that having a high EQ is at least as important as having a high IQ. Study after study shows that children with skills in emotional intelligence are happier, more confident, and more successful in school. Equally important, these skills become the building blocks for our children to become responsible, caring, and productive adults.

WHY EMOTIONAL SKILLS MUST BE TAUGHT

Skeptics wonder why it is necessary to teach children about emotions. They ask, "Don't emotions just come naturally to children?" The answer is "no," not anymore.

Many scientists believe that our human emotions have evolved primarily as a survival mechanism. Fear helps protect us from harm and tells us to avoid danger. Anger helps us overcome barriers to getting what we need. We find joy and happiness in the company of others. In seeking human contact, we find protection within a group as well as the opportunity to mate and insure the survival of the species. Sadness over the loss of an important person sends signals for that person to return, or a forlorn attitude can help attract a new person who can act as a substitute for the person who left.

But while our emotions were adaptive for our primitive ancestors, modern industrial life has presented us with emotional challenges that nature did not anticipate. For example, while anger still plays an important function in our emotional makeup, nature did not anticipate that it could be so easily provoked by sitting in a traffic jam, watching television, or playing video games. Certainly, our evolutionary development could not take into account the ease in which a ten-year-old could find a handgun and shoot a classmate over a perceived insult.

Seattle-based psychiatrist Michael Norden makes a passionate argument for us to recognize how modern times have taken a toll on our emotions and to some extent thwarted their evolutionary intent. He writes:

> No longer do most of us live in villages of a few hundred or less, as Stone Agers did, but rather in teeming cities that compose a global village of nearly six billion. These cumulative stresses of modern life have set off an avalanche of depression, anxiety, and insomnia. Less obvious are diverse problems such as weight gain and cancer. Most [of us] self-medicate [to keep our emotions in check] using anything from caffeine to cocaine; virtually no one remains untouched.

The emotional and social skills that are presented in this book were designed to help you take up where nature left off in raising children who are better able to handle the emotional stress of modern times. If a hectic and hurried life has made your children prone to irritability and anger, you can teach them to recognize and control these feelings. If fear of crime or frequent moves has isolated your children from the benefits of living in an open and cohesive community, you can teach them the social skills to make and keep intimate friends. If your child is upset by a divorce or remarriage, anxious when confronting new situations, or complacent about his schoolwork, you can teach him the specific EQ skills to help him cope with and overcome these normal problems of growing up.

CHANGING YOUR CHILD'S BRAIN

Perhaps what is most interesting about taking a role in your children's emotional education is that you are literally changing your children's brain chemistry, or more accurately, teaching them ways to control their brain functioning themselves. As we shall see, emotions are not abstract ideas that psychologists help us to name, but rather they are very real. They take the form of specific biochemicals that the brain produces and to which the body then reacts.

While most of us are not prone to thinking of emotions as chemical reactions, you have only to think of what happens when you drink an alcoholic beverage or several cups of coffee. You may not realize it, but the foods you eat also interact chemically with your emotions. "Feel good" foods like chocolate and ice cream trigger the brain to release serotonin and endorphins, biochemicals that the brain associates with a sense of well-being. That's why we typically crave these foods when we are blue.

But we don't have to ingest anything to produce the biochemical equivalents of emotions. The most important premise of this book is that you can teach your children ways to alter the biochemistry of their emotions, helping them to be more adaptive, more in control, and just plain happier.

LET A SMILE BE YOUR UMBRELLA

Serotonin is just one of the chemicals, called neurotransmitters, that make up our emotional reactions by conveying emotional messages from the brain to various parts of the body. Serotonin has received particular attention in the last ten years because of its role in helping us deal with stress and its significance (via the drug Prozac) in the treatment of depression, obsessive compulsive disorders, and other psychiatric disorders. But psychiatrist Michael Norden argues, in his book *Beyond Prozac,* that we can train our brains to naturally produce serotonin by such simple means as a healthier diet, increased exercise, and getting the appropriate amount of sleep (an estimated half of American adults do not get the full eight hours of sleep required for the body to function properly).

The importance of serotonin to a child's emotional life cannot be overestimated, since it influences many body systems (body temperature, blood pressure, digestion, and sleep, to name a few). It can help children deal with all kinds of stress by inhibiting an overload of input to the brain. Increased levels of serotonin are associated with a decrease in aggression and impulsivity. And yet the production of serotonin may be just a smile away. Robert Zajonc and his colleagues point out that when you smile, your facial muscles contract, decreasing the blood flow to nearby vessels. This cools the blood, which lowers the temperature of the brain stem, triggering the production of serotonin. When we tell our children to "just smile" and things will seem better, we are absolutely right. Little things make a difference.

TRICKS, SKILLS, HABITS, AND GAMES: THE RECIPE FOR A HIGH EQ

Our new understanding of neuroanatomy and developmental psychology presents many opportunities for parents to help their children develop a high EQ, and you will hopefully find dozens of useful ideas to help your children as you read through these pages. Some of the ideas I present are what I refer to as tricks—simple ways that can have an instant effect on changing your children's behavior. For example, when I work with children prone to fighting with others, I teach them the "turtle technique." I once worked with Sam, a seven-year-old who seemed to be reported daily for fighting on the playground. I told Sam that when he found himself about to fight, he should imagine that he was a turtle withdrawing into his shell. He should keep his arms at his side, his feet together, and he should lower his chin down to his neck. He should do this while he slowly counted to ten, breathing deeply with each count.

A technique like this can be simple and fun for young children to learn, but it is really a psychological trick. When Sam's arms and legs were held together, he could neither hit nor kick. When he counted to ten, breathing deeply as he counted, he sent a message to his brain to ease up on producing the biochemicals associated with aggression (called catecholamines) that would increase his arousal and likelihood to fight. When he lowered his chin to his chest, he would have to break eye contact with his presumed adversary. In doing so, he lost the will to fight (it is virtually impossible to fight with someone that you do not see).

Other activities you will learn in this book are really emotional and social skills that you can teach your child. Skills take more time to learn and involve some degree of practice, but once they are acquired, they become second nature. For example, reading nonverbal cues—like facial expressions, gestures, and postures—is a skill that children can easily acquire. Since studies tell us that nearly 90 percent of emotional communication is conveyed nonverbally, this skill can greatly improve your child's ability to understand the feelings of others and react appropriately.

You will also find suggestions on how to steer your child toward developing habits that will increase her emotional intelligence. For example, teaching your child relaxation and imagery techniques as a way to handle pain and psychological stress is a habit that may have profound positive effects throughout her life. These techniques do not just distract children from physical pain, but actually stimulate their bodies to produce a natural analgesic. They also lower blood pressure and stimulate centers in the brain that activate the body's immune system.

Many of the tricks, skills, and habits that you find throughout this book are presented in the form of games and other fun activities. It was Anna Freud, daughter of Sigmund Freud and a famous child therapist in her own right, who explained that "play is the work of children." Throughout my career, I have taken this adage to heart, teaching children new emotional and social skills through fun and challenging games. Games are a particularly good way to teach EQ skills, because children like to play them over and over again. Through games, we can give children the opportunities to learn and practice new ways to think and feel and act, and by participating in these games, we can become an integral part in the emotional learning process.

As you read the pages of this book and try the games and activities with your children, there are really only three things that you need: time, interest, and a desire to enjoy the challenges of raising children. These are the essential ingredients of raising a child with a high EQ. Good luck!

■ ACKNOWLEDGMENTS ■

Having written a book on emotional intelligence, it seems only fitting that I begin by acknowledging those people who have given me the emotional support I needed to complete this project. I am very grateful for the constant support, interest, and encouragement of my wife, Beth Shapiro. Her feedback as an experienced school psychologist was particularly valuable. My mother, Frances Shapiro, has been supportive of everything I do, for so many years, that I sometimes think I might take her for granted. But I never do. My daughter, Jessica, has been an inspiration for this book, for at every age she has had an exceptionally high EQ, adding immeasurably to my life and to the lives of others as well. I would also like to acknowledge the constant help of two friends and colleagues, Beth Ann Marcozzi and Gary Lynch, who have supported my writing by taking many of the day-to-day burdens of running a business off my shoulders.

Next I would like to acknowledge the dozens of researchers and writers whose work has been mentioned in this book, and in particular Dr. Daniel Goleman, author of *Emotional Intelligence*, who has popularized this important concept and made it part of the common vernacular. I would also like to acknowledge the influence of the work of William Damon, Stephanie Thornton, Jerome Kagan, Paul McGhee, John March, Paul Ekman, and Nancy Eisenberg, as well as the other authors and researchers mentioned in this book.

Finally, I would like to thank those people who have

helped in getting this book published: my editor at HarperCollins, Joëlle Delbourgo, and her assistant, Leigh Ann Sackrider; my agent, Robert Tabian; my copy editors and readers, Susan Golant and Hennie Shore; and my researcher, Tanya Freeman.

■ PART 1 ■

Introduction

• 1 •

Emotional Intelligence: A New Way to Raise Children

For the children in Miss Ansel's preschool class, it was a very special day. This is not to say that every day wasn't special in the room of brightly colored murals with the huge play locomotive that doubled as a reading area and the cubicles full of books and toys. But today, the class would have an important visitor, who would play a fun game with them in which everyone got a turn.

Barry, a four-year-old, was the first one selected to play this game, which was intentionally designed to be too difficult for the children. The visitor, a researcher in child development, showed Barry a shiny metal ball that sat on a platform attached to a tower. "It's like a little elevator," he said. "You have to raise the platform to the top of the tower without the little ball falling off."

On Barry's first try, the ball fell off almost immediately. The second time around, it fell off again and rolled off the table, onto the floor, and into the corner. On the third try, Barry was able to raise the ball about a quarter of the way up the tower before it fell off. His fourth try was no better than his first.

"Do you think that you're going to be able to do this?" the visitor asked in a neutral tone.

"Oh, yes!" Barry replied enthusiastically as he tried again.

Barry was typical of the rest of the children in his preschool class who participated in this experiment on self-motivation. Although each child tried repeatedly to raise the ball and failed, each child reported that he or she could eventually master the task.

Young children are naturally self-confident, even in the face of insurmountable odds and repeated failure. As the originator of the tower experiment, Deborah Stipek, notes, "Until the age of six or seven years, children maintain high expectations for success despite poor performance on past trials . . . they almost invariably expect to get the platform to the top, even though they barely got the platform off the base without the ball falling off on four previous trials."

The qualities that the children of Miss Ansel's preschool class demonstrated—persistence, optimism, self-motivation, and friendly enthusiasm—are part of what has come to be known as emotional intelligence. Emotional intelligence, or EQ, is not based on how smart a child might be, but rather on what we once called personality characteristics, or just "character." Studies are now finding that these social and emotional skills may be even more critical to life success than one's intellectual ability. In other words, having a high EQ may be more important to success in life than a high IQ as measured by a standardized test of verbal and nonverbal cognitive intelligence.

WHAT IS EMOTIONAL INTELLIGENCE?

The term "emotional intelligence" was first used in 1990 by psychologists Peter Salovey of Harvard University and John Mayer of the University of New Hampshire. It was used to describe the emotional qualities that appear to be important to success. These can include:

- Empathy.
- Expressing and understanding feelings.
- Controlling one's temper.
- Independence.
- Adaptability.
- Being well-liked.
- Interpersonal problem solving.
- Persistence.
- Friendliness.
- Kindness.
- Respect.

It was Daniel Goleman's 1995 best-seller, *Emotional Intelligence,* that propelled this concept into public awareness, placing it on the cover of *Time* magazine and making it a topic of conversation from classrooms to boardrooms. The implications and significance of EQ even reached the White House. "I'll tell you what's a great book," President Clinton told reporters at the Tattered Cover Bookstore in Denver, Colorado, on an unscheduled campaign stop, "this *Emotional Intelligence.* It's a very interesting book. I love it. Hillary gave it to me."

The excitement over the concept of emotional intelligence begins with its implications for raising and educating children, but extends to its importance in the workplace and in virtually all human relationships and endeavors. Studies show that the same EQ skills that result in your child being perceived as an enthusiastic learner by his teacher, or being liked by his friends on the playground, will also help him twenty years from now on his job or in his marriage.

In many studies of corporate America, adults do not appear to be that different from the children they once were, and the social workings of the job are reminiscent of playground politics. This does not come as a surprise to human resource consultants who have been saying for years that "people skills" are important at every level of a company's operations, from the sales call to the boardroom. But the extent to which EQ skills can affect the workplace is still surprising. For example, Alan Farnham reported in an article in *Fortune* magazine about a study done at Bell Labs to find out why some scientists were performing poorly at their jobs in spite of intellectual prowess and academic credentials equal to their high-achieving colleagues. The researchers studied the E-mail patterns of all the scientists and found that the employees who were disliked because of poor emotional and social skills were being ostracized by their colleagues, much the way the nerd or the show-off is left out of games on the playground. At Bell Labs, however, the playground was the electronic chat rooms, which were used, in part, to gossip, but also as a place where people exchanged important professional information and sought advice when they were stuck on a project. The study concluded that it was the social isolation, presumably due to a low EQ, that led to diminished work performance.

Even though emotional intelligence has only recently

become a part of the public vernacular, research in this area is hardly new. In the last fifty years, there have been thousands of studies exploring the development of EQ skills in children. Unfortunately, few of these findings have found their way into practical applications, largely due to a schism between the academic world of carefully planned statistical paradigms and the two-headache-a-day world of the frontline teacher and mental health professional. But we can no longer afford to raise and educate our children based merely on intuition or "political correctness." Just like medicine or other "hard" sciences, we must look to a body of knowledge to make the informed decisions that will affect our children's day-to-day well-being. Brown University professor William Damon forcefully explains this in the preface to his book *The Moral Child:*

> Scientific research on children's morality has a great potential to aid us in our pressing desire to improve children's moral values. This is an untapped potential, however, because most of this research is either unknown to the public, ignored as irrelevant or debunked as ivory-tower nonsense. . . . [In part] the scholarly work on children's morality is obscure because it has remained embedded in academic journals and scattered throughout disparate professional writings.

We can also look to the schools for practical information about the effectiveness of teaching social and emotional intelligence. Although there is controversy among educators as to the merits of bringing mental health issues into public education, for the past two decades, hundreds of millions of dollars have been spent on teaching social and emotional skills. The legitimization of teaching these skills in schools can be traced back to a single act of Congress, Public Law 94–142, the Education for All Handicapped Children's Act. This groundbreaking legislation states that all children in the United States have the right to a public education regardless of any disability or handicap and any and all problems that impede a child's ability to learn must be addressed by the school system. The school psychologists and special education teachers who worked to implement this law were among the first professionals to link what we are now calling EQ with academic performance and school success. As a result of their efforts, you can now look to the wide variety of techniques and myriad programs that have been developed for children with special needs and apply them to your child at home.

EQ VS. IQ

Social scientists are still arguing about exactly what makes up a person's IQ, but most professionals agree that it can be measured by standardized intelligence tests such as the Wechsler Intelligence Scales, which gauge both verbal and nonverbal abilities, including memory, vocabulary, comprehension, problem solving, abstract reasoning, perception, information processing, and visual-motor skills. The "general intelligence factor" derived from these scales—what we call IQ—is considered to be extremely stable after a child is six years old and usually correlates with other tests of aptitude such as college admission tests.

The meaning of EQ is muddier. Salovey and Mayer first defined emotional intelligence as "a subset of social intelligence that involves the ability to monitor one's own and others, feelings and emotions, to discriminate among them and to use this information to guide one's thinking and actions."

They object to the use of the term EQ as a synonym for emotional intelligence, fearing that it will mislead people into thinking that there is some accurate test to measure EQ or that it is even a measurable construct at all. But the fact remains that although EQ may never be measured, it is still a meaningful concept. While we cannot readily measure most personality and social traits—such as kindness, self-confidence, or respect for others—we *can* recognize them in children and agree to their importance. The popularity of and media attention given to Goleman's book attests to the fact that people intuitively understand the meaning and importance of emotional intelligence and recognize EQ as an abbreviated synonym for this concept, much the way they recognize that IQ is a synonym for cognitive intelligence.

EQ skills are not the opposite of IQ or cognitive skills, but rather, they interact dynamically on a conceptual level and in the real world. Ideally, a person can excel both in cognitive skills and in social and emotional skills, as some of our greatest leaders have. According to Duke University political scientist James David Barber, Thomas Jefferson had a nearly perfect blend of personality and intellect. He was known as a great and empathic communicator, as well as a true genius. In other great leaders, a high EQ seems to have been enough. Many people considered Franklin Delano Roosevelt's dynamic personality and unbridled optimism as one of the most important factors in leading the country through the Depression and World War II. Oliver Wendell Holmes, however, described Roosevelt as having "a second-class intellect, but a first-class temperament." The same has been said of John F. Kennedy, who, according to many historians, led the nation as much with his heart as with his head.

Perhaps the most important distinction between IQ and EQ is that EQ is much less genetically loaded, providing an opportunity for parents and educators to pick up where nature left off in determining a child's chances of success.

IQ IS UP, BUT EQ IS DOWN

The second half of the twentieth century has seen an unparalleled interest in the welfare of children and a recognition by us as parents that our day-to-day interactions can have a profound influence on our youngsters' lives. Most of us seek to provide enrichment opportunities for our children, assuming that making them smarter will also give them a better chance at being successful. We start explaining the world to our kids when they are just a few days old, begin reading to them when they are just a few months old, and it is not uncommon these days to see children sitting at a computer keyboard long before they can speak in full sentences.

Recent studies suggest that we have done an unprecedented job in making our children smarter, or at least they perform better on standardized IQ tests. According to James R. Flynn, a political philosopher at the University of Otago, in New Zealand, IQ has increased over twenty points since it was first measured in the early part of this century, a finding that defies what we know about evolutionary patterns. Although the precise reasons for this rise (now known as the Flynn Effect) are not clear, and to some extent can be explained by better neonatal care and overall health awareness, Flynn notes that at least part of this increase has resulted in changes in parenting since World War II.

Yet paradoxically, while each generation of children seems to get smarter, their emotional and social skills seem to be plummeting. If we measure EQ by mental health and other sociological statistics, we can see that in many ways today's children are much worse off than those in previous generations. The Children's Defense Fund, a nonprofit advocacy group for children, gives us the following profile of a day in the life of America's youth.

Every day:

- 3 youths under twenty-five die from HIV infection and twenty-five are newly infected.
- 6 children commit suicide.
- 342 children under eighteen are arrested for violent crimes.
- 1,407 babies are born to teen mothers.
- 2,833 children drop out of school.
- 6,042 children are arrested.
- 135,000 children take guns to school.

These statistics are based on what we can see, but the statistics on the emotional problems of children, which may not surface for years to come, are just as disturbing. In his book *The Optimistic Child,* psychologist Martin Seligman reports on what he describes as an epidemic of depression that has increased nearly tenfold among children and adolescents in the last fifty years and is now occurring at an earlier age. According to the National Mental Health Association, nearly 7 percent of American children are estimated to have a significant mental health problem, although only 20 percent of these children receive any form of treatment.

A NEW WAY TO LOOK AT RAISING CHILDREN

Many social scientists believe that the problems of today's children can be traced to the complex changes in social patterns that have occurred in the last forty years, including rising divorce rates, the pervasive and negative influence of TV and the media, the lack of respect for schools as a source of authority, and the diminishing time that parents spend with their children. Accepting for a moment that societal changes are inevitable, the question becomes, What can you do to raise children who are happy, healthy, and productive?

The answer may surprise you. You must change the way that your child's brain develops.

THE NEUROANATOMY OF EMOTIONS

To fully understand how new findings about emotional intelligence can affect the way that you parent, we must first take a short course in the neuroanatomy of emotions.

Scientists often talk about the thinking part of the brain—the cortex (sometimes referred to as the neocortex)—as distinct from the emotional part of the brain—the limbic system—but, in fact, it is the relationship between these two areas that defines emotional intelligence.

The cortex is a folded sheet of tissue, about three millimeters thick, which envelops the large cerebral hemispheres of the brain. While the cerebral hemispheres control most of the body's basic functions like muscular movement and perception, it is the cortex that gives meaning to what we do and perceive.

The cortex, literally the "thinking cap" of the brain, has put us on top of the evolutionary ladder. Although lower primates like cats, dogs, and mice possess a cortex and are capable of learning from experience, communicating, and even making simple decisions, their cortexes have only minimal function when compared to ours. These animals cannot plan, think abstractly, or worry about the future.

Because our large cortex is the most distinguishing feature

of humans, it is the part of the brain that has been most close-ly scrutinized. The medical community has primarily learned about the human brain when one is damaged by an injury or disease. The cortex has four lobes, and damage to a specific lobe will result in a specific problem. The occipital lobe, for example, located at the back of the head, contains the prima-ry visual area of the brain. A wound to this area may wipe out part of a person's visual field and, depending on the extent of the injury, even cause blindness. Damage to the temporal lobe, on the other hand, located just behind the ear on the other side of the head, will cause a problem in long-term memory. Understanding the cortex and its development helps us com-prehend why some children are gifted while others are learn-ing disabled, why some children excel at geometry and others can barely spell the word.

While the cortex is considered to be the thinking part of the brain, it also plays an important part in understanding emotional intelligence. The cortex allows us to *have feelings about our feelings.* It allows us to have insight, analyze why we are feeling a certain way, and then do something about it.

Take the example of what happened with Phyllis when six of the most popular girls in school came over to the lunch table and sat with her. This was a very unusual occasion, because most of these girls had never even spoken to Phyllis before, much less chose to eat lunch with her. They chatted about the common things that eleven-year-old girls talk about—new clothes, boys, TV shows—and Phyllis just lis-tened. Then Nance, one of the brassier girls, turned and said, "Phyllis, we were talking yesterday, and we were trying to decide of all the girls in our grade, who was the ugliest. Who do you think it is?"

Phyllis surveyed the cafeteria slowly, thinking that her answer should be a very good one. Her eyes fixed on Rosa.

Rosa had stringy, unkempt red hair. She had a long, pointy nose, a thin face, and her teeth stuck out, making her look like a rabbit. "I think it's Rosa," Phyllis said to the group, a little too eagerly. "She's horrible looking, isn't she?"

"Nooo," Nance said, "that's not what we decided. We decided that it's you, that you're the ugliest." She said this as casually as if she were commenting on the weather.

Phyllis felt a knot in her stomach, like someone had just grabbed her insides and twisted them. The blood drained from her face, and for a moment she thought she might be sick. But that moment passed. "So it was a trick," she said to herself, "just a trick to make me feel bad." She realized that her nausea was being replaced by anger. She felt the tension in her upper arms and noticed that she was making a fist with each hand.

Phyllis looked up from her lunch tray, observing that the girls had gone back to their conversation, but each had one eye on her to see her reaction. She looked directly at Nance and said with as much assurance as she could muster, "I guess everyone makes mistakes." She then picked up her tray and walked away.

Phyllis's cortex, the part of her brain given to insights, helped her analyze the situation and her response. Her snappy comeback and her decision to leave with her dignity intact indicate a victory of her thinking brain over her emotional brain. Her ability to control her reaction—to understand that she was tricked and save face—meant the difference between this incident becoming an embarrassment that would soon be forgotten or a trauma that might leave permanent scars.

The emotional and logical parts of the brain often serve different functions in determining our behaviors, and yet they are completely interdependent. The emotional part of the brain responds more quickly and with more force. It alerts us when our children might be in danger, even before we can determine exactly what that danger is. The cortex, on the other hand, specifically the prefrontal lobes, can act as a damper switch, giving meaning to an emotional situation before we act on it. In Phyllis's encounter with the cruel teasing of her classmates, she was able step back and observe what had happened, putting in check her rage and humiliation.

At one time not so long ago, neurosurgeons felt they could treat mental illness by surgically removing part of a person's cortex, not realizing the subtle ways in which the thinking and the emotional brain coexist. According to Judith Hooper and Dick Teresi, authors of *The Three-Pound Universe*, over 40,000 prefrontal lobotomies were done in the United States alone during the 1940s and 1950s. The intention of these lobotomies was to treat aggression and hyperemotional states, but in many cases, boring into a patient's frontal cortex with a surgical pick and mallet and cutting the nerve fibers to the rest of the brain only turned patients into emotional zombies. "Without an intact frontal cortex," they write, "a human being may appear normal at first glance, but hang out with him for a while and you notice he's emotionally shallow, distractible, listless, apathetic, and so insensitive to social contexts that he may belch with abandon at dinner parties."

The limbic system, which is frequently referred to as the emotional part of the brain, lies deep within the cerebral hemispheres and has the primary responsibility of regulating our emotions and impulses. The limbic system includes the hippocampus, where emotional learning takes place and emotional memories are stored, the amygdala, which is considered the brain's emotional control center, and several other structures.

Although neurologists have been able to assign specific

emotional functions to specific parts of the brain, it is really the interaction of the various parts that defines emotional intelligence. For example, let's imagine for a moment that you are home one night, washing up to go to bed, and the doorbell suddenly rings. You immediately get a rush of adrenaline, alerting your amygdala to be aware that some danger might be present. Cautiously, you open your door and your favorite movie star (or author, politician, sports celebrity, etc.) is standing in front of you, explaining that he (or she) has a flat tire in front of your home and is in need of some help. It is the hippocampus that would recognize this person as someone to get excited about, triggering the amygdala to rush in with the appropriate mixture of surprise, delight, awe, and perhaps lust. But the cortex would remind you that this object of your affection has a name and a reason for being there, which is probably not to look you up. It would also be the cortex that would allow you to say something that didn't sound stupid. Thinking about the future, the cortex would come up with the idea of getting an autograph or having a picture taken with your newfound friend.

The third component of the neurological system that relates to emotional intelligence is in many ways the most interesting, for it involves the way that emotions are biochemically conveyed to various parts of the body. Some truly groundbreaking research is taking place in this field. In the last fifteen years, scientists have been able to identify strings of amino acids, called neuropeptides, which they believe are the biochemical correlates of emotions. The neuropeptides are stored in the emotional brain and sent throughout the body when an emotion is felt, telling the body how to react. It was these brain chemicals, also referred to as neurotransmitters, that made Phyllis feel as if she were going to be sick when Nance and her friends insulted her. During the visit from the

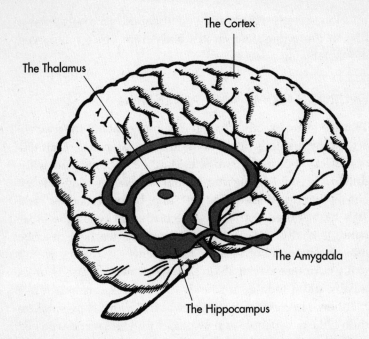

The cortex is the thinking part of the brain, and helps control emotions through problem solving, language, imagery, and other cognitive processes. The limbic system is considered the emotional part of the brain, and includes the thalamus, which relays messages to the cortex; the hippocampus, believed to play a role in memory and making sense out of our perceptions; and the amygdala, the emotional control center.

celebrity, these same neurotransmitters would cause the dryness in your mouth, the flush on your face, and the tightness in your abdomen associated with excitement. With every emotional reaction, the brain sends out these chemicals to a complex system of receptors, which are spread throughout the body. As we shall see in Chapter 23, besides acting as emotional messengers, these same neuropeptides may also play a part in protecting your child's body from viruses and even life-threatening diseases.

NEUROANATOMY AND PARENTING

To understand exactly what all this implies about the way we act as parents, let's take a look at two classmates, Matthew and Micky, both six years old. Matthew is timid and withdrawn. He comes home from school nearly every day in tears. His mother describes him as "afraid of his own shadow," and says he has been that way since birth. Micky, on the other hand, is chatty and likable. Although his teachers describe him as a natural-born leader, his parents say that he wasn't really born that way at all. In fact, when they describe him as a baby and a toddler, it sounds like he was very much like Matthew. He cried whenever he was left with a baby-sitter, he didn't like new people or new places, and he sat and watched while the other children romped on the playground.

As infants, both Matthew and Micky would be described by Harvard psychologist Jerome Kagan as being "behaviorally inhibited" or timid, one of four temperaments which Kagan believes characterize humans at birth. Kagan has theorized that a child's temperament reflects a specific innate emotional circuitry in the brain, a blueprint for his present and future emotional expression, as well as his behavior.

According to Kagan, a timid child is born with an easily aroused amygdala, possibly because of an inherited predisposition to having high levels of norepinephrine or other brain chemicals that overstimulate this control center of the emotional brain. Through years of research, he has found that two-thirds of children born timid grow up to be like Matthew: shy, withdrawn, and more likely to become anxious, phobic, and socially inhibited as they mature. These children apparently do not develop the neural pathways between the amygdala and the cortex to allow the thinking part of the brain to help the emotional brain to calm itself.

But about a third of the children that Kagan studied seemed to have tamed their overexcitable emotional brains, and like Micky, by the time they were in kindergarten, they were as outgoing and socialized as any other child. The difference in these children was the way their parents had responded to their timidity since they were infants, a difference that Kagan postulated *literally changed the development of their brains.*

The mothers of the still timid children took a protective stance toward their infants—they sheltered them from things that upset them and soothed them when they cried. But the mothers whose children outgrew their shyness felt that their kids should learn to cope with what upset them. While empathic toward them, they did not reinforce their crying and worries. Rather, they set firm limits and insisted on obedience. Kagan hypothesized that the neurochemistry of the children who outgrew their timidity changed because their parents continually exposed them to new obstacles and challenges, while the children who were not challenged kept the same brain circuits and so remained emotionally overreactive.

GOING AGAINST THE GRAIN

Kagan's study and others like it show that although our children are born with specific emotional predispositions, their brain circuitry retains at least some degree of plasticity. They can learn new emotional and social skills that will create new neural pathways and more adaptive biochemical patterns. To make these changes, however, you may have to question some of your natural parenting instincts and act in ways that may run counter to the normal habits of your lifestyle. The following are just a few examples of how parents, as well as teachers and mental health professionals, are learning to question their intuitive responses:

- Psychologists often recommend helping children talk about their emotions as a way to understand the feelings of others. But words account for only a small part (less than 10 percent) of how we attach meaning to emotional communication. Humans interpret emotional messages from a much more primitive part of their brain, and, as we shall see in Chapter 21, teaching children to understand the meaning of posture, facial expressions, tone of voice, and other body language will be much more effective in enhancing their understanding of their emotions and those of others.

- Children who are traumatized are typically treated as extremely vulnerable, and it is conventional wisdom to give them time to sort out their emotions in a supportive and nurturing environment. But recent advances in cognitive-behavioral psychology suggest that a more immediate and direct approach to desensitizing the effect of the trauma, which involves stimulating calming centers in the brain, will be more effective in preventing psychological symptoms such as nightmares and anxiety reactions. This technique is discussed in Chapter 23.

- Developing a child's self-esteem through constant praise and reinforcement, as advocated for over twenty-five years by followers of the humanistic psychology movement, may actually do more harm than good. As we shall see in Chapter 7, helping children feel good about them-

Many aspects of teaching EQ skills are counterintuitive. For example, most parents feel that their first obligation is to protect their children from distress, but protecting children when they don't need it will do more harm than good.

selves only has meaning if those feelings are attached to specific achievements and the mastering of new skills.

- Stress has been cast as an evil byproduct of our hurried technological society, a natural enemy of childhood. But protecting children from stress may be one of the worst things we can do. As we saw in Kagan's studies of timid children (and I further discuss this in Chapter 18 on teaching children to be persistent), learning to cope with life's difficulties causes children to develop new neural pathways, which can make them more adaptable and resourceful.

A DEVELOPMENTAL UNDERSTANDING OF EQ

The developing brain is observable to us in the ways that our children change physically, cognitively, and emotionally as they age. Our youngsters' neurological development creates a window of time in which they are preprogrammed to enter a specific stage and master it. We are usually very aware of our children's physical time clock, eagerly recording how they learn to sit by the time they are six months old, walk between the ages of twelve and eighteen months, and use the potty by themselves between two and a half to three years of age. If our children do not reach these physical milestones within a few months of the anticipated time, we are rightfully concerned and usually consult our pediatricians.

Similarly, we are aware of the major milestones in our children's cognitive development. Most toddlers say several words by the time they are eighteen months and speak in simple sentences by the age of two. Preschoolers learn their letters and numbers between the ages of five and six, and they can read simple sentences and do simple addition and subtraction by the time they are seven. Between ages eight and nine, our children develop the ability to memorize the dreaded multiplication tables, but geometry and algebra are reserved for middle school, because the ability to think in abstractions does not typically develop until children are between eleven and thirteen.

Most of us are less aware of the stages created by the development of the emotional brain, which shall be the prime concern of this book. Each EQ skill that we examine has its own developmental timetable, and although this varies much more than physical or cognitive development, in most cases it is just as predictable.

The fact that many of us do not anticipate changes in our children's emotional development, the way we look for changes in their physical and cognitive development can contribute to many preventable problems.

Take, for example, Miss Ansel's preschool class mentioned at the beginning of this chapter. You will remember that even though the four-year-olds failed on each attempt to balance a marble on a rising platform, they remained optimistic and confident that they could accomplish this task in spite of their failures. As we shall see in Chapter 17, children are developmentally preprogrammed to be confident in their abilities, at least until the age of seven. Up until this age, children do not distinguish effort from ability, and as long as they try, most believe that they will eventually succeed. By the time they enter the third grade, however, children's cognitive maturity enables them to make a more realistic assessment about what they can accomplish and what they cannot. They begin to realize that some children have more or less ability than they do. They realize that if they are to be as successful as their classmates with more aptitude, they will have to expend more effort.

The realization that effort can compensate for ability becomes a critical factor in children between the ages of eight and twelve, and may be one of the key ingredients in raising children who can persist in the face of difficulty. If we anticipate this developmental change and reward our youngsters' efforts rather than just their achievements from the time that they first enter school, they are more likely to have good study habits and other work-related skills.

HOW THIS BOOK CAN HELP YOU

Although there is wide agreement on the importance of teaching children EQ skills, this is the first book to systematically examine how these skills develop during childhood and explain, practically, what you can do to raise children with a higher degree of social and emotional intelligence. Unlike many other parenting books, this volume is not about my opinion as a psychologist as to what might help your child. Rather, it is grounded in research conducted all over the country at universities, hospitals, and clinics. Despite the fact that this research comes from diverse fields such as neuroanatomy, child development, social anthropology, education, and psychology, the composite results are unequivocal: EQ skills such as interpersonal problem solving, persistence, friendliness, and empathy are teachable, and they can make a difference in the quality of your child's life for years to come.

I have organized the components of emotional intelligence into six areas: skills related to moral behavior, thinking, problem solving, social interaction, academic and work success, and the emotions. Each general area is then further subdivided into specific EQ skills such as self-motivation, making friends, empathy, realistic thinking, and so on. By the time you finish this book, you will have a clear sense of what your child's EQ is and how you can help him or her to develop it.

THE "GOOD ENOUGH PARENT"

In reading this book, you will find many suggestions on what you could do differently with your child—perhaps too many. It is not my intention to make you feel that you are doing everything wrong, nor do I intend to overburden you with an idealized way to raise children. I assume that as a concerned parent you will read this book, take what seems relevant, and perhaps change a thing or two in the way you raise your children.

There is no such thing as the perfect parent, but many psychologists use the term the "good enough parent" to describe those who provide enough of what their children need to equip them with the building blocks for social and emotional growth and provide opportunities for them to continue their development outside of the family.

Another important perspective to keep in mind is that even a single change can have a profound effect on your child's life. In a book of this nature, it is easier to talk about EQ skills as if they were discrete, like riding a bike or learning to roller skate, but this is not the case at all. Nearly all the EQ skills that I present are interrelated, and teaching your child one skill will engender change in other EQ areas as well. For example, in Part VI, I discuss the EQ skills that are important to school achievement and suggest cooperative activities to take the pressure off children to succeed. But teaching your children cooperative skills can also help them learn to control their anger or get along better with authority figures, and these same cooperative skills will be particularly useful in helping your child develop friendships. In other words, emphasizing just one aspect of emotional intelligence in your home will have a snowball effect. Once you start, things just keep changing for the better.

▪ 2 ▪

Becoming a
High EQ Parent

Researchers studying how parents react to their children have found that there are three general parenting styles: authoritarian, permissive, and authoritative. Authoritarian parents set out strict rules and expect them to be obeyed. They believe that children should be "kept in their place," and they discourage them from voicing their opinions. Authoritarian parents try to run a household based on structure and tradition, although in many cases their emphasis on order and control becomes a burden to the child. In her book *Raising a Responsible Child,* Elizabeth Ellis writes, "Many studies suggest that children from authoritarian and rigid controlling families don't fare so well. . . . They tend to be unhappy, withdrawn, and have difficulty trusting others. They have the lowest levels of self-esteem [as compared to children raised by parents who are less controlling]."

The permissive parent, on the other hand, seeks to be as accepting and nurturing as possible, but tends to be very passive when it comes to setting limits or responding to disobedience. Permissive parents do not make strong demands, nor do they even have clear goals for their children, believing that kids should be allowed to develop according to their natural inclinations.

Authoritative parents, by contrast to both authoritarian and permissive parents, manage to balance clear limits with a nurturing home environment. They give guidance, but they are not controlling; they give explanations for what they do while allowing children to have input into important decisions. Authoritative parents value their children's independence, but hold them to high standards of responsibility to family, peers, and the community. Dependency and babyish behavior is discouraged. Competence is encouraged and praised. As you might expect, in study after study, authoritative parents are deemed to have the style that is more likely to produce children who are self-confident, independent, imaginative, adaptable, and well-liked—kids with high degrees of emotional intelligence.

While these broad definitions are useful for research purposes, in many ways they are too simplistic. In reality, it is not uncommon to find families in which one parent is authoritarian while the other is permissive. These parents may actually balance each other out in the way that they raise their children. In other families, we see parents who are authoritative in some aspects of their child-rearing, but too permissive in other areas. They might better be described as overindulgent rather than permissive, although according to Elizabeth Ellis, the net effect is the same. According to Ellis, the average American parents may love their children a little too much for their own good, finding it difficult to refuse them nearly anything they want.

DEVELOPING AFFIRMATIVE CARING

Caring for children and indulging their every whim are two very different things. Affirmative caring means giving children emotional nurturance and support in a way that is clearly recognized by the child. This type of caring is more than praise for a good grade on a test, or a hug and a kiss good night. It involves an active participation in the emotional life of your child. As we shall see, this involves playing with your younger children or participating in activities with your older children in a way that is not very different from what children experience in professional counseling.

Research also suggests that an open and caring relationship with your child will have the long-term effect of increasing your child's self-image, coping skills, and possibly even his health. A study presented by psychologists Linda Russek and Gary Schwartz to the March 1996 meeting of the American Psychosomatic Society shows just how important building a positive relationship with your children can be to their future. These researchers reported on a study started thirty-five years ago when eighty-seven Harvard University men, all around twenty years old, were asked to give written assessments about how caring and supportive their parents were.

After examining these same participants thirty-five years later, with the men now in their mid-fifties, it was found that the participants who had as college students described their parents as more loving had fewer serious illnesses in middle age, including heart disease and hypertension, independent of key risk factors such as family history, age, and smoking. As might be expected, the young men who had perceived their parents as unjust became the middle-age men with the most serious physical illnesses.

Studies like this emphasize the important role that we have in our children's mental and physical health. An increasing trend among child therapists is to train parents to engage in play therapy with their children, emphasizing acceptance and positive regard. In the 1960s, Bernard Guerney, then a professor at Rutgers University, pioneered techniques in training parents to act as surrogate therapists for their troubled children, concluding that many children had problems not because their parents were malicious or disturbed, but because their parents lacked the inherent skills to develop a positive relationship with their kids.

More recently, Dr. Russell Barkley, one of the nation's leading experts on attention deficit disorders in children, suggests, in his book *Taking Charge of ADHD*, that parents of "difficult" children spend twenty minutes of "special time" each day with their children as a way to virtually assure that they will get the benefits of affirmative caring. While this is particularly important for children with attention deficit disorders—who typically receive too much negative attention and criticism from teachers, peers, and family members—it is a good prescription for all children (although, in most cases, having "special time" two or three times a week would be more realistic).

For children under the age of nine, Barkley suggests that parents set a particular time period to participate with their child in a play activity. During this time, parents should create a nonjudgmental atmosphere of interest, enthusiasm, and acceptance. According to Barkley, the general principles of "special time" include:

1. Praise your child for appropriate behaviors (e.g., "That's a huge tower that you're building!"), but be accurate, honest, and avoid excessive flattery.

2. Demonstrate your interest in what your child is doing by participating in the activity, describing what you see, and reflecting his or her feelings whatever they may be (e.g., "You seem to really like having those two guys wrestle with each other. But you don't look angry, so I guess that you're just having fun wrestling.").

3. Don't ask questions or give commands. Your job is to
    observe and reflect what you see, not to control or guide.

If your children are between the ages of four and nine, try
to schedule a play period at a regular time several days a
week, making sure that this time is respected and consistent.
For children over the age of nine, it would be too awkward to
schedule rigid playtimes, but rather you should look for
opportunities to spend similar nonjudgmental time with your
children in age-appropriate activities.

AFFIRMATIVE DISCIPLINE

Very few parents have trouble learning the principles of affirmative caring, but affirmative discipline is another matter. By
affirmative discipline, I simply mean that you need to have
thought-out, predictable, and age-appropriate ways to
respond to your children's misbehaviors.

What would you do in the following situation?

The saleswomen in the small jewelry store were
frozen in place, as were most of the customers. In
the middle of the store on the busiest day of the holiday season, a five-year-old boy was having a full-
blown tantrum, flailing and kicking, screaming at
the top of his lungs, dangerously close to a glass
case of fine jewelry. His mother, apparently as oblivious to the surroundings as her son, sat down next
to him cross-legged in a lotus position and began a
conversation. "Now Benji, you need to talk to me
about what is wrong instead of just crying. I can't
understand what the problem is if you are crying. I
know you're upset, but you have to tell me what's

bothering you if you want me to do something about it."

"I'll tell you what's bothering me," the store owner muttered under her breath, wondering if she had the nerve or the strength to heave both the mother and her son out of the store. Instead, she just watched and waited, wondering what this mother must be thinking about the effect this incident was having on her son.

The mother in the jewelry store was under the mistaken belief that children should always be reasoned with and given choices, even when they misbehave beyond accepted social limits. As William Damon writes in his book *Greater Expectations: Overcoming the Culture of Indulgence in Our Homes and Schools*, "All young people need discipline in both a positive and a constraining sense. If children are to learn productive skills, they need to develop discipline in order to make the most of their native talents. They also need to encounter firm and consistent discipline whenever they test the limits of social rules (as every child will do from time to time)." In fact, it is impossible to develop a parenting style that enhances your children's EQ without also having a consistent and effective way to discipline them. But as many teachers and counselors will tell you, this is an area in which many American parents have the most trouble. While there are hundreds of books on how best to discipline your child, effective discipline really boils down to just a few simple principles and strategies:

1. Make clear rules and limits and stick to them. Write them down and post them if you can.

2. Give warnings or cues when your child is beginning to misbehave. This is the best way to teach him self-control.

3. Shape positive behavior by reinforcing good behavior with praise or affection and ignoring behavior that is designed to simply get your attention.

4. Educate your child as to your expectations. Generally speaking, parents do not spend enough time talking to their children about values, rules, and why these values and rules are important.

5. Prevent problems before they occur. According to behavioral psychology, most problems occur as a result of a specific stimulus or cue. Understanding and eliminating these cues will help you avoid situations that trigger misbehavior.

6. When a clearly stated rule or limit is broken, intentionally or otherwise, follow up immediately with an appropriate punishment. Be consistent and do exactly what you said you would do.

7. When a punishment is necessary, make sure that it is commensurate with the rule infraction or misbehavior (let the punishment fit the crime).

8. Be comfortable with a range of discipline techniques. The most frequently recommended ones include:

   A. *Reprimands:* This is the first thing that parents must do, and it is used often enough. See Chapter 7 for a discussion of how to reprimand your children so that their behavior changes without their developing resentment toward you or a negative self-image.

   B. *Natural consequences:* This strategy refers to letting your children experience the logical consequences of their misbehavior in order to see why a particular rule is important. For example, a child who dawdles when his mother is trying to rush him to catch the school bus might be made to walk to school and explain to the principal why he was late. (However, natural consequences may sometimes be unrealistic or even dangerous, as when you want to teach your youngster not to run into the street, or why he shouldn't play with fire.)

C. *Time-out:* Perhaps the most commonly prescribed discipline technique, time-out involves putting your child in a neutral, unstimulating corner for a short period of time (one minute for each year of the child's age). This can also be effective when children misbehave in public places.

D. *Taking away a privilege:* When children are too old to go into a time-out corner, parents usually take away a privilege. TV time, video game time, and phone time seem to work best. Avoid taking away a privilege that would also remove a developmentally important experience for your child. For example, it would be better to make a teenager's curfew earlier for a month than to keep her from going on an overnight school trip.

E. *Overcorrection:* This technique is often recommended for quick behavioral change. When your child misbehaves, he must repeat the correct behavior at least ten times or for up to twenty minutes. For example, if your son came home from school, threw his coat and books on the floor, and ignored your greeting, you would require him to go back outside and reenter the house appropriately ten times, each time giving you a cordial greeting, putting away his books, and hanging up his coat.

F.   *A behavioral point system:* For chronic problems, most psychologists recommend a system in which children can earn points for clearly defined positive behaviors. These points can then be "cashed in" for immediate and/or long-term rewards. Misbehaviors result in the subtraction of points.

As we shall see throughout this book, research strongly suggests that if you want to raise a child with a high EQ, you are better off being too strict than too lenient. In a *USA Today* survey of 101 former Academic Team All Stars—high school seniors selected annually for high academic performance, talent, and community service—49 percent of the students described their parents as stricter than other parents.

THE GREATEST OBSTACLE TO RAISING A CHILD WITH A HIGH EQ

The problem that we have in setting limits for our children is made crystal clear when we examine our children's television habits. In my opinion, televisions, like cigarettes, should come with a warning label from the United States Surgeon General. Although watching TV does not result in the immediate physiological harm as with cigarettes, one could argue that it is a significant factor in the rise of childhood obesity, which is now estimated at nearly 14 percent, and obesity certainly contributes to major illnesses and a shortened life.

Although TV may not be physically addictive, its ability to form a psychological addiction is hard to question. In a survey by *Peoplepedia*, an encyclopedia of facts on American habits, over 1,000 people were asked what it would take to induce them to give up TV. A surprising 46 percent reported that they would not do it for less than $1 million dollars, and

25 percent of those surveyed said that they would not give up TV even for that amount.

While television in itself is not bad, it is the passive time spent in front of the TV that stunts the growth of EQ skills. The average American child watches twenty-four hours of TV a week—that's a day a week! In fact, our children spend more time watching TV than they do in any other activity except sleeping. By the time the average child is five years old, he or she has spent as much time watching TV as the average college student does attending class over a four-year period!

Although experts have long maintained that excessive TV-watching is not good for children, many parents' own

How do you want your child to learn about the world, by watching or by doing? Television may be the single greatest deterrent to developing social and emotional skills.

addiction to television is partially responsible for their inability to monitor their children's time in front of the TV—it's a little like asking an alcoholic to enforce sobriety. Many parents have found that TV is a very inexpensive baby-sitter. But if you are serious about raising children with a high emotional intelligence, you must set strict limits on your child's television watching.

My advice is to put your family on a TV diet of perhaps two hours a day (this should include rented videos and video games, as well). This applies to everyone in the family, not just the children. Sit down with your kids with a TV schedule in hand and give them guidance in selecting the shows that they want to watch (and of which you approve). A great deal of TV watching just fills time, and as you shall see, there really isn't that much that children get excited about.

While you may need at first to structure your child's TV free time, she will eventually become creative with it once she is weaned off the television. The next step is to plan activities that take the place of watching TV. Pull the board games out of the closet, go to the library and get some books, make a list of art projects and hobbies that can be worked on, enroll your children in sports programs. As you will see in Part VIII, I do not consider time on the computer to be equivalent to watching television, for it is active rather than passive and has a great deal of potential for teaching EQ skills. Even so, computers only offer a world of virtual reality and cannot give a child the feel of a hug or the smell of a ball field, so computer time should be limited as well.

WHERE TO BEGIN

If you are like most readers of parenting books, you will probably begin by looking for information that is of particular concern to you or your children rather than reading the book straight through. The following checklist was designed to help you see how much you are already doing to raise an emotionally intelligent child and what new things might be done. The purpose of this checklist is not to see how high you can score, but to direct you to the parts of the book that will help you the most in raising children with a high EQ.

The Parent's EQ Checklist

Do you hide serious problems from your child?

____Yes   ____No

No.
Most psychologists feel that parents should not hide serious problems even from very young children. Children are much more resilient than many people realize and benefit from realistic explanations of problems (see Chapter 6).

Do you discuss your own faults openly?

____Yes   ____No

Yes.
In order to become realistic in their thinking and expectations, children must learn to accept their parents' positive attributes as well as their flaws (see Chapter 9).

Does your child watch more than twelve hours of TV a week?
____Yes   ____No

No.
The average American child actually watches twenty-four hours

of TV a week, and this is far too much. This passive activity does very little to promote EQ skills. Violent TV shows are particularly problematic for children who have trouble controlling their anger (see Chapter 2).

Do you have a home computer?

____Yes   ____No

Yes.
At one time, psychologists and sociologists thought that computers and computer games would have a detrimental influence on a child's social development, but the opposite seems to be true. Children (and adults) are finding new ways to use computers and on-line services that actually increase EQ skills (see Chapters 24 and 25).

Do you consider yourself an optimistic person?

____Yes   ____No

Yes.
Studies show that children who are optimistic are happier, more successful in school, and actually physically healthier. The primary way that your children develop an optimistic or a pessimistic attitude is by watching and listening to you (see Chapter 7).

Do you help your child cultivate friends?

____Yes   ____No

Yes.
Researchers in child development believe that having a "best friend," particularly between the ages of nine and twelve, is a critical developmental milestone in learning to have intimate rela-

tionships. Teaching friendship skills should begin when your child is a toddler (see Chapter 14).

Do you monitor the violent content of your child's TV-watching and video games?

____Yes   ____No

Yes.
While there is no clear evidence that watching violent TV programs or playing violent computer games leads to aggressiveness in children, it does desensitize them to the feelings and concerns of others (see Chapter 2).

Do you spend fifteen minutes a day or more with your child in unstructured play or activities?

____Yes   ____No

Yes.
Unfortunately, today's parents spend less and less time with their children. Spending time playing with younger children or in unstructured activities with older children enhances their self-image and self-confidence (see Chapter 2).

Do you have clear and consistent ways to discipline your child and enforce rules?

____Yes   ____No

Yes.
A significant number of problems that children experience today could be forestalled by authoritative parenting. Authoritative parenting combines nurturance with consistent and appropriate discipline. Many parenting experts believe that overly permissive parents are the cause of an increasing number of childhood

problems, including defiance and antisocial behaviors (see Chapter 2).

Do you participate in community service activities with your child on a regular basis?

____Yes   ____No

Yes.
Children learn to care about others by doing, not just by talking. Community service activities also teach children many social skills and help keep them out of trouble (see Chapter 3).

Are you truthful and honest with your child, even about painful subjects such as an illness or the loss of a job?

____Yes   ____No

Yes.
Many parents try to protect children from stress to preserve their childhood innocence, but in reality this does more harm than good. Children who haven't learned to deal effectively with stress become vulnerable to more serious problems as they grow older, particularly in their relationships (see Chapter 4).

Do you teach your child how to physically relax as a way to cope with stress, pain, or anxiety?

____Yes   ____No

Yes.
You can teach relaxation training to children as young as four or five. This will not only help them cope with immediate problems, but may even help them live longer and healthier lives (see Chapter 23).

Do you step in when your child is having difficulty solving a problem?

____Yes   ____No

No.
Research suggests that children can solve problems much earlier than we once suspected. When your children learn to solve their own problems, they gain self-confidence and learn important social skills (see Chapters 10 and 11).

Do you have regular family meetings?

____Yes   ____No

Yes.
Modeling is the single most important way that children learn emotional and social skills. Family meetings are an ideal way to teach children problem-solving skills and how to function in a group (see Chapter 15).

Do you insist that your child always show good manners toward others?

____Yes   ____No

Yes.
Good manners are simple to teach and extremely important in school and for social success (see Chapter 16).

Do you take time to teach your children to see the humor in everyday life, even in their problems?

____Yes   ____No

Yes.
An ever-increasing number of studies show that a sense of humor is not only an important social skill, but it is a significant factor in a child's mental and physical health, as well (see Chapter 13).

Are you flexible with your child's study habits and need for organizational skills?

____Yes ____No

No.
There are many ways that you need to be flexible, but study habits and work skills are not among them. To become successful in school and later in work, your children need to learn self-discipline, time-management, and organizational skills (see Chapter 18).

Do you make your child keep trying even when he complains that something is too hard or even when he fails?

____Yes ____No

Yes.
One of the most important ingredients in becoming a high achiever is the ability to overcome frustration and give a persistent effort in the face of failure. In general, American parents do not require enough effort from their children (see Chapter 18).

Do you insist that your child maintain a healthy diet and daily exercise?

____Yes ____No

Yes.
Aside from the obvious physical benefits of a good diet and exer-

cise, a healthy lifestyle plays an important part in the biochemistry of your child's developing brain (see Chapter 23).

Do you confront your child if you know that they are not being truthful, even if it is a small matter?

____Yes   ____No

Yes.
Children's understanding of honesty changes as they grow older, but truthfulness should always be emphasized in the family (see Chapter 4).

Do you respect your child's privacy, even if you suspect she is doing something harmful to herself or others?

____Yes   ____No

No.
When raising children, privacy and trust go hand in hand. At every age, children should understand the difference between what can be kept private and what you need to know (see Chapter 4).

Do you let your child's teacher handle motivational problems in school without becoming involved?

____Yes   ____No

No.
Motivating children to achieve begins in the home. Studies from other cultures suggest that the more parents are involved in their children's education, the more likely children are to succeed (see Chapter 17).

Do you think that you should be more tolerant of problems in your children because you have the same (or similar) problems?

____Yes   ____No

No.
It is not surprising that children often have the same problems as their parents. If you are struggling with serious issues like depression or a bad temper, you should seek ways to change your own behavior as well as your child's (see Chapter 7).

Do you leave your child alone if they don't want to talk about something that is making him or her angry or upset?

____Yes   ____No

No.
Very few children like to talk about what is upsetting them, but from an emotional intelligence perspective, you should strongly encourage your children to talk about their feelings. Talking about problems and giving words to feelings may change the way a child's brain develops, forming links between the emotional and the thinking parts of the brain (see Chapter 20).

Do you believe that every problem has a solution?

____Yes   ____No

Yes.
Children, as well as adolescents and adults, can be taught to look for solutions instead of dwelling on problems. This positive way of viewing the world can enhance your child's self-confidence as well as her relationships (see Chapter 11).

PART 2

The Moral Emotions

For the last four decades, everyone from elementary school principals to preachers to presidents have wrung their hands about the crisis in the moral development of our children, but things don't seem to be any better. As shocking as the statistics may be, the stories behind them are even worse.

There is the fourteen-year-old who brutally beat a classmate to death with a baseball bat and then went to a friend's house for a snowball fight, offering to show him the bloody body. There is the nine-year-old in Kissimmee, Florida, who pushed his three-year-old neighbor into a swimming pool and watched as the toddler drowned. Another nine-year-old Florida boy recently held his mother hostage with a penknife to her throat, threatening to kill her unless she returned to their local Burger King restaurant to exchange the puppet he had received with his lunch.

These statistics and newspaper headlines reflect only the most serious problems. The inadequate moral development of children—one could say the lack of a fully developed conscience—affects every aspect of our society: the harmony in our homes, the ability of our schools to teach, the safety of our streets, and the integrity of our societal values.

Successful moral development means having emotions and behaviors that reflect concern about others: sharing, helping, nurturing, altruistic behavior, tolerance toward others, and a willingness to follow societal rules. In order to become a moral person, Brown University professor William Damon, considered to be one of America's foremost experts on the moral development of children and adolescents, suggests that children must acquire the following emotional and social skills:

- They should adopt and understand what distinguishes "good" from "bad" behavior and develop habits of conduct that are consistent with what they perceive as "good."

- They should develop concern, regard, and a sense of responsibility for the welfare and rights of others. They express this concern in acts of caring, benevolence, kindness, and mercy.

- They should experience negative emotional reaction, including shame, guilt, outrage, fear, and contempt for the breaking of moral rules.

The desire to care for and about others, even to the point of self-sacrifice, is undoubtedly part of our genetic coding. We can observe countless examples of moral behavior not only in primates, but in much less developed animals. Soldier ants and termites frequently expose themselves to danger to draw attention from the others when their colonies are attacked. Female birds have been observed feigning injury and moving away from their nests in an attempt to distract a perceived enemy from their offspring. Numerous species have been known to adopt animals from other species and raise them as their own.

According to scientists, the often misunderstood rat, frequently vilified in movies and literature as dirty and evil, is actually one of the most nurturing of all animals. In one test of interspecies adoption, an experimenter found that rats readily adopted baby mice and baby rabbits. They tried to adopt baby kittens and fought the experimenters when they tried to remove the kittens from their nests. The rats were unsuccessful at suckling the kittens despite their vigorous attempts.

History as well as day-to-day experience reveals numerous instances of how humans care for each other. But in spite of our genetic predisposition toward being concerned for others, studies of different cultures show that moral development can readily be influenced by child-rearing practices and values. In her book *The Caring Child*, Arizona State University professor Nancy Eisenberg describes the Ik people of Uganda as a "love-less people," where any form of caring and generosity was perceived as a weakness. The only real value in the Ik society was placed on food, or "ngag," which is synonymous with "goodness." A good person was therefore a person who had a full stomach. The quest for food was so important to the Ik that it even overrode concern about their closest relatives. It was not uncommon for sons to steal food from their aging and sick parents, even if it meant that they would starve to death.

Other cultures such as the traditional Hopi Indians of

Arizona show examples of extraordinarily high levels of moral development. The Hopi were taught that cooperation among members of the tribe was essential for survival, since all aspects of the universe are interdependent. From birth, Hopi children learned that nothing was more important in life than having a "good heart," which was achieved by focusing on the welfare and happiness of others.

A variety of negative emotions motivate children to learn and practice prosocial behaviors, including:

- The fear of punishment.
- Anxiety over social disapproval.
- Guilt over failing to meet one's own expectations.
- Shame and embarrassment over being caught at doing something that is unacceptable to others.

The two major positive emotions that shape a child's moral development are empathy and what we might call the nurturing instinct, which includes our capacity for love. We will consider the positive forces that shape your child's conscience first, because positive parenting is more consistent with our Western child-centered culture. However, it would be a mistake for parents to ignore the fact that negative emotions, particularly shame and guilt, are also important aspects of building their child's character. We shall consider the significance of the negative moral emotions in Chapter 5.

▪ 3 ▪

Encouraging Empathy and Caring

Dwaina Brooks was studying homelessness in her fourth-grade class. Like most children her age, it was a topic more of interest than one that affected her life. Then one day on her way home from school, she stopped to talk to a homeless man and asked the simple question, "What do you need?"

"I need a job and I need a home," he replied matter-of-factly. Dwaina knew that she couldn't give him those things, so she asked, "Is there anything else you need?"

"I'd love a really good meal," he replied, and Dwaina felt that was something she could help supply.

After three days of shopping and planning, Dwaina, with the help of her mother and two sisters, made more than 100 meals, which they drove to a nearby homeless shelter. Nearly every Friday night for a year, Dwaina and her family did the same. Soliciting donations from the community and the help of her classmates, Dwaina made thousands of meals for the homeless in Dallas.

As she explained her philosophy to a reporter from USA Today, "Each of us should have some kind of concern in our hearts for other people. . . . And we owe it, too. There isn't one of us who hasn't been helped by someone else. You should always be ready to give back what people have given you."

Dwaina exemplifies what it means to be empathic—she was able to put herself in another's shoes. Indeed, she was more than empathic, because once she recognized what her homeless neighbor was feeling, she was willing to act on his behalf. She has helped hundreds of people as a result.

The payoff in teaching children to be more empathic is enormous. Those with strong empathic capacities tend to be less aggressive and engage in more prosocial acts, such as helping and sharing. As a result, empathic children are better liked by peers and adults and have more success in school and on the job. It is not surprising that empathic children grow up to have a greater capacity for intimacy in their relationships with their spouses, friends, and children.

THE STAGES OF EMPATHY

Developmental psychologists point out that there are actually two components to empathy: an emotional reaction toward others, which normally develops in the first six years of a child's life, and a cognitive reaction, which determines the degree to which older children are able to see the point of view or perspective of someone else.

We can see emotional empathy in most infants throughout the first year of life. Babies will turn to watch another child who is crying and will frequently start to cry as well. Developmental psychologist Martin Hoffman refers to this as "global empathy" because of the child's inability to distinguish between himself and his world, interpreting every other baby's distress as his own.

Between the ages of one and two, children enter a second

stage of empathy in which they can clearly see that another person's distress is not their own. Most toddlers intuitively try to reduce the other's distress. However, because of their immature cognitive development, toddlers are not sure exactly what they should do, leading to a state of empathic confusion, as illustrated in the following example:

> Sara showed such empathic confusion when her playmate, Melanie, suddenly began to cry. At first, it looked as though Sara would break into tears herself, but then she stood up, put down the blocks she had been playing with, and began to pet Melanie.
>
> When Melanie's mother entered the room and scooped Melanie in her arms to see what was wrong, this only caused her daughter to wail louder. Seeing that Melanie was still in distress, but now having another person to deal with as well, Sara began to softly stroke Melanie's mother's arm. Deciding that Melanie was wet, her mother took her out of the room, leaving Sara alone and apparently unsatisfied with the results of her ministries. Sara walked over to a stuffed bear and began petting the bear, occasionally petting her own arm as well.

Some children seem to be born with more empathy than others. Psychologists M. Radke-Yarrow and A. Zahn-Waxler report that in a study of toddlers, some responded to other children's distress with an expression of empathic feelings and direct attempts to help, while others just looked on and expressed interest rather than concern. Still a third group showed a negative reaction to other children's pain—some withdrew from those who were crying and others even scolded or hit the complaining child.

As their perceptual and cognitive capacities mature, children increasingly learn to recognize the different signs of another's emotional distress, and they are able to match their concern with appropriate behaviors.

The age of six marks the beginning of the stage of cognitive empathy—the ability to see things from another person's perspective and act accordingly. Perspective-taking skills allow a child to know when to approach an unhappy friend and when to leave him alone. Cognitive empathy does not require emotional communication (such as crying), because a child has by now developed an inner reference point or model for how a person might feel in a distressing situation, whether or not he shows it.

Kevin, age eight, for example, decided to stand outside the corner market while his mother shopped for their dinner. He saw a woman, about his grandmother's age, loaded down with shopping bags and heading toward the door. Instinctively, he opened it. "Thank you, young man, aren't you sweet?" she responded to his considerate gesture.

Moments later, a young mother approached the door, balancing a shopping bag and her blanketed baby. Again, Kevin swiftly opened the door, and he was gratefully thanked. Then came a man with a painter's cap holding a cup of coffee, then another older woman, then two teenagers talking. Kevin opened the door for each person and was thanked by each in turn. Kevin could imagine how these individuals were feeling, even though they said nothing, and he acted accordingly. He was using his cognitive empathy skills.

In late childhood, between the ages of ten and twelve, children expand their empathy beyond those that they know or directly observe to include groups of people whom they have never met. In this stage, called abstract empathy, children express their concern about people who have less advantages than they do, whether they live on another block or in another country. When kids do something about these perceived differences by performing charitable and altruistic acts, we can assume that they have completely acquired the EQ skill of empathy.

WHAT YOU CAN DO TO HELP YOUR CHILD BECOME MORE EMPATHETIC TOWARD OTHERS

As we have seen, empathy, the basis of all social skills, comes naturally to the vast majority of children. It may surprise you that most studies do not show significant differences in the

Kindness and consideration are part of your child's genetic coding, but if these traits are not nourished, they will disappear.

empathic behaviors of boys and girls. In general, boys are as helpful as girls, but tend to be more eager to do physically helpful or "rescue" type activities (such as helping another child learn to ride a bike), whereas girls are apt to be more psychologically supportive (such as comforting another child who is upset). Neither social class nor family size seem to be related to empathic behaviors, although older siblings appear to be generally more helpful than their younger counterparts. More helping behavior tends to occur between siblings when there are larger differences in their ages.

Given this level playing field and our children's natural urge to be helpful and thoughtful, we might expect to find much more frequent and consistent empathic behavior than we do. When children are unkind, thoughtless, and even cruel, most of the time we can trace the reasons for this "unnatural" behavior back to the home. If you want to raise a child who cares for and about others and whose behaviors are consistent with these feelings, here is what you can do.

"RAISE THE BAR" ON YOUR EXPECTATIONS FOR CONSIDERATE AND RESPONSIBLE BEHAVIOR IN YOUR CHILDREN

In some families, religion plays an important part in the moral development of children. Although most religions require children to memorize a list of moral rules like the Ten Commandments, this simple memorization and recitation seems to have little effect on their behavior. The way that parents live out their religion's value system in their day-to-day lives is what is effective in influencing children. Some religious communities are particularly effective at teaching children to be concerned about other people.

For example, in his book *Raising Your Child to Be a Mensch*,

Rabbi Neil Kurshan defines the Jewish emphasis on concern for others. He writes, "[The word] 'menschlichkeit' [means] responsibility fused with compassion, a sense that one's own personal needs and desires are limited by the needs and desires of other people. A mensch acts with self-restraint and humility, always sensitive to the feelings and thoughts of others. As menschen we feel a genuine passion to alleviate the pain and suffering of those around us."

Rabbi Kurshan bemoans the fact that the word "mensch" has largely disappeared from American Jewish culture. He describes an incident in which he asked a class of tenth-graders to define the term, only to be met by puzzled stares of confusion. Then one boy, waving his hand vigorously, explained that "it's a pretty woman who likes to flirt with men."

"No," the Rabbi explained confusedly, "that's not it." He went on to give an appropriate definition. It only occurred to him later in the day that this boy had given him his definition for the word "wench."

Kurshan attributes the disappearance of "menschlichkeit" from all levels of society to diminished parental expectations, even to the point that parents actually fear their children's disapproval and rejection. He explains, "Over the years I have met couples who hide five or ten dollars in their dresser for their children to find because they fear their kids will otherwise steal a lot more from their purse. I know parents who do not set a curfew because they fear their children will ignore them, and parents who bite their tongues when their children call them 'morons' or 'idiots' to their face."

If you want your children to become more empathic, caring, and responsible, then you must *expect* this of them. You must make your family rules clear and consistent and not waiver from them. You must *require* them to be responsible.

Children as young as three should be expected to clean up after themselves and even help with simple chores like setting the table. Chores and other responsibilities should increase with age and should not be contingent on rewards, not even on an allowance. Children should be expected to help around the house because helping others is the right thing to do. Getting an allowance and learning how to handle money is an entirely separate matter.

If you want your child to be thoughtful, considerate, and responsible, there is one simple thing you must do: raise the bar on your expectations. It is easy to be a permissive parent. It is easy to make your child's bed or do his homework for him. But to raise more responsible children, parents must become more responsible themselves, and they can begin by overcoming their denial that spoiling children will not harm them. It will.

TEACH YOUR CHILDREN TO PRACTICE "RANDOM ACTS OF KINDNESS"

The Roman statesman Cicero once wrote, "In nothing do men more nearly approach the Gods than by doing good for their fellow man."

One of the simplest and most effective ways to teach children empathy is to practice "random acts of kindness." This national movement was spearheaded by the book *Random Acts of Kindness,* which contains anecdotes of how simple acts of thoughtfulness and consideration profoundly affect people's lives. A college student received anonymous mystery postcards from a friend's mother that made his first few months away from home easier. A woman left a broken lamp on the bus, and the bus driver went out of his way to return it, fixing it first. A recent widow got out of her car and sobbed by the side of the road, because a Christmas trip with her teenagers was such a disappointment. A complete stranger stopped her car, held and comforted the woman, and invited her family back for tea and a tour of the town's Christmas lights.

What was so intriguing to the editors of *Random Acts of Congress* at Conari Press, who continue to be flooded by stories of kindness, was how the simplest good deeds could become life-altering events for people. They write in the preface to a second volume of letters: "From the vantage point of having read so many people's stories . . . kindness emerges as one of the most powerful tools at our disposal as we go through our lives. Its power not only is easily accessible to anyone who cares to use it, but it also can never be diminished; rather it expands with every action."

Today is as good as any other day to make kindness a family project. Purchase a "blank" journal at the stationery store and record an act of kindness every day for each person in the family. An act of kindness can be as simple as holding the door for someone or making a call to an ill friend. As kindness becomes a habit, you will find that children can't get enough of it. They will go out of their way to perform more altruistic acts.

INVOLVE YOUR CHILD IN COMMUNITY SERVICE

Many schools across the country are beginning to require community service as a condition for high school graduation. According to a 1994 survey by the Educational Research Service, more than 30 percent of U.S. public and private schools currently mandate—or plan to in the near future—community service as a requirement for graduation. This requirement ranges from 40 hours in Laguna Beach, California, to 240 hours in St. Louis, Missouri. But the fact that schools must mandate community service in order to fulfill their obligation to graduate responsible citizens is a sad commentary on how families have failed. While some religious groups practice community service as part of their religious commitment, the vast majority of children do not experience the sense of belonging and meaning that comes when people are regularly involved in organized efforts to help those with less advantages. Although most parents convey this value to their children, it is really only deeds that have an impact.

Committing yourself and your family to regularly helping others in organized projects will not only teach your children to be more concerned about others, it will also teach them social skills, the importance of cooperation, and the value of perseverance and following through. These are all skills that contribute to a high EQ

If you are not a member of a religious or community service group that involves children in at least biweekly community service, there are several good resources to help get you started. These include *The Kids' Guide to Social Responsibility* and *The Helping Hands Handbook.* These and similar books suggest activities such as:

• Working at a soup kitchen.
• Joining an organization to save endangered species.
• Pitching in on neighborhood clean-up projects.
• Reading to elderly people at a nursing home.
• Tutoring young children.
• Making dolls for sick children.

If you contact your local newspaper, you can learn about dozens of worthy projects going on in your community. One will certainly appeal to you and your child. The key factors to remember in making community service a part of your children's lives are:

- Choose something meaningful to you and your children.
- Keep your commitment a priority in your life. Don't let interest fade.
- Participate in the project with your children as much as possible.

EQ SKILLS TO REMEMBER

- In teaching children to care for others, there is no substitute for experience; talking is simply not enough. As we shall see throughout this book, certain EQ skills, particularly those that involve your child's relationships with others, can only effectively be taught to the emotional brain.

- Although the language and logic of the thinking brain are important in teaching values to your child, they will not shape your child's behavior like the feelings of pride and belonging that accompany acts of caring for and helping others.

· 4 ·

Honesty and Integrity

As all parents know, children tell lies almost as early as they begin to talk—sometimes earlier.

Two-and-a-half-year-old Lara, for example, spilled her bowl of cereal when her mother left the room to answer the phone. When her mother returned, she asked in annoyance, "Lara! Did you spill your cereal?" In spite of the fact that no one else was in the room, Lara vigorously shook her head and answered, "No."

It is usually so obvious when young children lie that parents find it hard not to laugh. When Mark's father noticed that a chocolate Easter bunny was suddenly missing its head, he sought out his three-year-old son to explain this mystery. Although Mark's face and hands were covered with chocolate—at seven in the morning—he told his father that he had no idea who had eaten the candy.

Lara and Mark knew what they did was wrong and that it would make their parents angry, but they did not fully understand that lying was also wrong. At two and three, children have neither the cognitive nor the language development to see that there is a direct link between what they say and what they do. To toddlers, behaviors are much more important than words, which often have vague and multiple meanings.

But by four years of age, children begin to understand that lying with the intent to mislead is bad. In fact, most children at this age or slightly older become fanatical about the truth, reacting with moral indignation if they perceive that their parents, brothers, sisters, or friends have in any way misled them. A person's intentions are not as important as the truth or falsity of a particular statement, as in the case of Michael and his father, Jeff.

Jeff: Uh-oh, it looks like it's raining. I'm afraid we won't be able to go to the ball game.

Michael: (age five) You said that we would go today!

Jeff: Yes, I know, but it's raining, and the ball game will be called off.

Michael: (his eyes filling with tears) But you said we would go! You said it! If we don't go, that's lying!

Jeff: No, it's not lying. I can't help it if there is no game. I want to go, but there is no game to go to.

Michael: (now starting to cry) But that's lying. You said we would go, and now you're lying 'cause we can't go.

Most of your children's EQ skills improve as they grow older, but this is not the case when it comes to being truthful. In a study on how children's perceptions of lying change with age, 92 percent of five-year-olds said that lying was always wrong, and 75 percent said that they had never lied. But by age eleven, only 28 percent said that lying was always wrong, and none of the children claimed that they had never told a lie. As children grow older, they begin to differentiate and grade the types of lies that people tell, considering some worse than others. A lie that is told simply to avoid punishment is the worst kind ("I lost my watch, so I couldn't help being late for school."), while a lie told to spare someone's feelings is not so bad ("I really like your new glasses. They make you look smart."). An altruistic lie, which is told to help someone else, is nearly always perceived as forgivable and even honorable ("It's my fault Tommy got dirty. I told him to walk through the mud because it was a shortcut.").

According to Paul Ekman, author of *Why Children Lie*, there are a variety of reasons why children are untruthful, some understandable and some not. Younger children most frequently lie to avoid punishment, to get something they want, or to get admiration from a peer. Adolescents are more likely to lie to protect their privacy ("I just went out, I didn't see anybody."), to test authority ("We're not getting a final in history this semester. You can call Mr. Nathanson if you like!"), or to avoid embarrassment ("They canceled the Halloween dance, so I didn't need to get a date, anyway!").

But while lying is often understandable from a developmental point of view, it can be a problem when children lie habitually or lie about things that are important to their welfare. As Ekman writes, "Lying about serious matters is not a problem just because it makes it more difficult for parents to do their job. Lying erodes closeness and intimacy. Lying breeds distrust, it betrays trust. Lying implies a disregard for the person deceived. It can become nearly impossible to live with someone who lies often."

Studies of children who are chronic liars show that they frequently participate in other forms of antisocial behavior as well, including cheating, stealing, and aggressiveness. This is in part due to the fact that children who lie typically make friends with other children who are dishonest, and they develop a peer group that believes it is acceptable to lie to anyone outside the group. Ekman also points out that children who lie frequently become the victims of a "horn" effect, the opposite of the familiar "halo" effect. When we begin to perceive that our children lie, we unconsciously assume that this behavior is characterological, and we start to expect other forms of antisocial behaviors. In many cases, this becomes a self-fulfilling prophecy, and our children live up to our worst expectations.

It is also worth noting that children of divorce are more susceptible to problems related to honesty and truthfulness. When parents separate, children may lie to their friends about the separation as a way to deny what has happened, avoid embarrassment, or feed their own fantasies that their parents will get back together again. They may lie when confronted by one parent to protect the other, particularly when one begins to date, or they may lie to the stricter parent about lax rules in the more permissive household in an attempt to preserve what they believe are extra privileges.

The more bitter the divorce and the more acrimony between the parents, the more likely children will develop a habit of self-protective lying. This may contribute to why children of divorce more frequently have problems in their adult relationships. If you have been recently divorced, you should be particularly aware of how your actions and choices will affect the moral development of your children.

WHAT YOU CAN DO TO TEACH CHILDREN THE IMPORTANCE OF HONESTY

Research shows that children who lie most are more likely to come from homes in which parents frequently lie. In addition, children who come from homes with minimal supervision or where there is parental rejection are more frequently dishonest.

Although few parents would say they never lie, you should be aware of the direct and indirect effects that lying

Humans have an enormous capacity for self-deception. Parents can help their children face the consequences of their actions by being direct and clear about their expectations.

has on your kids. Certainly, there is never a good reason to lie to your children. This doesn't mean you should tell them everything—there are many things they don't need to know—but there is no need to tell them a fabrication. If something is private or beyond your children's understanding, tell them just that.

Make the importance of honesty a continuous topic of conversation in your home. To help insure that this becomes a part of your child's moral education, read stories that stress honesty, such as in William Bennet's *The Book of Virtues,* or the books recommended in the American Library Association's *Best of the Best for Children.* For an up-to-the-minute listing of value-oriented TV and radio programming, as well as audio and video cassettes, you can look to KIDSNET, a nonprofit clearinghouse for quality educational entertainment. Its recommendations are available on-line through CompuServe.

BUILDING TRUST

Although trust does not usually become a hot subject with children until they are preteens, it is never too early to begin talking about this issue. Trust games were popular in the humanistic psychology movement of the 1970s, and are still part of many warm-up exercises for team-building, therapy, and self-help groups. Some trust-building activities, which also happen to be fun, include:

Leading the Blind (ages seven and up): In this classic trust-building exercise—used for years in building group interdependency in counseling groups, sports teams, and management training—you blindfold your child and lead him around a room. As you go around furniture, avoiding obstacles that children normally take for granted, your child will increasingly depend on your physical guidance. At first, your child may resist the feeling of helplessness and dependency, but gradually he will begin to accept and even enjoy it. The real fun begins when you reverse the roles, and your child or adolescent begins to lead *you* around the room without the ability to see where you are going. Like any skill-building activity, it is important to discuss the skills of trust and interdependence before and after the actual activity.

Backwards Fall (ages five and up): Stand behind your child and instruct him to just fall backward. Catch him under his armpits. Then reverse roles. Your child may be too small to catch your backward fall, but unless there is an extreme size difference, you can usually demonstrate this on your spouse in front of your children. Kids enjoy and learn from seeing their parents trust each other.

The "Secret" Game (ages seven and up): This game is an enjoyable and emotionally challenging way to build trust and encourage openness. Begin by asking each member of the family to write down a secret on a piece of notebook paper. Then each person should fold up the paper, write his or her name on the outside, and put it in a bowl. Each player picks a secret with someone else's name on it.

As all the players hold on to someone else's unopened secret, go around the room and have each player tell of a time when they trusted someone with something important. Then go around again, and each player must tell of a time when someone else betrayed a trust. Players get one point when they respond to each of these statements, but they have the option to "pass" if they like.

For the third round, each player in turn asks the person who wrote the secret he is holding whether it should be read. If the person who wrote the secret responds "no," then it is returned to her unopened. If the person responds "yes," then it is read, and the person who wrote the secret gets a point for talking about it.

RESPECT YOUR CHILD'S PRIVACY

Mary Ann Mason Ekman suggests that just as parents must teach children to respect their privacy, they must also respect the privacy of their children and certainly their adolescents. In a chapter entitled "How Can Parents Cope with Kids' Lies?" in her husband's book, she writes: "One of the greatest strains between parents and children is the child's ever-increasing need to become independent, and therefore more secretive, and the parents' equally strong but opposing need to protect, control and guide." She advises parents to make a checklist of what they really "need to know" and what is appropriate for them "not to know," a list that naturally changes as the child grows older.

You could introduce a checklist—like the one in the table below—to your child of eight or nine, before privacy becomes part of a power struggle. You could use it as a way to broach the issue of your child's right to privacy versus your responsibility to protect and guide. Review it annually, at the beginning of the year, or around your child's birthday. The more trust and openness, the less your children will need to deceive.

EQ POINTS TO REMEMBER

Here are some things to remember in trying to raise a responsible child who cares for and about others and addresses life's challenges with honesty and integrity.

- Teach the value of honesty to children when they are young and be consistent with your message as they grow older. Children's understanding of honesty changes, but yours shouldn't.

- You can make honesty and ethics a topic of conversation from very early on by choosing books and videos to share with your child, playing trust-building games, and understanding your child's changing needs for privacy.

The Children's Privacy Chart			
Date	Age	What Parents Need to Know	Things That Are Private

· 5 ·

The Negative Moral Emotions: Shame and Guilt

When Ambrose Robinson found that his ten-year-old son had taken a candy bar from a convenience store, he made him return to the store and apologize to the clerk as well as to the customers. Having accepted the apology, the clerk tried to give David back the candy, but his father would not let him take it. "He cannot have it," he told the clerk. "It is not his candy." Ambrose then took both David and his brother home and spanked them both—David for the crime and his brother for going along with it.

Twenty years later, David Robinson—the NBA's most valuable player in 1995, a classical pianist, computer whiz, and community activist—recalled, "I'll never forget the feeling I had standing behind the desk after being exposed as a thief. It left a lasting impression on me. That was my father's way of showing me what kind of person I didn't want to become. After that, stealing was no longer an option for me."

This anecdote was recounted by David Robinson in an introduction to his parents' book, *How to Raise an MVP (Most Valuable Person)*. David Robinson shares the belief with his parents that children are more effectively taught the difference between right and wrong in families where parents are strict rather than permissive. Only a generation ago, most parents might have reacted very similarly to Mr. Robinson upon finding that their child had stolen even something of small value, but in the last twenty years, there has been a steady movement toward avoiding punishment for all but the most egregious misbehavior. As Brown University professor William Damon notes in his book *Greater Expectations: Overcoming the Culture of Indulgence in Our Homes and Schools*, "We are living in a time when the 'child-centered' ethic has become a justification for every sort of overindulgent child-rearing practice. [This philosophy] has spawned a host of permissive doctrines that have dissuaded parents from enforcing consistent discipline in the home . . . [The] once valuable premise of child-centeredness has been used (or misused) to encourage self-centeredness in today's children and adolescents."

As we shall see in this chapter, our understanding of emotional intelligence supports Damon's viewpoint that our culture has moved too far in trying to protect children from things that they do not need to be protected from. To put it simply, too much understanding and sympathy toward some children may be as harmful as too little.

Some people trace the overindulgence of the current generation of middle-class American children to the 1945 publication of Benjamin Spock's book *Baby and Child Care*. Spock based his advice on the then popular psychoanalytic theories of Sigmund Freud and other progressive thinkers of the day such as John Dewey and William Kilpatrick, all of whom were reacting to the restrictive, repressed, and rigid child-rearing practices of the Victorian Age. It was their belief that many, if not all, neurotic problems could be traced back to parents who withheld love and affection and/or suppressed their children's "normal" sexual and aggressive impulses.

Judging from the popularity of Spock's book, which sold over 24 million copies during the three decades that the baby boomers were growing up, it was clear that this was a message that parents recovering from the war years wanted to hear. Before the publication of Spock's baby book, there was still a widespread belief that the rigid control of children was a good thing. The Children's Bureau, a federal agency that gave advice to mothers on child-rearing, advocated that babies should be fed, bathed, and tucked in to bed on a precise, minute-to-minute schedule, regardless of their age or individual needs.

As Spock's babies grew up and became young, rebellious adults in the 1960s and 1970s, the shift toward a more permissive lifestyle served to reinforce the benefits of permissive parenting. The human potential movement, led by such idealists as Carl Rogers and Virginia Axline, purported that each individual had the right and power to fulfill themselves in their own way. Based on respect and faith in the capacity of the individual, it was believed that the inherent goodness of children would invariably be revealed once restrictive obstacles and expectations were removed and children were allowed to express their feelings and needs.

In retrospect, this belief in the inherent goodness of the individual appears to have been naive, and yet today's children are still being raised on what we know are mistaken principles, as exemplified by many advocates of the self-esteem movement. Martin Seligman, a prominent psychologist who has spent decades studying the life-shattering effects of depression, criticizes those who believe that increasing a child's self-esteem can cure such epidemic social ills as teenage pregnancy, drug use, and gang warfare. As an example of this misplaced Pollyannaism, he points to the California legislature's establishment of a self-esteem task force to promote self-esteem throughout the state school system and actress Shirley MacLaine's plea to the president of the United States to establish a cabinet level department of self-esteem.

But from what we are now learning about emotional intelligence, the most significant mistake made by advocates of permissive parenting and education has been to unwittingly make "good emotions" the heroes of our psyche and "bad emotions" the villains. From an evolutionary perspective, every human emotion has developed for a purpose, and removing the negative emotions from our understanding of child development is like removing one of the primary colors from a painter's palette—not only is that single color lost, but millions of shades of complementary colors are also lost. In addition, as we shall see, negative emotions like shame and guilt are indisputably more powerful than positive ones in terms of emotional learning and behavioral change.

THE VALUE OF SHAME

Although Americans are not comfortable with the emotions of shame and guilt and mental health professionals have traditionally viewed them as impediments to mental health, we cannot deny their effectiveness in guiding children toward prosocial behaviors. Shame is defined as a form of extreme embarrassment that results when children feel they have failed to act according to other people's expectations. Guilt occurs when children fail to meet their internalized standards of behavior.

Shame makes an indelible impression on children, much more so than incidents involving positive feelings. According to theories of neuroanatomy, the extreme emotions brought on by shame short-circuit the normal ways that the brain registers information and stores memories. Extreme emotions appear to detour around the thinking part of the brain, the cortex, and electrify the emotional control center of the brain, the amygdala, which is the seat of emotional learning and memory. Thus any experience in which extreme emotion is involved will have both a more significant immediate effect on your children's behavior as well as a more long-term effect on their personality development.

If you are unconvinced of the power of negative emotions such as shame or guilt, try this simple experiment. On your watch, time how long it takes you to recall three incidents from your childhood in which you were embarrassed to the point of shame. Did you have an "accident" in front of your classmates or friends? Did your parents say or do something to shame you? Did other children tease you about your appearance? Rate each incident on a scale of one to ten, with ten being very powerful and one being very weak. Now remember three positive incidents in which you were proud of something you did to help someone. Again, rate each incident on a one to ten scale. If you are like most people, it took you three to five times longer to recall positive emotional experiences, and you rated their power as less than a third of the negative emotion.

In many cultures, shame is an appropriate way of punishing antisocial behavior. Although we may look down on societies that practice public shaming, we must also recognize that these cultures tend to have significantly less crime and social unrest. Undoubtedly, part of our discomfort in using shaming in our child-rearing techniques is our unfamiliarity

Making your child feel ashamed of his or her antisocial behavior is a legitimate way to change this behavior. The "negative" moral emotions of shame and guilt can be used constructively to shape your child's moral behavior.

with it. In countries like Japan, shame and dishonor are integrated into the traditional values and morals of the country. Confessions, even humiliating ones, are seen as the most direct route to repentance.

Given the rise in senseless and heartless crime in the United States, particularly among teenagers, some members of our justice system are beginning to reconsider shaming as both a punishment and a deterrent to victimless crimes. For example, District Judge Ted Poe of Houston, famous for his unusual sentences, made a teenager who had vandalized thirteen schools go back to each one and apologize to an assembly of the student body, answering questions about why he did it. In other jurisdictions around the country, men who have been convicted of frequenting prostitutes have been ordered to literally sweep up the crime-ridden area of town where they were caught; men who were convicted of failing to pay child support have had their names and faces posted in local post offices and even on the Internet; and convicted spouse abusers were made to apologize to their wives in court, as well as in front of women's groups.

USING SHAME

Should shaming be considered as part of our normal child-rearing practices? Can "negative" moral emotions be reintroduced into our culture to address our moral crisis? The answer to both of these questions would be "yes" in two cases:

1. Shame should be invoked when a child has no emotional reaction after doing something of which he should be ashamed.
2. Shame should be considered as a legitimate behavior-changing strategy when less dramatic forms of discipline have failed.

William Damon, in his book *The Moral Child*, gives one example of how shame might be used with children who do not appear to have acquired emotional empathy. Damon describes a program designed to enhance empathic motivation in delinquents who showed little or no remorse for their crimes, even when their victims were physically injured. In a small group setting, each delinquent is required to discuss his antisocial behavior and face disapproving feedback from his peers and the therapists leading the group. Their intentions are to provoke shame and even disgust. As Damon notes, "Such methods are effective because they leave an emotional as well as a cognitive legacy for their participants."

John Braithwaite, a professor of social science at the Australian National University in Canberra and an advocate of shame as a punishment for antisocial acts, notes an important caveat to using shame as a punishment. Braithwaite explains that shaming can only be considered humane if it not only expresses community disapproval, but also includes forgiveness and reacceptance. He uses the term "reintegrative shaming" to emphasize that this form of punishment should be neither an expression of anger nor a form of retribution, but rather a ritual that elicits the appropriate level of remorse in the wrongdoer and forgiveness in the community or family.

THE USES OF GUILT

Based on internal standards and expectations rather than on being "caught" by others, guilt is actually a more powerful and longer lasting moral motivator than shame. Although comedians bemoan the lifelong neurotic effects of guilt, most psychologists would agree that guilt has its uses. Donald Miller and Guy Swanson, in their studies of children's responses to illustrated pictures, distinguish neurotic guilt, in which one punishes oneself for unwarranted and irrational reasons, from interpersonal guilt, which arises out of concern for another's opinion and serves to reduce self-criticism and enhance a child's personal relationships.

Many studies suggest that interpersonal guilt, what we might truly call the "conscience," is more effective at controlling children's behaviors than any external threat or fear. In fact, when we can stimulate our children's guilt, they are apt to have an even stricter interpretation of rules and the consequences for breaking them than we might have.

For example, when Bruce, age seven, was caught cheating on a spelling test, his parents asked him how he thought he should be punished. In tears, Bruce suggested that he should have his video games taken away for three months, that he should not be allowed to watch TV for one month, and that he should have to do extra chores until the school year was over. This was a much more severe punishment than his parents had envisioned, but on the advice of the school counselor, they accepted it.

The research of Donald McAbe, a professor at Rutgers University, suggests that guilt continues to be more effective than fear of punishment in influencing moral behavior well past childhood. In a study of cheating conducted at competitive private colleges, McAbe reports that as many as 78 percent of students admit to cheating at least once. But in schools with an honor code—where students sign a pledge not to cheat, take tests without proctors, and have input into how to deal with campus dishonesty—this statistic drops to 57 percent.

HOW AND WHEN TO USE THE "NEGATIVE" MORAL EMOTIONS APPROPRIATELY

If we accept the fact that shame and guilt are normal and powerful aspects of our children's emotional lives, the question then becomes one of how to use them to foster our youngsters' moral development without causing undue harm. The following are some general recommendations that show how you can use shame and guilt constructively to guide your children toward honest, ethical, and caring adulthood.

1. Have consistent rules and consistent punishments when the rules are broken. Make sure that your punishments are fair, immediate, and effective.

2. When children over the age of ten break important rules and seem undeterred by your punishments, ask them to list their own punishment for each rule. Then agree on a neutral mediator (such as a friend of the family, aunt, or uncle) to determine which punishments will work best. If he or she is willing, you could even ask the mediator to monitor the punishment. In most cases, this will stimulate your children to have higher expectations for themselves and make them more likely to live up to those expectations.

3. React more harshly when your child does something that hurts someone else. For example, if your child doesn't hand in a report on time, she hurts her chance of getting a good grade, but it is only she who must suffer the consequences. On the other hand, if she comes home two hours past her curfew, she causes you extreme distress, and this calls for more extreme measures. If your child's irresponsible actions hurt someone else, don't be afraid to express your own strong feelings along with an appropriate punishment. If this upsets your child, don't be quick to comfort her. Feeling guilty will prevent her from being thoughtless the next time.

4. Make a big deal out of apologies. Written apologies should be combined with oral ones. If your child's apology is insincere, don't give up easily, but rather keep

increasing the requirements of the apology until he responds emotionally.

My client Arthur's eight-year-old son was rude to him whenever Arthur made any request. For instance, when Arthur said, "It's time to clean up and get ready for dinner," Kevin would reply, "Why should I? I'll eat dinner when I'm ready."

I advised Arthur to have Kevin write out the sentence "I will show respect to my father and mother" the next time he was rude. The second time, Kevin had to write the sentence twice. Then three times, and so on. While he wrote this, I instructed Arthur to stand resolute behind Kevin's desk and make sure that he finished each assignment completely and legibly.

Arthur reported that it took ten incidents for Kevin to start showing some emotion to this punishment. But as he was midway through the ten sentences, he began to weep and fell into his dad's arms. Arthur did not comfort his son, but led him back to finish his writing. After that, the boy's behavior drastically improved in all areas.

For the past thirty years, mental health professionals and educators have for the most part been reluctant to recommend the negative emotions—shame and guilt—as a way to raise healthy children. They have seen far too many cases of emotional abuse, sometimes with results even worse than physical abuse, to feel comfortable even suggesting that parents consider these strategies. But from a viewpoint of emotional intelligence, any excess may do harm to a child. Children have different emotional strengths and weaknesses, just as they have different cognitive or academic strengths and weaknesses. The rule of thumb in raising children should always measure what is in their best interests and what can be done to insure their development into happy, successful, and responsible adults.

EQ POINTS TO REMEMBER

- Shame and guilt are not emotional villains. When used appropriately, they are important ways that parents can teach children moral values.

- The appropriate use of shame and guilt will depend on the temperament of your child, but your use of them can reintegrate your child into the support of the family.

PART 3

EQ Thinking Skills

Unlike any other species of animals, humans have the capacity to manufacture and control their emotions by simply thinking. The development of the neocortex, the part of the brain that controls language and logical thought, allows us to have thoughts about our feelings and to actually change the feelings themselves. If a student perceives that he is anxious before taking a test, he can think of ways to calm himself. If a sprinter feels that she is lethargic and unmotivated, she has the ability to think herself into focus and quicken her reaction time as she bolts off the starting block.

For almost a century, psychotherapists have known that the mind can make us physically ill, and they have developed numerous methods to reverse this process. We are now finding that the thinking part of our brain can *prevent* both physical *and* emotional problems. Anyone can learn these techniques, without years of extensive therapy.

The techniques I discuss in the following three chapters are culled from some of the most exciting findings in modern psychology. As a group, they are classified as cognitive therapies, because they are based on the assumption that our thoughts, or cognitions, are the easiest way to change the way we feel.

Many of the theories and strategies I present in this chapter have been developed for high-risk children, but today, there are few children who don't fall into this category. Before we became an industrial society, parents taught their children to distinguish plants they could eat from ones that would harm them, how to shoe a horse, or how to cultivate a field. Children today need different survival skills. Parents need to teach their children to use their intellect as well as their emotional and social skills to cope with an increasingly complex array of personal, family, and societal stresses.

▪ 6 ▪

Realistic Thinking

The human capacity for self-deception is almost boundless, making it difficult to overestimate the importance of teaching children reality-oriented thinking. Our emotional brain appears to have the ability to don a suit of armor on order to protect its most fervent desires from attack by the logical brain. As a result, we are continually doing things that we shouldn't. For example, we know that cigarette smoking is associated with debilitating disease and early death, and yet 23 percent of the population still smokes and nearly 3,000 children and teenagers take up the habit every day. We know that wearing a seat belt will make it more likely that we survive a collision, and yet nearly a third of drivers feel that it is too much of an inconvenience. Anyone who has ever entered a relationship he knew was self-destructive, gotten into a car with a driver he knew was intoxicated, or simply spent more money than he could afford has practiced the fine-tuned art of self-deception.

The fact that we so frequently do things that are not in our best interest suggests that evolution has taken a wrong turn in developing the so-called "logical" part of our brains. Fortunately, that can be remedied. Children can be raised to act both in their own best interest and in the interest of others.

LIVING IN DENIAL

Mariane really hated her new school. She would rather do almost anything than study, and talking to her boyfriend, David, on the phone for four or five hours a night was certainly more interesting than world history. Her teachers knew that Mariane wasn't motivated to learn and graded her accordingly.

Mariane knew that her parents would be very disappointed when they saw her grades. They would probably punish her severely, so she had a simple solution: She hid her report card when it came home in the mail. Strangely enough, this seemed to work. With three children in three different schools and demanding, stressful jobs, Mariane's parents missed the fact that she never got a report card.

Then on May 10, just a month before the end of school, the principal called Mariane's parents to see why they had not responded to his letters. The resulting meeting was a shock for Mariane's parents and a signal that denial had ceased to work for the family.

We frequently conspire unconsciously with our children to avoid a painful truth—even when faced with hard facts. For example, in August of 1996, the findings of a government sponsored survey showed that 10.9 percent of teenagers admitted to using drugs, an alarming 105 percent increase from 1992. This included a 183 percent increase in the monthly use of LSD and other hallucinogens and a 166 percent increase in monthly cocaine use.

Some experts blame this alarming increase on "permissive and lax" parents who used drugs themselves as teenagers and reason that since they went on to lead productive lives, why make a big deal out of the "recreational" drug and alcohol use of their own teenagers. But this reasoning, what some may see as a justification for being permissive, does not take into account the more sobering statistics regarding early drug use. During the same period of increased drug use, there was a 96 percent increase in emergency room admissions related to marijuana use for twelve- to seventeen-year-olds and a 58 percent increase in emergency room admissions related to heroin use.

As humans, we are all subject to denial and rationalization. Millions of otherwise reasonable adults get into cars each day without buckling their seat belts, or they light up a cigarette and pretend that there are no adverse health effects to just one cigarette. Some of us are more prone to hide our heads in the sand than others, but to the extent that we want to raise physically and emotionally healthy children, we must learn to face reality.

CLEARING OUR HEADS

The opposite of self-deception is realistic thinking—seeing the world exactly as it is and responding with appropriate decisions and behaviors. Many of us neglect to teach our children this EQ skill, and may even teach them the opposite. By trying to protect our children from the "harsh realities" of life, we are really reinforcing this denial.

Rather than trying to protect children from a problem, we can help them most by being truthful, no matter how painful the situation may be. As we explain the situation to our kids, detailing the facts from our point of view, they learn that we have the emotional strength to examine and cope with even the most distressing situation. This implicitly sends the message that they can do the same.

For example, in one of the most widely read self-help books for children, *The Boys and Girls Book About Divorce*, child psychiatrist Richard A. Gardner explains that kids have to rely on themselves to cope with their parents' divorce rather than assume that their parents will always act in their best interest. Current research suggests that his advice should be taken.

After studying sixty families with 131 children for up to twenty years following a divorce, Judith Wallerstein found that many parents delude themselves into thinking that divorce is a temporary crisis, resolved after one or two years. But Wallerstein's research suggests that this is not the case. Divorce has lasting effects on children that can cause trauma long after they have grown, even when there did not seem to be any serious problems at the time of the divorce. Wallerstein refers to this as the "sleeper effect."

According to this study, many of the problems that children carry with them are due to the "overburdened child" syndrome. At the time of a divorce, parents frequently have a difficult time in separating their children's needs from their own, giving less time, less discipline, and generally being less sensitive to their children, even though they often report that they have never felt closer to them. Wallerstein reports that in the tenth year of her study, 25 percent of the mothers and 20 percent of the fathers had not gotten their lives back together after a decade of divorce. A diminished level of parenting also continued. The children in approximately 15 percent of families were judged to be "overburdened" by their parents' inability to fulfill their roles as parents or even to take care of their own needs. These children were then deemed at risk for serious psychological problems, often mirroring their parents' dysfunction.

In his book, Richard Gardner tells his young readers that while most parents love their children very much and try to do the right things for them during a divorce, parents sometimes fail—they do and say things that are not good for their children, and children must learn to recognize this and make decisions that are in their own best interests.

For example, the Martinellis went to the school counselor to discuss how they could best tell their six-year-old daughter Tina about their divorce. Loving parents, they both wanted to say and do the right things. The school counselor gave them several books to read and went over some of the most important things to say and not to say. She reassured them that Tina would be fine if they continued to work together for her best interests.

It was only two weeks later that the incidents began. Mr. and Mrs. Martinelli screamed at each other in the school parking lot. Mr. Martinelli pulled Tina crying out of his wife's car. There were nightly calls to the teacher, threats of not returning Tina after a visit, and more. With each incident, the Martinellis met again with the school counselor, still for the most part seeming reasonable and concerned about their daughter. When the counselor decided it would be best to begin meetings with Tina herself, Tina came to the sessions reluctantly. She said nothing. She told the counselor, "I just don't want to think about it."

Gardner tells children that some parents even confuse their children about their love for them. He explains that parents may *want* to love their children, they may *say* that they love them, but their actions say something else. Gardner advises children:

Most parents love their children very much. [But] sometimes parents who love their children very little or not at all say that their love for them is very great. This can be very confusing. For this reason, what a person says is sometimes not a good way of learning whether he really loves you.

The father [who is no longer living at home] usually loves his children very much, wishes he could live with them, and is very, very sorry to leave them. However, a few fathers who leave home really don't love their children, or they love them very little.

Sometimes a divorced father doesn't love his children, and yet the mother tells the children that he loves them even though she knows that he doesn't. . . . She really thinks that she's doing the best thing for her children by telling them that their father loves them even though she knows that it isn't true.

Gardner teaches children that they can find out for themselves whether a parent loves them or not by realistically looking at what they do, not just what they say. He tells them to:

- Look at how much your parents *try* to be with you. Sometimes parents can't be with you for good reasons, but they should let you know that they are making a real effort.

- Look at how much your parents go out of their way to help you when you're in trouble and how much concern and sympathy they show when you're sick or hurt.

- See if your parents are pleased with the things that you learn and do. Parents who love their children are proud of them and let others know about their children's accomplishments.

- See how much your parents enjoy doing things with you. When you love someone, you enjoy doing things with that person.

- See how your parents act when they are mad at you. All parents get angry at their children some of the time, but if they are angry at you *most* of the time, every day, then they might not love you in the way that children need to be loved.

- See how much your parents like to hold you and hug you. As you get older, parents are not as physical with their children, but everyone needs to be hugged and held sometimes, and that is an important job of parents.

Gardner does not believe that a child's judgment can be infallible, but he does believe that children must learn to evaluate their situation realistically and act in their own best interest. Children cannot learn this if parents are secretive or dishonest about real problems. He warns parents:

- Don't hide your feelings.
- Don't hide your faults.
- Don't be afraid to tell children the truth.

WHAT YOU CAN DO TO RAISE CHILDREN WHO CAN LOOK AFTER THEIR OWN INTERESTS BY THINKING REALISTICALLY

Clearly, the most important thing you can do to help your child develop a pattern of realistic thinking is to be honest and truthful. There is no benefit in protecting children from stress and unavoidable pain; you are actually doing them a disservice.

But modeling realistic thinking and truthfulness can only be effective when you take the time to talk to your child. As I have noted in Chapter 2, American parents spend less and less time simply talking to their children. Families watch TV while they eat their dinners. In the car, they listen to the radio or make sure that their kids have something "to do" while they drive. In 1982 the perennial puppeteer, Shari Lewis, reflected the mood of the country when she wrote a book that she perceived to be an answer for the harried parent, *The One-Minute Bedtime Story*, followed by other "one-minute" books such as *The One-Minute Bible Story* and *The One-Minute Scary Story*.

Helping parents do things faster is not really the answer to what children need. The most critical ingredient for raising an emotionally intelligent child is your time. Ms. Lewis's point of view is particularly distressing, considering the importance of storytelling to a child's development. For decades, psychologists have promoted the positive effects of reading and telling children stories. It is a particularly good way to teach children realistic thinking, as stories can show children how people realistically solve their problems.

Many people don't realize the extent to which stories influence our behavior and even shape our culture. Think about how stories from the Bible teach the fundamentals of religion and rules for conduct. Think of the fables and parables that molded your values. Think of how stories about your national, cultural, or family history have shaped your attitudes about yourself and others.

Stories are particularly effective in influencing the way our children think and behave, because they like to hear or read them over and over again. This repetition, combined with your children's imaginations and the inestimable power of your presence, makes stories one of the best ways to influence their thinking.

In his book *The Competent Child*, psychologist Joseph Strayhorn, Jr. teaches parents to make up what he calls "positive modeling stories" that address their child's real-life problems or concerns. In these stories, the protagonist, who has similar traits to the child, models realistic thinking and problem solving in her thoughts, feelings, and behaviors. The protagonist may or may not be externally rewarded for exhibiting particular psychological skills, but she always rewards herself for being internally motivated.

Although some parents are natural storytellers and can spontaneously invent positive modeling stories once they understand the basic principles, most parents will wish to write down stories they can read to their children. In creating a positive modeling storybook, you should try to use the format and vocabulary level of other books your child enjoys reading or hearing. For younger children, you can illustrate the book with either drawings, computer clip art (see Chapter 24 to learn how computers can help you make professional-looking storybooks or stories where the characters actually move and talk), or photographs from an instant camera. Your children will enjoy participating in the design of the book, as well.

In choosing a theme for the book, consider a story line that is similar to, but not exactly like, a problem your child might be having. If you write a story using your child's name and exact situation, she may become anxious and upset, particularly if the problem is a serious one. As a result, she will probably express her anxiety by showing disinterest or boredom with the story, making it a frustrating experience for both of you.

Instead, write the story so that it is about someone "like" your child, creating a metaphor for her situation. The hero of the story could be another child, an animal, a being from outer space—any character with whom your child might identify.

In creating a positive modeling story, it is usually best to select a theme that contains familiar elements to your child. The following are some examples for story lines that have been written for children with common childhood problems. This synopsis was written for Annie, a six-year-old who was afraid of dogs:

> Barry lives next door to a very mean dog who barks all the time. He has heard that the dog bites children and even tried to eat a baby! Barry gets a book on dogs and reads about this kind of dog. He meets the dog and his owner when they are out for a walk and actually pets him! He learns from the dog's owner why dogs bark, what makes them mad, and what to do if a dog is bothering him.

When Miguel's family was displaced by a hurricane that severely damaged their home, the story summarized below offered the four-year-old some solace:

> Rover is a dog who lives in southern Florida, where there are many hurricanes. When his doghouse blew away, Rover had to go to a temporary shelter for homeless dogs. But Rover saw that there were other dogs at the shelter who temporarily had no homes, and he liked to chew a bone or two with them and run around the shelter yard. After a few weeks, his owners decided to move to a new home with a new doghouse. Rover was sad to leave his

new friends at the shelter, but thought about the friends he might meet in his new neighborhood.

This synopsis of a story was written for Stephanie, age nine, whose parents were in the middle of a raging divorce. It illustrates how some stories need to be more subtle, more removed from the direct experience of the child, so that they can be told without raising too much anxiety.

Diana lives in a faraway country, where there is always a war going on between the Purple People and the Green People. Diana lives with her parents, but one is purple and the other is green (Diana is exactly half purple and half green.) Since Diana cannot change her color or the colors of her parents, and because she cannot stop the war, she finds ways to cope with the situation and make peace with herself.

Here's the synopsis of a story for Natalia, age eleven, who was teased because she is overweight:

Helen Keller, Stevie Wonder, and Ray Charles meet in a bus station on their way to New York City. They discuss what it is like to be blind and look different from other people. They talk about times that were really bad for them and how they got through them. They talk so passionately that they miss their bus, but they catch the next one. They are happy to know they have each other as friends.

Once upon a time, there was a little girl, a lot like you...

Making up or reading positive modeling stories to your children is one of the simplest and most effective ways to teach them the importance of realistic thinking.

This technique is primarily used between the ages of three and ten, when children like to have stories read or told to them. When making up and reading these stories, Strayhorn suggests that parents create a friendly environment by:

- Picking a time when there are no significant distractions for the child.
- Picking a story that fits their child's attention span.
- Reading with enthusiasm and drama.

- Giving the child frequent eye contact while reading.

- Encouraging their child to interrupt with comments or questions.

- Making the time mutually gratifying rather than a chore.

- Encouraging younger children to be physically close.

- Using a tone of approval that signals the end of the story.

- Having their child discuss alternative endings to help him explore his own reasoning process.

Stories that you make up are always the most effective with children. However, if you are not comfortable creating stories, there are an ever-increasing number of positive modeling books for children about such diverse subjects as coping with fears, divorce, the illness of a parent, and so on. Many school and public libraries keep a list of these books for parents to borrow.

EQ POINTS TO REMEMBER

- Realistic thinking is the opposite of self-deception.

- Modeling stories are probably the best way to teach this skill, whether you read from books already available or stories that you make up.

- Your children will ultimately learn to think realistically about their problems or concerns if you do the same. Do not hide the truth from your children, even if it is painful.

Optimism: An Antidote to Depression and Underachievement

Sharon, a poised six-year-old, showed up for a photography shoot fifteen minutes early. "You know what," she told the photographer on being introduced, not waiting for an answer, "I went to Disney World last year and rode every ride twice!"

"That's nice," responded the advertising executive who was coordinating the shoot. "Now why don't you sit over here? We're going to test the lighting."

"You know what," Sharon said as she took her place in front of the lights, "I started modeling when I was just four, 'cause my sister Holly did it, and I saw her do it, and I said I want to do it, and my mom said, 'Okay, you can do it,' and so now I do it, but Holly doesn't."

"Oh?" responded the executive, caught up in the enthusiasm of this chatty girl. "Do you like modeling?"

"I love it," Sharon replied, her face lighting up.

"That's the look I want," said the photographer, and somehow Sharon was able to keep the same smile while she continued to talk.

"I love it," she repeated. "I got to go to New York, and Mommy took me to a play, and I always meet people, and they take my picture, and I'm going to be in a real commercial, too. Holly doesn't like to do it anymore, and Mommy and me go together."

Optimism is more than just positive thinking. It is a *habit* of positive thinking or, as the Random House Dictionary defines it, "a disposition or tendency to look on the more favorable side of events or conditions and to expect the most favorable outcome."

Optimistic children like Sharon are a joy to be around. Their zest and zeal is contagious. But according to psychologist Martin Seligman, author of *The Optimistic Child*, optimism is much more than just an engaging personality trait. It may actually be a kind of psychological immunization against a host of life's problems. Seligman writes that in more than 1,000 studies—involving more than half a million children and adults—optimistic people were shown to be less frequently depressed, more successful in school and on the job, and, surprisingly, even physically healthier than pessimistic people. Perhaps most importantly, even if a child is not born with an optimistic disposition, optimism is an EQ skill that can be learned.

Seligman notes that until recently America was a nation of optimists: "The first half of the nineteenth century was the great age of social reform, whose cornerstone was the optimistic belief that humans could change and improve ... Waves of immigrants found an endless frontier, and 'rags to riches' was not for them an empty dream. Nineteenth-century optimists created the institution of universal schooling, founded public libraries, freed the slaves, rehabilitated the insane, and fought for women's suffrage."

Seligman believes that pessimism came into vogue initially as a reaction to the postwar boosterism of the 1950s, but was fed in the 1960s by the assassinations of some of our most hopeful leaders, Watergate, and, of course, the Vietnam War.

OPTIMISTIC VS. PESSIMISTIC THOUGHTS

In order to teach your child to be more optimistic, you must first distinguish between pessimistic and optimistic thoughts. According to Seligman, the major difference is the way that optimists and pessimists explain the causes of both good and bad events.

The optimist believes that positive, happy events are explained by things that are *permanent* (they will keep happening over time) and *pervasive* (they will keep happening in different situations). The optimist also takes the appropriate responsibility for making good things happen. If something bad happens, he sees it as temporary and specific to that situation, and he is realistic about whether he has caused the bad event.

> Andy is an optimistic child. When he found out that his family was going to move for the third time in three years, he was understandably upset. He liked his school, his friends, and his house, which was only two blocks from the community pool. But after some initial complaining, he started thinking about his new home, which was just one hour away from Orlando, Florida, home of Disney World, Epcot Center, and other great amusement parks.
>
> Andy knew his father had to move because of his job, not because of anything anyone had done. He also knew that his family was "good at moving."

They would keep in touch with old friends, and they always had a big party to meet new neighbors within a week of their arrival. Andy decided to use his experiences as a basis for an English essay. He called it "On the Move."

The pessimist thinks in opposite terms: Good events are *temporary*, bad events are *permanent*; good events are the result of luck or happenstance, bad events are more predictable. The pessimist also makes mistakes in assigning blame. He will tend to either blame himself for everything bad that happens or blame everyone else.

A pessimist may also be predisposed to "catastrophizing." While being prepared for the worst-case scenario is appropriate in dire circumstances, it is not appropriate in day-to-day life. The child who cries and sulks because she did not make the basketball team or her parents won't let her pierce her ears is deliberately distorting the significance of these events and synchronizing her emotional response to her distortion rather than reality. If you respond to your child's pessimistic view of the world rather than the logical one, you may reinforce her tendency to view events as bleakly as possible.

THE DANGER OF PESSIMISM

To Seligman, pessimism is not just a negative style of thinking, but a symptom of what he considers to be one of the greatest health threats to our children today: an "epidemic of depression." Basing his conclusions on four studies that gathered information from more than 16,000 people of every age, Seligman explains that, compared to people born in the first third of this century, a child today is ten times more likely to be seriously depressed. Even more disturbing, serious depression seems to be occurring earlier in the life cycle. He cites the findings of a survey of 3,000 nine- to fourteen-year-olds in which 9 percent of the children were determined to have a full-blown depressive disorder.

Fortunately, there is strong scientific evidence that pessimism and even depression can be changed by literally teaching children (or adolescents and adults) new ways of thinking. Aaron Beck and his colleagues at the University of Pennsylvania were the first to develop a systematic therapeutic program proving that the logical mind can be trained to control the emotional mind.

Beck believes that depressed people develop a habit of thinking that the future is bleak. He found that teaching patients to think differently diminishes their depressive symptoms.

Expanding on Beck's system of treating depression, Seligman and his team at the Penn Prevention Program at the University of Pennsylvania developed a twelve-week program to treat children at risk for depression. The Penn program taught these children different ways to think about themselves and new ways to solve interpersonal problems. It had an immediate effect. Before the program, 24 percent of the children in the prevention group and 24 percent of the children in the control group showed moderate to severe depressive symptoms. Immediately after the program, the prevention group was down to a 13 percent rate of depression, while the control group stayed about the same.

Bearing in mind that prevention was the major goal of the program, its real value had to be measured by its long-term effects. At a two-year follow-up, although 24 percent of the children in the prevention group began to show moderate to severe symptoms, twice as many in the control group—46 percent—were now symptomatic. In other words, the Penn program reduced the number of children who would have predictably developed depressive symptoms by 100 percent.

THE ADVANTAGES OF OPTIMISM

Fighting depression is only one of the benefits of teaching your child to be more optimistic; optimistic children are also more successful in school than their pessimistic peers.

> Teyonka Parker was named to *USA Today*'s All-Star Third Team in May of 1996. She graduated from the California Academy of Mathematics and Science with a 3.86 average, planning to attend prestigious Stanford University. Teyonka was also recognized for her work with inner-city youth and school leadership.
>
> But her accomplishments throughout high school can only be appreciated in the context of what she had to overcome. Her mother was addicted to crack, so Teyonka lived with a succession of relatives, shuttled from Mississippi to San Diego to Chicago and finally to Los Angeles. Of her three older brothers, two were serving time in prison on drug charges while she was a senior in high school.
>
> According to those around her, what distinguished Teyonka from other disadvantaged children who are much less successful was her attitude—a fierce determination to succeed. To Teyonka, adversity is simply an enemy to defeat. As she explained to a reporter: "If I had been born with a silver spoon in my mouth, I wouldn't have anything to overcome. I'd be walking along instead of striving along." But no words could be clearer than

Teyonka's last line on her application to Stanford: "Through my diligence, commitment and volition, I will take the world by storm."

HOW YOU CAN RAISE AN OPTIMISTIC CHILD

Optimism can be taught. Here are some guidelines and activities you can start with today.

Consider How You Criticize

Consider how you criticize your children. Seligman points out that there are right and wrong ways to criticize. This can have a significant effect on whether your child becomes optimistic or pessimistic.

The first rule in criticizing your child is to be accurate. Seligman writes: "Exaggerated blame produces guilt and shame beyond what is necessary to galvanize the child to change. But no blame at all erodes responsibility and nullifies the will to change."

Secondly, develop an optimistic explanatory style: Explain problems in realistic terms where the cause is seen as specific and changeable.

Take, for example, eight-year-old Suzie, who left her room a mess in spite of three requests by her parents to clean it up before going on a picnic with friends. Her parents were particularly upset, because they were showing the house to a real estate agent that morning. They had to scramble to clean up the room for her.

On Suzie's return that afternoon, her mother was visibly upset, and immediately took her daughter to her bedroom to explain why she was angry. Here are two versions of what Suzie's mother said. The first reflects an optimistic explanatory style, the second a pessimistic one.

Optimistic Style

"Suzie, you did something that really inconvenienced your father and me, and we are very mad." (Her mother's criticism is specific. She describes her feelings accurately.)

"We spoke to you three times about cleaning up your room, but each time you put it off." (Her mother describes the incident accurately and puts Suzie's problem in temporary terms.)

"Since you didn't clean up your room, and we had a real estate agent coming over, we had to clean it ourselves, which kept us from doing other important things. It is your responsibility to keep your room clean, not ours." (Her mother explains exactly what happened—the cause of the problem and the effect. She places blame correctly.)

"I'd like you to stay in your room for fifteen minutes and think about what I've said. Then I want you to tell me what you can do so that your room will stay neat and this won't happen again. Write down at least three ways to solve this problem." (This is a realistic period of time for an eight-year-old to ponder a problem. Suzie's mother has created a specific task for Suzie to master as a way to put closure on this problem.)

Pessimistic Style

"Why are you always so inconsiderate? I'm furious at your behavior!" (The word "always" implies that the problem is global and will never change. The emotional reaction is exaggerated and will produce too much guilt.)

"I told you a million times to keep your room clean, but you never listen! What is the matter with you?" (Suzie's mother describes the problem as pervasive—"a million times"—as well as global—"you never listen"—in order to induce guilt.

She further implies that there is something permanently or characterologically wrong with her child.)

"The real estate agent came over this morning and it was nearly a disaster! They say the first impression someone gets of a house can make all the difference in the world. You could have blown us getting a good agent! That kind of thing can knock thousands of dollars off the sale of a house! This could mean that we can't afford the new house!" (Suzie's mother describes the problem in catastrophic terms. She implies that

When you criticize or reprimand your children, you are influencing whether they will see the world optimistically or pessimistically.

Suzie's single inconsiderate act could wreak havoc on the family's well-being.)

"Now I want you to stay in your room and think about what you've done." (The punishment is unclear and nonspecific. This gives Suzie time to brood and feel guilty. There is no opportunity for her to learn or do anything to remedy her mistake.)

Using Yourself as a Model

Your children will model themselves after your behavior—they will absorb both your good and bad points. If you are a pessimist, your children may think this way, too. If you want them to derive the benefits of optimistic thinking, then you must change the way you think.

It is not easy to change the way you think, but it can be done if you understand that pessimistic thinking is a habit and treat it as such. You can use the form below to practice changing negative thoughts into realistic positive ones. The middle column will help you identify what types of distortions (specific vs. pervasive, assignment of blame, catastrophizing) you are making. You can also use this form with children over the age of ten to help them more realistically and optimistically evaluate their problems.

Thought Ping-Pong (ages eight and up)

Thought Ping-Pong is a game that pits optimistic thoughts directly against pessimistic ones. It is designed to help you and your children be more aware of your automatic negative voices and then dispute them. This is a cooperative game where everyone plays together toward a common goal. As in other cooperative games, everyone wins or everyone loses.

Changing Negative Thoughts to Positive Thoughts

Write Your Problem Here:_____

Negative Statement	Type of Distortion	Positive Statement

To conceptualize this game, think of cartoons you have seen in which an angel sits on one shoulder of a character and a devil sits on the other. The angel and the devil then proceed to make their case about what the character should do (although in a cartoon, the final choice is just as likely to be wrong as right).

To play this game, you need three people who begin by sitting next to one another on a couch or three adjoining chairs. You will also need two index cards, one with a "+" written on it and one with a "−" written on it.

Begin the game with the youngest player sitting in the middle. The next oldest player holds the minus card and the oldest player holds the plus card.

The person in the middle states a problem that he or she is having. Then the person holding the minus card says something negative or pessimistic about that problem. Next the person with the plus card says something to dispute the negative comment. Remember that it must not just be a positive statement, but it must be realistic and "provable." For example, a comment like "You can do anything that you set your mind to" is too vague and not really true. Nobody is good at everything. Similarly, a comment like "Just go for it" is just a form of cheerleading. Optimism is *not* cheerleading. It is a positive and realistic way of looking at a problem.

For example, let's say that the problem is: "I am doing poorly in science class."

Negative Comment

   You're no good at science. Why bother trying?

Positive Comment

   If you study more or do an extra project, you can bring up your grade.

Negative Comment

Science is boring, and the books we are using are too hard.

Positive Comment

You can find books that will make it more interesting, or maybe even a computer program that would explain it. You can ask for help from someone who knows it well and is a good teacher.

Negative Comment

Let's face it, no matter what you do, you'll still get a poor grade. You already have three failures.

Positive Comment

Even if you get a poor grade this time, you can balance it out with a good grade in your reading. If you read two extra books, you can get an "A."

The person sitting in the middle who presented the original problem acts as the "judge." He should write down each negative and positive comment on the score sheet, circling each positive comment only if it is both accurate and realistic. Each round should last five minutes, and then the players should switch roles, with the player in the middle stating a new problem that he or she has and again writing down the positive and negative comments of the other two players. The game should continue for about twenty minutes. If thirty realistic positive comments have been written down in that time period, then the "team" has won the game.

EQ POINTS TO REMEMBER

For a variety of reasons, the current generation of children is more prone to being pessimistic than any generation before. This increase in pessimism has made children more vulnerable than ever to the debilitating effects of depression and the associated problems of poor school performance, lack of friends, and even physical illness. You can help your child by remembering that:

- Children can be taught to be more optimistic as a way to inoculate them against depression and other mental-health and physical problems.

- Optimism comes from realistic thinking as well as from opportunities to meet and master age-appropriate challenges.

- You must be more optimistic in the ways that you relate to your children. Children learn most readily by observing what their parents do and say.

· 8 ·

Changing the Way Children Act by Changing the Way They Think

At universities and research centers throughout the country, scientists are finding that teaching people to change the way they think can actually alter their brain chemistry. These breakthrough methods are referred to as cognitive behavior modifications, because they focus on changing the links between what we think and what we do, following the general principles of behavioral psychology.

Just one example of the research involves one of the most mysterious and debilitating of mental illnesses, obsessive-compulsive disorder or OCD. Children, adolescents, and adults with OCD drive themselves and others to distraction with their irrational thoughts and behaviors.

> Barry was a seven-year-old with OCD. He had to look inside every parked car that he passed to see if the interior light was on. His father told his therapist that it took nearly an hour to walk the three blocks from their house to the playground, because

Barry had to check every car and would throw a tantrum if he was not allowed to do so. Barry also spent hours watching the digital clock in his kitchen change its numbers, and had to compulsively watch *Wheel of Fortune* on TV to see the wheel spin. He could not leave the house unless he had on one article of clothing that was red and one that was blue.

Other children (and adults) with OCD become obsessed with cleanliness. They cannot use public toilets, they avoid touching doorknobs, and they may shower a dozen times or more a day. One teenage girl I know washed her hands so frequently that they ulcerated. Obviously, this kind of ritualistic behavior and obsessive thinking causes chaos in the lives of the child and all those around her. In many cases, these children are unable to leave the house for months at a time.

CHANGING BRAIN CHEMISTRY

Recent research on people with OCD shows that they have a different brain chemistry than those without the disorder. Research psychiatrists Jeffrey Schwartz and Lew Baxter at UCLA injected a glucose-like substance into volunteers with and without OCD. Using a new brain-scan technology, they found that patients with OCD consistently showed more energy use in their orbital cortex, the underside of the front of the brain.

It is not surprising that certain kinds of medication (including Prozac) can change the way the nerve cells transmit information and energy, reducing OCD symptoms. But as Dr. Schwartz has reported in his book *Brain Lock*, cognitive-behavior modification can produce the same chemical changes in the brain as psychoactive drugs. Similar research has also found that changing the way people think can be as effective as medication in treating depression, phobias, anxiety disorders, and certain psychosomatic disorders.

In this chapter, we will look at specific cognitive-behavior modification techniques that have been used with a wide range of psychological and physical problems. You may find these techniques useful with problems that your children already have, such as a fear of going to the dentist or doctor. But many of these techniques will be even more important to your child in the future. The imagery skills that will help your child when she gets a tetanus shot today will help her when she experiences childbirth twenty years from now. The same cognitive skills that can help your child take a spelling test today will help him take his SATs or perform under the pressure of his job.

These skills are particularly important to children when they face problems or conflicts. Psychiatrist John March, head of the Child and Adolescent Anxiety Disorders Program at Duke University, tells children to build a "tool kit" of strategies that, he explains, they will always have with them, because the tool kit is in their minds. Your child's tools could include any of the ideas discussed in this book, but for now, we will just discuss cognitive or thinking skills that have proven to be effective with children experiencing a variety of difficulties.

DEFINING A PROBLEM AS THE "ENEMY"

The first step in most forms of cognitive psychotherapy is to have children differentiate themselves from a problem that they are having. The child must see the problem as outside of himself. Duke's John March tells children to see their problem as their enemy, to give their problems a name, and to go to war against the problem.

For example, at age five, Josh had many phobias. He was afraid of elevators, escalators, bridges, tunnels, the dark, loud noises, and more. His therapist pointed out how all these fears were making life very difficult for Josh, and that he was virtually "under attack" by his fears.

"You have to think of your fears as your enemy," Josh's counselor explained, "and your enemy is attacking you from every direction! When you go out, there is a bad guy behind every door. You've got to look and be careful and fight back! It's not the elevator or the escalator that is your enemy, it is your fear of these things.

"Now we need a name for these fears, this enemy. It is a very bad enemy to do this to a nice kid like you, and I'm getting mad just talking about it! I hate this enemy, don't you? What shall we call this enemy that is making you so unhappy?"

Josh was wide-eyed, watching his normally mild-mannered therapist work himself up, preparing for a fight. "I'm not sure what I would call him," Josh explained. He thought a little more and asked, "How about the Beast-Man?"

"The Beast-Man is a good name," the therapist replied. "What do you think of when you hear that name?"

"I don't know," Josh said softly, "it's just a name."

"Well, we don't want 'just a name,' we want an awful name. We want a name that makes you mad! A name that makes you furious! A name that makes you a warrior!" With each sentence, the therapist became more animated and resolute. "Now, what's a name that really makes your blood boil? Give me a name that makes you angry just to say it. Give me a name for your rotten, no-good enemy—your unfair, stupid, mind-your-own-business fears!"

"Robert!" Josh exclaimed. "I'll call my enemy Robert! I hate Robert, he was a big, fat bully that used to pick on me and call me a baby and sit on me and pull my hair! I hate him!"

"Robert," repeated the therapist, obviously pleased at Josh's new fighting spirit, "yes, that sounds like a good name for your enemy. Watch out fears named Robert! We're going to get you!"

REFRAMING A PROBLEM AND WRITING IT OUT OF YOUR CHILD'S LIFE

Psychologists call the process that Josh went through "reframing." Having children think about an internal problem as outside of themselves gives them a new way to look at it, a new frame of reference. In addition, naming a problem as an enemy serves to motivate your child to do something new. He realizes, sometimes for the first time, that *he* is not bad. Rather, it is the problem controlling his behavior that is bad.

The next step, according to New Zealand psychologists Michael White and David Epston, is for children to *write* a problem out of their lives. These authors developed a cognitive approach they call "narrative therapy," which uses a variety of written activities to help increase the distance between children and their problems. Narrative therapy helps children see that, by their choices and behaviors, they are metaphorically writing the stories of their lives. If a child like Josh is fearful, then that fear influences every chapter of the story of his life. If there is a chapter about starting school, the fear is in it. If there is a chapter about going away to camp, the fear is in it. But White and Epston explain that just as children can write the story of their lives with a problem in every chapter, they can also write the problem out of their lives. They note how something as simple as a written declaration can motivate a child to completely change his attitude and behavior. For example, they describe how fourteen-year-old Daniel, who suffered from life-threatening asthma, was helped to write a declaration of independence from his asthma. Daniel was described as a trusting and easygoing adolescent who was passive in dealing with his medical condition. His therapist explained that Daniel must see his asthma as a "trickster" who would do him harm if he got a chance. Through letters to his therapist, along with occasional meetings, Daniel committed himself to understanding what caused his asthma attacks, knowing what could prevent them, and being watchful for the "tricks" his medical condition might play on him. Previous to the therapy, Daniel's parents explained that they felt 99 percent responsible for dealing with Daniel's asthma, and they thought their son was only alert to the problem 1 percent of the time. The intent of the therapy was to make Daniel 100 percent responsible for coping with his problem.

The essence of cognitive therapy is to get children (or adults for that matter) to think about their problems in a new way until they begin to believe these new thoughts. These new beliefs then promote different feelings and behaviors.

The Problem Battle Plan is a written exercise that you can use to help your children externalize and attack their emotional problems and conflicts. It is appropriate for any problem that your children should have some control over: fears, anxiety, habits, learning problems, and so on. You can use this form to externalize the problem and then join forces to solve it. Obviously, if problems are severe or chronic, a professional therapist or counselor should also be consulted to develop a more sophisticated plan of attack and give you and your child more support.

Problem Battle Plan

Your Personal Battle Plan Against a Problem That Is Making You (or Others) Miserable

Name your enemy (your problem):

_____

_____

_____

What type of war are you going to fight? Describe different strategies:

_____

_____

_____

Sneak attack (Approach the problem in a new and tricky way. Surprise is a key element.):

_____

_____

_____

All-out battle (Name as many ways as you can think of to attack the problem.):

_____

_____

_____

Guerrilla warfare (Anything goes!):

_____

_____

_____

Where will the battle be staged?

_____

_____

_____

When is the best time to fight?

_____

_____

_____

Who are your allies? (Who are the people you can trust to help you solve the problem? How are they going to help?)

_____

_____

_____

Designate a problem-free zone (a time when and a place where you can rest from the fatigue of battle):

_____

_____

_____

Enemies can be sneaky. What do you think your enemy might do to undermine your best plans?

_____

_____

_____

What is in your peace treaty? What can you live with and what can't you live with?

_____

_____

_____

How will you know when the war is won?

_____

_____

What will the future look like now that the war is over?

_____

_____

_____

SELF-TALK

Unlike any other animal on Earth, humans have the capacity to talk to themselves and carry on inner dialogues. But in studying the way that our thoughts influence our feelings and behaviors, researchers have found a tremendous variation in how children use their capacity for inner speech. These differences may be a defining element in our mental functioning.

According to child development theorist Lawrence

Kohlberg, children go through five stages of using language to talk to themselves. At first, their private speech can be described as a form of self-entertainment, as they repeat words or rhymes. In the second stage, speech is directed outward, and toddlers can frequently be heard describing their own activities, making remarks to themselves as if they were talking to someone else in the room. But between the ages of five and seven, most children develop a self-guiding speech, and they can be heard asking themselves questions and coaching themselves through a course of action. In the fourth stage, this self-guiding speech begins to become internalized thought, and children can be observed muttering to themselves or mouthing the words of their thoughts without making a sound. In the fifth stage, the child's inner dialogue is entirely silent, although studies have shown that children will continue to show subvocal tongue movement as they think.

While Kohlberg's developmental stages are common to most children, psychotherapists have found that some do not use inner thoughts to help them cope with problems. They are either impulsive and literally do not think before they act, or their thoughts are simply not directed, but instead are vague, self-contradictory, or even self-defeating. Teaching children to cope with difficult situations by talking to themselves will have both short-term and long-term positive effects.

Many therapists promote "self-talk" as a way to learn new behaviors. Some programs use self-coaching to teach children to plan ahead and control their impulsive behaviors. Other therapists teach children to talk to themselves to cope with stressful problems and reduce anxiety. In his book *Positive Self-Talk for Children,* Douglas Bloch advises parents to script a series of statements that help children accept their strengths and limitations, say "no" to drugs and other temptations, control their anger, and cope with a wide variety of difficult situations. For example, the following script was developed for Isaac, who was being picked on by a bully:

> "Bullies are scared people who like to scare others. I can handle Tim [the bully]. I can easily say, 'Leave me alone,' in a firm voice. I let Tim know what the consequences of his behavior will be. I know how to get help if I need to."

The idea behind this strategy is to have your child repeat the statement so many times that he begins to believe it. This does, in fact, happen.

Although the rote repetition of a phrase may seem a simplistic psychological strategy, there is no question that this has an effect. Performers talk to themselves before going onstage to deal with stage fright, women experiencing childbirth "coach" themselves through labor, passengers afraid of flying repeat the statistics of air-travel safety as a way to ease their anxiety.

We can understand this phenomenon from the perspective of brain physiology. Repeating thoughts generates activity in the neocortex, the higher brain center, which then inhibits the emotional brain from releasing hormones and other chemical messengers that would have signaled the body to respond with an increased heart rate or queasy stomach. Our children can learn this inhibitory response over time so that a particular situation, say anxiety over taking a test, triggers an internal dialogue (an appropriate, adaptive response) rather than a physiological response (a maladaptive state). A child is then able to talk himself through the test, rather than get upset by it.

MAKING POSITIVE SELF-TALK AUTOMATIC

As you may remember from a high school or college psychology course, through reinforcement you can pair many different behaviors with different kinds of stimulus if the reinforcement is strong enough and the new behavior is repeated over and over again—that's how Pavlov got his dogs to salivate when they heard a bell. Unfortunately, it is not easy to provide adequate reinforcement or repetition when you ask children to memorize something.

Chris, a learning disabled and overweight ten-year-old, came to see me with a variety of problems. He didn't get along with his stepfather, his grades were poor, and he hated his younger brother, who seemed to do everything perfect. But what troubled him most was the way his classmates picked on him without mercy on the playground. Nearly every day, Chris left school in tears, giving his tormentors even more reason to tease him.

Chris and I had met for several sessions, talking about his attributes and trying to build his self-confidence. Although he was a poor speller, he was good in math. Although he was poorly coordinated at softball and basketball, he was a good swimmer. We made up a list of ten things he was good at, and I asked Chris to memorize this list for our next session. I told him that we would role-play some situations in which he was teased, and that if he could repeat his list of positive qualities in his mind, it would help him endure the teasing.

As I might have expected, when the next session came and I asked Chris if he had memorized his list, he unhesitatingly told me that he had lost it almost the minute he left my office. "Okay," I said, "we'll try again," and I gave him another copy of the list.

On the next visit, this same scene was repeated. This time, Chris had a slightly better excuse for not having memorized the list, but the net effect was the same. I knew that I was caught in Chris's cycle of defeat. As so frequently happens when we try to help someone else, I underestimated the power of the human capacity to resist any change, even one for the better.

I was fortunate on two counts: I had a copy machine down the hall and Chris's mother had a good sense of humor. I excused myself for a minute, put a new list in the copier, and by the end of the session handed Chris and his mother a stack of 300 copies of his list of positive qualities. At the next session, Chris's mother explained to me how she had wallpapered his room with the lists. They were all over his walls, the ceiling, the bathroom mirror, virtually anywhere Chris could look. Needless to say, Chris had memorized the list, and now the role-playing could begin.

As Chris's story illustrates, memorizing positive statements is an arduous task for many children. When it involves an area of conflict in which there are already natural resistances, it becomes more difficult still. Nevertheless, there are ways that you can get this technique to work. One of the easiest and most effective, as we shall see in Chapters 24 and 25, involves using computers, which make repetition easy and fun.

IMAGERY

Dwayne was an eight-year-old boy with sickle-cell anemia. He was referred to me because of his refusal to go for his frequent blood checks and his terror at the thought of having to have a transfusion. I told Dwayne that I could teach him how to use his brain to numb his arm so that he would barely even feel the needle. "This is something that many people have learned to do over the centuries, from magicians to medicine men to great heroes," I said.

"The brain works like a giant computer command center," I explained. "When we want to walk or talk, it sends a message to our legs or to our mouth and tells these muscles what to do. It controls parts of our bodies without us even having to think about it. For example, it tells our hearts to pump blood faster when we exercise and our stomachs to digest the food when we are finished with a meal."

Then I asked Dwayne, "Did your hand or foot ever 'go to sleep,' so that it almost felt like it wasn't a part of you?"

"Sure," he said, "that happens to me lots of times."

"What if I teach you how to make movies in your mind that would let your brain put parts of your body to sleep, but it would be under your control? What if whenever you want it to, you could make your arm go 'numb' and you would hardly feel it if you need to have a shot or give blood?"

I asked Dwayne to hold his arm up in the air, shut his eyes, and count slowly up to 100. As he counted, I instructed him to relax his muscles, breathe deeply, and imagine himself sitting in front of a fire on a very cold winter's day in an easy chair with a blanket thrown over him (before Dwayne had come, I had turned up the air-conditioning in the office to give his imagination a little help).

"Now, I want you to imagine yourself going outside," I said soothingly, "taking some snow from the ground, and packing it into a snowball. It's cold, isn't it? Now take the snowball and put it right on the spot on your arm where the nurse puts in the needle to take blood. Can you feel how numb your arm has become? It's like you can hardly feel it? Go ahead and pinch the skin on that spot. Can you feel anything?"

"Just a little," Dwayne responded hesitantly. "I can just feel it a little."

"That's right," I responded, "and with practice, you can do this whenever you want. You can make your arm numb, so that you never have to be afraid of a shot or giving blood. Cool, huh?"

"Yeah," Dwayne said, pinching his arm again, "it really is numb!"

Anyone who has ever awakened from a dream in a cold sweat, sheets and covers askew after running from some imaginary monster, knows the power of the mind to create images that, under certain conditions, cannot be distinguished from reality. Even in a waking state, we can ask people to imagine a frightening experience and their heart rates will accelerate. If we ask them to imagine they are placing their hand on a hot surface, we can even measure an increase in skin temperature and blood volume.

Between the ages of three and four, children develop the ability to create a picture in their minds and even run it like a movie. This ability to create images is particularly strong in childhood, but then apparently fades in most of us by late adolescence.

Imagery can be an important tool in reducing psychological and physical distress. By distracting the thinking part of the brain, images may directly weaken the nerve impulses that distress evokes. The intense concentration we use to form an image may then be a key factor in triggering an internal pain-suppressing system. According to Patricia McGrath, author of *Pain in Children*, this type of distraction is not simply a diversionary tactic in which children don't pay attention to the presence of pain, but rather it actually reduces the pain, creating a natural analgesic.

You can teach your child to form mental images as a way

Imagery does not just distract the child's attention, but may actually trigger a pain-suppressing system in the brain, creating a natural analgesic.

to help cope with a wide variety of situations. When she falls and scrapes a knee, she can imagine a bag full of ice being placed on the sore to numb it. If she is afraid of dental pain, she can learn to close her eyes, relax, and imagine that she is being swept away for a ride on a magic carpet. If she is sick to her stomach about reading a poem in front of her class, she can imagine that the air is filled with magical, invisible "power stars," which she can swallow for confidence and to make her stomach relax.

There is no question that imagery training works in controlling severe and chronic pain, often even better than medication. In a research study teaching children to cope with migraine headaches, Dr. Karen Olness, a professor of pediatrics at Case Western University, explains: "Although we don't know the specific cause of migraine, we do know from controlled studies that regularly practicing a relaxation imagery exercise results in far fewer migraines than taking a conventional medicine for the same purpose. Children trained in self-regulating techniques did far better than the children with medication, and certainly better than children who were on placebo and received no medication at all."

Simply giving children the tools they can use to control their pain and stress may be a significant factor in why these techniques work. Many studies show that when people perceive that they have some control over stress, it bothers them much less. Years ago, as an undergraduate at New York University, I was a lab assistant for psychologist Dr. David Glass, who was researching the effects of noise pollution. In those studies, we found that simply giving subjects a button that could turn off a loud noise improved their performance of a routine task. These subjects also rated the noise as much less distressing than those who did not have a button. In other research, cancer patients who are allowed to give themselves their own injections of morphine, versus those who received it from a doctor, reported better pain control, even though they actually used less of the narcotic.

CHOOSING AN APPROPRIATE IMAGE

When you instruct your child to think of an image to cope with a particular pain or stressor, choose one that is both age-appropriate and complementary to the particular problem. The following are some images that different children have used to overcome their problems:

- *Fear of dogs:* The child is watching a barking dog as Superman stands next to him. The child approaches the dog under the watchful eye of the man of steel, who coaches him on how to proceed. The dog then becomes friendly and the child is unafraid.

- *Headaches:* The child sees his headache as a pounding drum. He visualizes cool "magic" blankets being wrapped around the drum until it is muffled.

- *Asthma:* The child envisions his bronchial tubes as flat balloons. He imagines that magic pumps are placed within each balloon, which make them expand, and breathing becomes easier.

- *Anxiety and frustration over a difficult homework assignment:* The child imagines that his pencil is enchanted, but loses its power if it is not directly touching the paper. The pencil talks to him and encourages him to keep trying for a specified time period.

TEACHING YOUR CHILDREN TO USE IMAGERY

If you take the time to teach your children to use imagery to cope with physical and psychological distress, you will be teaching them skills that will last a lifetime, reducing a great deal of unnecessary suffering.

Begin by explaining what you are doing and why you are doing it. It is important even for young children to know that this is a tool that they can put in their tool kit and that it is a part of staying healthy, just like a nutritious diet and exercise.

I find it helpful to tell children about how the best athletes in the world use imagery to perform feats that no one thought possible. An Olympic canoeist visualizes the course of the river before she navigates it. There are rocks and white water everywhere, but she skillfully maneuvers around them. When it is time for the race, she makes quicker turns and wins. A batter learns to practice his swing in his mind several times a day and just before he is called to bat. His hitting average soars nearly 20 percent.

It is easy to get excited about the power of imagery and convey this enthusiasm to your child, because these stories, and thousands like them, are all true. Dr. Shane Murphy, sports psychologist for the U.S. Olympic Committee and author of *The Achievement Zone*, reported in a study done at the Olympic Training Center in Colorado Springs that over 90 percent of these elite athletes used imagination to enhance their sports skills. In one experiment, Murphy reports asking a group of college students to practice their golf putts for seven consecutive days. One-third of the students were told to visualize themselves making their putts before every attempt, one-third were told to visualize themselves missing the putt, and one-third did not do any visualization training. The group that practiced positive imagery improved by 30 percent by the end of the week, while the group that did not practice visual rehearsal only improved 10 percent. In an unexpected result, the group who visualized themselves missing the putt actually decreased their accuracy by 21 percent, even after a week of practice.

Before you teach your child this EQ skill, try using imagery yourself for a minute or two. Sit back, close your eyes, breathe deeply, and imagine yourself on an isolated beach, lying quietly on the warm white sand. Make the experience as real as possible, consciously engaging every one of your senses. Can you feel the warm sand? Smell the salt air? Hear the sound of the waves coming in on the shore or the seagulls flying overhead? Can you taste a cold vanilla ice-cream bar and feel it in your mouth?

The most powerful images trigger sensory memories, creating what hypnotherapists refer to as a "waking dream." Now rate your image on a one-to-ten scale, with ten being "almost exactly like being on the beach" and one being "a vague and incomplete picture of the beach." If your score was seven or above, you almost undoubtedly enjoyed this five-minute vacation.

Now have your child sit in a comfortable chair in a quiet place where you won't be interrupted. Before introducing the image, have him breathe slowly and deeply. Have him relax his muscles until you can see that his body has lost all its tension.

Describe in detail the scene that you want your child to imagine. He should not just "picture the scene," but involve every sense in creating an image that is as close to real life as possible. When guiding your child to see the image, take your time in describing each detail. Speak slowly, but with emotion, like you are telling a fascinating story. Remember that he is creating a picture in his mind with each of your suggestions, so give him time to do this.

Images are more meaningful to children if they are created using elements they already enjoy. The following is an image told to Mike, a seven-year-old who had night terrors. It was designed to help him initially fall asleep, as well as to calm himself if he woke up from a nightmare. One of Mike's favorite activities was fishing by a lake with his father.

You are walking in a forest. As you walk deeper and deeper into the forest, you feel more and more relaxed. There is a cool breeze, and you can smell the pine needles and hear the light crunch of the leaves on the ground as you walk. After a while, you get to your destination: a lake where Daddy is waiting with fishing poles already in the water. You and Daddy sit in chairs and watch the surf from the lake come and go. The sun is setting and it is getting dark. The lake is so quiet, you can almost hear the fish swimming in it. You are so relaxed and content that you drift off to sleep.

Like every EQ skill, imagery must be practiced if it is to be effective. As Dr. Murphy explains to athletes as well as to boardroom executives, the mind is like a muscle—it only becomes stronger with exercise. If your child has chronic health problems, there are few things that work as well as imagery in teaching pain control, particularly when it is combined with other relaxation/distraction techniques. Imagery is a skill that all children should learn, just as they should learn good manners, how to make friends, or how to assert their rights.

OTHER WAYS YOU CAN HELP YOUR CHILD HARNESS THE POWER OF IMAGERY

The procedure I have described for training your child to use guided imagery is simple and straightforward, but there are also other activities, grounded in the arts, that can have the additional benefit of exposing your child to music and art appreciation and reinforcing his aesthetic awareness.

1. Tell your child to close his eyes and listen to a variety of nonvocal music (symphonic, jazz, New Age). Talk about what image the music evokes.

2. Show your child images of abstract art and ask him to look for shapes that remind him of something. Then have him draw a picture based on one shape.

3. Ask your child to stare at a picture with many details (like a Norman Rockwell painting) for about a minute. Then ask him to close his eyes and see the picture in his mind's eye, trying to remember as many features of it as possible.

4. Cover your child's eyes and let him smell several different things around the house (an orange, perfume, a plant). Then have him draw a picture that includes the object that each of these smells came from.

5. Ask your child to remember a pleasant event from her past. Then have her close her eyes and describe the scene with as much detail as possible.

In many ways, the "thinking" EQ skills described in this chapter are the easiest to teach, because they are most accessible. On the other hand, they typically involve more repetition than other types of emotional and social skills, and may seem unnatural or awkward. However, their benefits are indisputable if you take the time and energy to teach them to your children.

EQ POINTS TO REMEMBER

- Children over six can learn to talk to themselves as a way to increase their attention span and improve their performance, acting as if they were their own coach.

- If self-talk techniques are to be effective, they must be conditioned into your child's thinking and behavioral repertoire through repetition and reinforcement.

- You can use guided imagery to teach your children to cope with pain and discomfort, as well psychological distress.

- The earlier you teach your children to use these skills, the more effective they will be.

- Repetition is essential for your children to master these thinking skills, so make them enjoyable and reinforce them with your own interest and enthusiasm.

PART 4

Problem Solving

A five-year-old witnesses his father injuring himself with a power saw and runs into the house to call 911. A seven-year-old, tired of her father picking her up late for her weekend visits, buys him a watch with an alarm for his birthday and sets it before she gives it to him to ring an hour before she is scheduled to be picked up. A ten-year-old, distraught because his cousin was wounded in a drive-by shooting, writes the mayor and the chief of police about his worries, urging them to put more policemen in the area. He gets a personal letter back from the mayor promising him that this will happen.

We often do not give our children full credit for their capacity to solve problems. Too frequently, we jump in to help before help is really needed or we assume our children should have decisions made for them. When given the opportunity and encouragement, however, our kids are capable of looking at all sides of an issue and solving very complex problems, improving the quality of their lives, as well as the lives of others.

Some parents may not take the time to teach problem-solving skills, naively believing that childhood should be as free from problems as possible. As one parent put it when he learned that problem-solving training was part of his child's kindergarten class curriculum, "He's only a little kid! He's got plenty of time ahead of him for dealing with problems."

What this parent didn't realize is that the ability to solve problems is an inherent part of growing up. Our children become problem-solvers in the first few months of life. Their intellectual and emotional growth is driven by the problem-solving process. But like other EQ skills, a child's ability to solve problems is age-specific. We need only observe a child trying to solve a new problem to appreciate the developmental urgency of the problems at hand:

- The infant spends hours trying to get her thumb into her mouth, often misjudging and stabbing her nose or forehead, until she eventually, contentedly, succeeds.

- The one-year-old works hard to balance three blocks in a tower, at first baffled, then frustrated and on the verge of tears. If the blocks are taken away, though, the child has a tantrum.

- The three-year-old insists on tying his own shoes, ignoring the fact that he is in the middle of the aisle in a grocery store with harried shoppers squeezing their carts around him to get by. He refuses to be distracted from his task until he masters it and will loudly protest to the parent who interferes, even for his safety.

Parents who define their own happiness or success as having fewer problems to worry about may find it hard to understand that children actually enjoy the problem-solving process. Watch a group of eight-year-olds building a fort in the backyard as they draw plans; gather cardboard boxes, lumber, and rope; and rummage through the garage or the basement for anything that can enhance their architectural fantasies. They may forget about lunch and ignore the drizzling rain. They will be visibly unimpressed with their parents' skepticism about the final outcome. In many cases, children will show more excitement and enjoyment over solving the problem of building the fort than in actually playing in the structure itself.

Another common misconception is that problem solving has much more to do with intellectual development (IQ) than with emotional and social skills (EQ). The eminent developmental psychologist Jean Piaget assumed that logic, first concrete and then abstract, is the critical element in problem solving, tying it directly to age and a child's intellectual gifts. But a growing body of evidence suggests that social experience and familiarity with the problem may be the more critical factors.

In her book *Children Solving Problem*, Stephanie Thornton, a professor of psychology at the University of Sussex, quotes a wide range of research studies that suggest children are much more adept at problem solving than once was thought. She concludes that successful problem solving depends less on how smart children are and more on their experience. Thornton explains that previous research on how children learn problem-solving skills, including the work of the world-famous Jean Piaget, relied on tests where children were unfamiliar with the type of problem that was presented to them. For example, not many two- or three-year-olds can answer an abstract problem such as:

1. If A is true, then B is true.
2. A is true. What follows?

But few three-year-olds would have trouble with this same inferential concept if it were stated as:

1. If you behave on the shopping trip, you can have an ice-cream cone.
2. You were good on the shopping trip. What is going to happen?

Young children can solve fairly complicated problems when they are couched in terms that are familiar and concrete, even though they would fail at these same problems if they were presented in an abstract, factually inaccurate, or hypothetical manner.

Indeed, even adults have difficulty with logical problem solving if they cannot draw on prior knowledge and beliefs about the real world. This makes sense if we think about how much familiarity adds to our ability to reason. Suppose you had to give someone directions to a specific location in your hometown versus giving that same person directions in a city that you visited once or twice. Both problems are the same from a strictly cognitive point of view, and yet with one, you have the information and experience available to solve the problem.

This principle holds true as we teach our children to solve their interpersonal problems. With every positive problem-solving experience we can give our children, we build a storehouse of facts and experiences on which they can draw to solve the next problem. Thus we are creating pathways for problem solving that begin with their natural developmental drives, but which connect and reconnect through knowledge and experience.

· 9 ·

Teaching by Example: Your Role in Making Your Child a Problem-Solver

When children watch us calmly discussing a problem, reasoning things out, and weighing alternative solutions, they naturally begin to value and imitate this behavior. On the other hand, if we become irritable, argumentative, depressed, or overwhelmed by our problems, or if we pretend that the problems will just go away or take care of themselves, what can we expect our children to learn?

For a variety of psychological reasons, some parents may not model problem-solving skills in the home, in spite of the fact that they are capable problem-solvers at work or in the community. Consider the reactions of Dan, father of three, a pharmacist at a chain superstore. Dan works nine- and sometimes ten-hour days. He also takes courses toward a Ph.D., in the hope that he might one day land a research position with a pharmaceutical company. Dan is proud of his ability to handle "anything that comes down the pike." He considers himself cool-headed and rational, the man to call when a problem arises.

But at home, he feels that he should have time off from problems. He tells his wife that he wants his home to be a sanctuary, a place for rest and recharging his spirit.

However, when he arrives from work at 6:30 P.M., his wife explains that dinner will be late. "Late! Late again?" he says. "Can't I get my dinner on time once a month?" At dinner, his oldest daughter announces that she got a "C" on a spelling test. "Well, if you studied like I told you to," Dan growls, "you would have gotten an 'A,' wouldn't you? Nobody wants to do their job around here. Everybody takes the easy way. I've got a headache." He storms away from the table.

It is a great mystery why we so often treat casual acquaintances and even strangers better than those we love. And yet with effort, this does not have to be. As community psychologist Dr. Louise Hart explains in *The Winning Family,* when parents take responsibility for their roles as leaders in the family, they provide excellent models for their children. To your children, you are a person with tremendous power—even more than the president! Hart explains that there are six leadership qualities that parents need to exhibit in order to maintain happiness and individual esteem in the family:

1. You must have vision, direction, and goals.
2. You must communicate your leadership effectively.
3. You must keep the family focused on the goals.
4. You must consider the needs of others.
5. You must support progress.
6. You must expect success and get it.

Do you demonstrate to your child how to solve problems through your day-to-day words and actions? Think of a recent problem you had that affected your family. Were you late pay-ing bills? Did you have an illness that kept you from some of your normal activities? Did one of your children misbehave? Now, using the chart below, check off the statements that describe how you solved the problem.

Parent's Problem-Solving Checklist

_____   Did you try to think of several strategies to solve the problem?

_____   Did you clearly define the problem?

_____   Did you allow everyone involved in the problem to have a real say in its solution?

_____   Did you discuss the good and bad points of each idea, even those ideas that were not your own?

_____   Did you remain calm and refrain from blaming others?

_____   Did you make an honest attempt to have the solution work?

_____   Did you acknowledge other people's efforts in arriving at the solution?

_____   Did you make a backup plan in case the solution didn't work?

Did you check off more than half of these statements? If not, read on.

FAMILY MEETINGS

Few parents would argue the importance of helping children learn good problem-solving habits, but many do not make the time to do this. One way to guarantee that you have opportunities to model problem-solving skills for your children is by scheduling weekly family meetings. These meetings should be scheduled at times when everyone will be available. Making attendance at the family meetings mandatory—for parents as well as children—will give children the message that you take your role as a family leader seriously and you are committed to helping them develop emotional and social skills for success.

Typically, family meetings are scheduled to last for half an hour. As the leader(s) of the meeting, the parent(s) should insist on the following ground rules for all good meetings:

- Begin and end on time.
- Don't interrupt when someone else is talking.
- Don't criticize someone else's opinions or feelings.
- Give everyone a chance to participate, but don't force anyone to participate if he or she doesn't want to.

About half of the meeting should be spent on individual concerns and the other half on problems that affect the family as a group. Each person should have the opportunity to discuss and "think out" a problem that he or she is having. This is the opportunity for you to bring up your own issues that are appropriate for discussion in the family.

As you discuss a problem that you are having, model a five-step problem-solving procedure:

1. Identify the problem.
2. Think of alternative solutions.
3. Compare each solution.
4. Pick the best solution.

5. At the next meeting, report how the solution turned out and discuss any modifications that are needed.

For example, Mrs. Garvey was coming home every day from work with a headache and was uncharacteristically snappish with her children and her husband. In a family meeting, her ten-year-old asked what was wrong, and the mother of three explained that pressure at her job was making her stressed and anxious. Mrs. Garvey was a paralegal for a large law firm, and two of the lawyers she worked with had given her more work than could handle. She didn't want to complain, because she was up for a promotion, but both lawyers wanted her to make their work a priority. She tackled the problem at a family meeting using the five-step process:

1. Identify the problem: "I have more work than I can manage."

2. Think of alternative solutions: "I could a) tell both lawyers that I am overworked, b) bring work home at night and work weekends, or c) recommend that they hire a temporary worker and supervise that person."

3. Compare each solution: "The first solution just puts the problem on the lawyers, giving them more stress, which they won't like. The second solution will make things harder on me and my family. The last acknowledges the problem, provides a reasonable solution, and doesn't make work harder for me or anyone else."

4. Pick the best solution: "The third. In the short run, it will cost the firm a little money, but in the long run the work will get done quicker and more effectively."

It is easy to see how Mrs. Garvey's children could learn from watching her solve her problem out loud. They might then apply this process to their own problems and conflicts. As an added benefit, Mrs. Garvey makes the time to reason out her problem, sharing with her family why she has been irritable and giving them an opportunity to give her emotional support.

Once you have modeled the problem-solving process, your children should have the opportunity to discuss a problem if they wish. Younger children will need guidance in going through each of the steps, but you may be surprised at how quickly even five-year-olds catch on. Each person in the family may also ask for help from other family members. Children like to be given the opportunity to help their parents with important matters, and their opinions should be respected. Remember that problem solving is a process where there are not always right or wrong answers. It is also an activity that not only contributes to the emotional intelligence of your children, but builds a sense of family cohesiveness and support, as well.

EQ POINTS TO REMEMBER

- Younger children learn to become problem-solvers through experience. Challenge them to solve problems, rather than stepping in and solving them yourself.

- Develop an atmosphere of problem solving in your home through family meetings and by showing your children how you solve real problems in your own life.

· 10 ·

The Language of
Problem Solving

One of the most widely researched programs on teaching problem-solving skills was begun in the early 1970s by Philadelphia-based psychologists David Spivak and Myrna Shure. With over twenty-five years of clinical research behind it, the I Can Problem Solve (ICPS) program has demonstrated that even impulsive three- and four-year-olds can be taught to *reason* out instead of *acting* out their problems. Children have learned to ask to share a toy instead of taking it, to say that they are mad instead of fighting, and to speak up for themselves instead of withdrawing and sulking. Once learned, these skills persist. Research studies have shown that children taught ICPS training in preschool were less likely to have problems in kindergarten. Not only are children who are exposed to ICPS training less likely to be impulsive, insensitive, aggressive, or antisocial, they also achieve more in their academic curriculum.

The ICPS program begins with teaching young children six word pairs that form the building blocks for problem-solving skills. You can use these word pairs playfully to get your children to begin using them regularly and associating them with a fun activity. That makes your children more likely to use them when it is time to deal with an interpersonal problem. These word pairs will help your children think about whether they should do their homework *now* or *later*, what happened *before* a fight and what happened *after*. The initial word pairs are:

is/is not

and/or

some/all

before/after

now/later

same/different

You can play word games with your children to reinforce the usage of this problem-solving language. Play the games as frequently as possible and in as many places as possible: in the dining room, in the grocery store, on a car trip . . . anytime you and your children are together. Naturally, any other adults who are with your children on a regular basis—teachers, baby-sitters, grandparents—can also play these word games. As with learning a foreign language, the more reinforcement and exposure children receive for using problem-solving language, the better.

The word games are designed to help young children see the differences in the word pairs, as in the following examples:

Mom: (in the grocery store) Let's play a game called "Is/Isn't" while we shop. Here's some cake. It is dessert, it isn't a main course. Here is an apple. Is it a main course?

Stacie: No, it isn't. It is a fruit. It's like a snack.

Mom: That's right. It isn't a main course. It is a dessert or
         a snack. Can you help me find something else that
         we can eat tonight for dinner, but isn't a main
         course?

Or if your child is a little older, you might initiate a conversation like this one on the way to school:

Dad: Do you remember the game of "Before and
         After?" Let's play it now to plan our day, okay?

Jeremy: Okay.

Dad: Are you going to do your homework before din-
         ner or after dinner?

Jeremy: Before dinner.

Dad: That's right. That's the rule in our house.
         Homework has to be completed before dinner. Do
         you have your snack at school before you meet in
         your reading group or after?

Jeremy: Before reading. Ms. Harvey says that a snack helps
         us to pay attention and not think about being hun-
         gry.

Dad: Oh? I didn't know that. That's a good idea. By the
         way, do you get hungry before or after you eat a
         big bowl of ice cream?

Jeremy: That's silly. Before you eat ice cream, of course.

For an older child, you could play these games while you
practice academic skills. This is a game of same/different,
which tests a child on basic math concepts:

Mom: Is 1 x 3 the same or different as 3 x 1?

Amy: It's the same.

Mom:	That's right. Good. Is 6 ÷ 2 the same or different as 12 ÷ 3?
Amy:	That's hard. Let me write it down . . . Oh, they are different numbers. Three and four are the answer. Yeah, different.
Mom:	Very good. Can you think of two multiplication problems that have the same answer? Like 2 x 4 = 8 and 1 x 8 = 8. Both answers are exactly the same.

USING WORD PAIRS TO SOLVE PROBLEMS

It may not be immediately clear how these basic word games relate to learning interpersonal problem-solving skills, but they are analogous to practicing scales before you learn to play the piano. The skills rehearsed in these word games teach your children the basic concepts for problem solving—where the "notes" are—and they teach quick thinking, much the way that scales on the piano teach finger dexterity.

Here is what happens when six-year-old Alex has learned these basic word games and he comes to his mother crying after being made fun of by his eleven-year-old sister and her friends:

Alex:	(crying) I hate Martha! She's so mean to me.
Mom:	(calmly) What happened before you started crying?
Alex:	Martha said I was a baby and I couldn't watch TV with her.
Mom:	And what happened before that?
Alex:	(slightly less upset) I came into the room and said that I wanted to watch TV with Martha and her friends, and that they were watching it all morning and now it was my turn.

Mom: I can see that you wanted to share the TV, which is good. But I don't think that the way you acted helped to solve your problem and get you what you wanted. Is the way you acted the same as just asking if you can have a turn at the TV or is it different?

Alex: (now no longer crying, thinks) I guess it's . . . different. I guess.

Mom: That's right, it is different. Do you think the way that you asked Martha was right or was it not right?

Alex: I guess it was not right.

Mom: Why do you think that?

Alex: Because Martha was mean to me and I cried.

Mom: Yes, that's true. But that isn't what I'm asking. Do you think that the way you asked was the right way?

Alex: No. I didn't say "please."

Mom: That's right. What else could you have done differently?

Alex: I could be nicer.

Mom: That's right. That would be the right way to do it. Now maybe you'd like to try again?

Once your children have learned and practiced the initial word pairs, you may wish to introduce a new group of word pairs, which can help them connect the causes and effects of their behavior:

good time/not a good time

    This is not a good time for me to read you a story. After dinner would be a good time.

if/then

If you do your homework when you get home from school, then you will be able to watch TV after dinner.

might/maybe

If I tease Billy, he might not want to play with me anymore.

Maybe he will share his toys with me if I am nice to him.

why/because

The reason why I don't have anyone to play with is because I didn't invite anyone over.

fair/not fair

It's fair that Brian gets to stay up later because he is older, but it's not fair when he gets to skip his chores because he is busy with baseball practice.

Once you begin to think in terms of using these word games, practice them frequently and use them consistently when your child has a problem. In order to remember them and cue him that this problem-solving language will be used, you might write them on index cards. Take the cards out when your child has a problem to solve. The sight of the cards will be a signal that this is the way the problem will be solved, and your youngster will eventually be able to use problem-solving language automatically. (This is actually a conditioned response. The very sight of the problem-solving card will trigger a learned behavioral pathway.)

Learning problem-solving skills is much like learning any other new skill: You need to practice more at the beginning to master it, until it becomes almost second nature. You might be asking yourself if this is really worth the trouble. Can simple games really help children that much? The answer is emphatically yes. The ICPS techniques have been used for over twenty-five years and have proven successful with thousands of children initially labeled as insensitive, impulsive, withdrawn, aggressive, or antisocial. When parents are committed to helping their children and make the time to do so, problems, even serious ones, get addressed and solved.

EQ POINTS TO REMEMBER

• By the age of four, you can start teaching children the language of problem solving.

• Begin with simple word games and then generalize these to situations in which your child presents you with a problem to solve.

· 11 ·

Solutions Training

Even very young children almost always have more than one potential strategy to solve a problem. A nine-month-old trying to put a square peg in a round hole will try to bang it in, twist it in, try a new hole, and possibly throw it away in frustration (which is one way to solve an unsolvable problem). However, by the time children begin formal learning, usually with the alphabet, they begin to perceive that there are "right" and "wrong" answers. They gradually begin to give less credence to their natural ability to generate alternative strategies and solutions.

When eight-year-old Marie was caught stealing lunch money out of the cubbies in her classroom while the other children were on the playground, she explained to her teacher that her mother had lost her job and didn't have enough money to pay for her lunch every day. She thought she would take a little from the children who had more money. When Mrs. Otis asked if there wasn't some other way to solve the problem, Marie held her head down in shame and began to cry. She felt that the teacher wanted the one "right" answer, and she didn't know what it was. Giving another "wrong" answer, Marie felt, would just make matters worse.

What Mrs. Otis *really* wanted was to have Marie consider

other possible solutions to her understandable predicament and discuss better ways to handle her problem than stealing. But Marie's natural ability to generate alternative solutions was far outweighed by her fear of further social rejection.

Marie's emotions, her shame at being caught, and her fear of rejection short-circuited her natural ability to see that there are usually many solutions to a problem. In *Children Solving Problems*, psychology professor Stephanie Thornton explains that when emotions are not involved, children instinctively learn many different strategies to solve a single problem. When a second-grader is given a simple addition problem like 5 + 3, she may use at least four different ways to solve the problem:

- Remembering the answer because she recognizes the problem.
- Counting out each of the numbers on her fingers.
- Counting only from the larger number (for example, taking the 5 for granted and then counting out three more fingers to get 8).
- Decomposing the larger number by remembering that 5 consists of 2 + 3, that 3 + 3 = 6, and that two more is 8.

Thornton explains that children of this age tend to vary these strategies, depending on how they see the complexity of the problem and their past associations with success. With repetition, children select the strategy that is most likely to work for each individual problem.

With interpersonal problems, the connection between the logical brain and the emotional brain may be short-circuited. In neurological terms, the amygdala loses its ability to form interconnecting pathways with the cortex, and so relies exclusively on its own "emotional logic." Emotional logic, which forms the basis of intuition, may be sufficient to solve some types of problems. But in many cases, particularly when strong emotions are involved, only the dispassionate help of the cortex can guide the brain toward finding realistic and effective solutions. When children practice finding solutions to their problems, they establish connecting pathways between the emotional and the logical parts of the brain.

HELPING YOUR CHILD SEEK OUT ALTERNATIVES

As in other aspects of learning problem-solving skills, generating solutions can be rehearsed in game format until it is an automatic reaction to encountering a problem. The Brainstorming Game involves having children generate as many solutions to a problem as possible and then picking the best ones. The emphasis is on helping children approach problems with more flexibility and creativity. It can be played anywhere, and it helps children of any age become more creative problem-solvers.

Several years ago, I was asked to talk to a kindergarten class about ways they could deal with an epidemic of teasing that sent several children home in tears nearly every day. To warm the children to the task of considering alternative solutions to this problem, I told them that we would play the Brainstorming Game. I asked each child to think of a new way to use the green, metal trash can sitting by the teacher's desk.

"It doesn't matter how silly your idea sounds," I explained. "The object of the game is to come up with as many ideas as possible. When you are trying to solve a problem, you need to consider all the solutions that are possible, then go back and pick the ones that are the best." I divided the class into teams. Each team would get a point for each new idea. I asked the kids to think of at least twenty ideas in five minutes. They came up with thirty-seven. Here are some of their ideas:

"Put your toys in it."

"Put it on your head like a hat."

"Make pee-pee in it."

"Use it for a bucket in the sandbox."

"Use it for basketball."

"Put dirty clothes in it."

"Put your baby sister in it."

"Put money in it, like a bank."

I wrote each of the ideas down, and then we went back and I circled the ideas that were good ones, ignoring the ones that were silly. I asked the group to play another round of the Brainstorming Game, but this time I asked them to come up with twenty things to do when children teased each other. Their list included:

"Tease back."

"Tell the teacher."

"Walk away."

"Find someone else to play with."

"Stick our tongue out."

"Ask them why they are teasing you."

Again, I wrote them all down and circled only the answers we thought were good ones. We then went on to discuss how these solutions might work in their classroom.

Like all EQ skills that involve logic and language in the thinking part of the brain, considerable practice is needed before children will automatically begin to see problems in terms of possible solutions. When the Brainstorming Game is played, it is usually best to play the first round or two with age-appropriate interpersonal problems that fictitious children might have, such as:

- Jamie and Jonathan wanted to watch different TV programs at the same time. What could they do?

- Beatrice was afraid to go to school, because the older girls picked on her. What could she do?

- Chris loved to play basketball, but he was the shortest kid in the class and was never picked for the team. What could he do?

Then the game should be played with problems that are taken directly from your children's day-to-day experiences, remembering that relevance is a key ingredient in learning new problem-solving skills. The Brainstorming Game is particularly useful when children are "stuck" on a problem. As they develop their problem-solving skills, they need to be able to build on past solutions and strategies, but they also need to be able to completely abandon former approaches that did not work and start from scratch.

Another game that can help your children practice generating different solutions to their problems is described by Myrna Shure in her book *Raising a Thinking Child*. Dr. Shure asks children to play a game of Solutions Tic-Tac-Toe as a fun way to structure the problem-solving process in a simple game format.

SOLUTIONS TIC-TAC-TOE (AGES FIVE TO TEN)

Begin by making a deck of twenty or more problem cards using standard three-by-five index cards. Each card should describe a real-life problem that is relevant to each of the players, like what to do when your sister takes your things or how to handle a test you know will be hard. The cards are then shuffled and the youngest player goes first, selecting the top card and reading the problem out loud. Then the children play a traditional game of tic-tac-toe, but they can only write down an "X" or an "O" when they offer a legitimate possible solution to the chosen problem. If a player cannot offer a good solution, he loses his turn. Obviously, the player who is not armed in advance with a storehouse of solutions will be at a significant disadvantage. When younger children play, you can act as the arbiter of what counts as a "good" solution.

The helpfulness of this simple game will increase if each player keeps track of all the solutions generated for each round of tic-tac-toe. Playing the game for at least ten rounds will facilitate the connection of one solution to another, increasing the competence and confidence of each of the players.

The skill of generating possible solutions is most effectively learned when your children practice it with other kids. As children watch and listen to others, they learn about shared assumptions and meanings, and in particular about what is and what isn't regarded as a good solution to a given problem.

Children can learn to solve their own problems when they are taught specific strategies and are given appropriate support.

SOLVING TOUGH PROBLEMS BY FINDING "EXCEPTIONS"

Even when children have practiced brainstorming, there are some problems that seem too difficult or long-standing for them to see a potential solution. In her book *Counseling Toward Solutions*, Linda Metcalf explains that one of the key elements in helping children learn to find solutions to their own problems is helping them see "exceptions" to the problems.

Metcalf points out that there is always some time when the problem doesn't exist. Children can be helped to see these times as holding the key to a successful solution. Looking at times when the problem *doesn't* exist is also a way of putting it into perspective. Children and adults frequently perceive their problems as being pervasive and ever-present, when in fact they almost always occur at specific times in specific ways. (See Chapter 7 for a discussion of ways to train children to think more optimistically.)

For example, Kristen described how she was mercilessly teased at school for being overweight and clumsy at sports. She frequently reported to her mother that "everyone at school hates me." But when her mother sat down to talk about the problem and analyze it with Kristen, she was able to see that it wasn't really "everyone," but rather three girls in the class of twenty-seven children. Her mother explained, "I know that these girls are nasty and mean to you, and that's wrong. Eventually they will probably find someone else to pick on, or maybe they will even become nicer, but that may take some time. In the meantime, there are twenty-four other children in your class who don't pick on you or tease you. Let's make a list of them and see which kids might be more like you and who you could be friends with."

In finding the "exceptions" to the problem, Kristen's mother opened a world of possible solutions. The original problem didn't go away, but Kristen began focusing on positive and possible solutions, rather than on the problem itself. Metcalf notes:

Every complaint pattern contains some sort of exception . . . global complaints are typical from people who feel hopeless and out of control. . . . When students talk about school being awful, ask, "When is it not as awful?" Opening up the possibility that to each problem there is an exception gives opportunities for people to see that they are in control more than they think. Many times, counting the minutes, hours, or days when a problem is not interfering with schoolwork or home makes it seem more solvable and less intrusive in one's life.

SHIFTING THINKING TO SOLVE PROBLEMS

Psychologist Stephen de Shazer, another prominent advocate of solution-oriented thinking, explains that these simple concrete problem-solving strategies can lead to major shifts in the way we perceive and experience problems. Many times we know the solution to a particular problem, but we don't know that we know it. It is as if our problems are behind a locked door and we don't have the key. A shift in thinking can unlock the door, so that past solutions to similar problems are again accessible.

As in any other skill area, from athletics to academics, increased practice in problem-solving skills will lead to increased confidence. Practice will help our children perceive themselves as problem-solvers. Sometimes just the perception of oneself as a problem-solver can actually increase one's ability. Researcher Robert Hartley studied how a group of disadvantaged children solved problems. He found them to be impulsive, poor planners and lacking the desire to either monitor their progress or correct their mistakes. But when he asked these children to solve the same kind of problems again, this time pretending they were the brightest children in the class, he found that they were instantly less impulsive, better at planning, and more motivated to monitor and correct their mistakes. Even more significantly, they were far more successful at obtaining correct solutions.

ENCOURAGING PROBLEM SOLVING IN OLDER CHILDREN AND ADOLESCENTS

The most sophisticated form of problem solving is referred to as means-end thinking. This type of problem solving depends on the ability to plan a logical sequence of actions that result in the attainment of a desired goal, and also includes the ability to derive insight from what is learned at each step, forestall or circumvent potential obstacles, and have available alternative strategies, when needed, to deal with obstacles to the goal. Means-end thinking includes the awareness that goals are not always reached immediately, the final goal may be modified from the original goal, and the timing of one's behavior is often relevant to success.

While you may associate this type of complex long-term problem solving with the adult world (and, indeed, you may know many adults who don't seem to have mastered it yet), children as young as twelve or thirteen frequently demonstrate an aptitude for means-end thinking. Popular adolescent role-playing and strategy games like Dungeons and Dragons and computer games like Myst can require extremely complicated planning and problem-solving strategies upon which children at this age seem to thrive.

However, far fewer children and adolescents apply these same problem-solving skills to their own lives. Stephanie Thornton might argue that this supports her thesis that problem-solving skills are acquired not so much by an orderly progression of cognitive development (as Piaget and other cognitivists have theorized), but by successive learning in a particular content area. She argues that logic is in itself just one of many strategies that people use to approach a problem, but that logic alone would not help a surgeon fix a dishwasher or a repairman remove someone's appendix.

It should therefore not be surprising that children and adolescents who might excel at algebraic logic or computers still need instruction and guidance in using means-end thinking to solve their personal and interpersonal problems. It also makes sense that they might need guidance in different areas of interpersonal problem solving, since each area requires a different pattern of emotional and logical thinking. Finding an after-school job that won't interfere with team practice, navigating a relationship with an inconsiderate boyfriend, publishing the school newspaper with writers who don't turn in their assignments on time—all of these problems may need some initial adult guidance.

SCAFFOLDING

The Russian psychologist Lev Vygotsky postulated that children learn problem-solving skills best when joined in a particular task by a skilled partner. Psychologists Jerome Brunner and David Wood have used the word "scaffolding" to describe the symbiotic relationship between an adult and a child as the youngster learns the specific mixture of skills and talents to work through a complex problem. In a scaffolded relationship, you ideally provide just enough of a framework so that your child can stretch himself, but not so much that you prevent him from acquiring the needed skills. After initially providing the structure or outline for means-end problem solving, you then gradually limit your guidance until your child is able to solve the problem independently.

The Prepare Curriculum by Dr. Arnold Goldstein, a comprehensive program to teach children "prosocial competencies," lists the following seven steps to teach older children to solve more complex problems in their lives:

1. Teach children the importance of stopping to think things through.

2. Teach children to identify and define the problem.

3. Teach children to gather information from their own perspective, including opinions, facts, and information that is not known.

4. Teach children to gather information from other people's perspectives, including what other people see, think, and feel.

5. Teach children to consider alternative strategies, including what can be done or said and what obstacles can be anticipated.

6. Teach children to evaluate consequences and outcomes, including how to decide among the various possible choices and anticipate what will happen in response to specific words or deeds.

7. Have children practice the entire problem-solving process, reinforcing each individual step and encouraging them to persist until they have a well-thought-out solution.

To help your older children or adolescents solve real-life everyday problems, be prepared to initiate a scaffolded relationship whenever a problem arises. To do this, you'll need to make the time in your busy schedule to regularly sit down with your children and discuss their interests and concerns. This will also make them see that their problems are as much a priority as your job deadline, household problems, or any other matter that may preoccupy you.

Older children will rarely turn to their parents to help them solve a serious interpersonal problem, unless the foundation for this relationship has been laid and they are confident that your help will reduce rather than exacerbate their concern and anxiety. To create a pathway between you and your children—a direct route they view as the easiest and most productive way to address a specific problem—demonstrate not only your willingness to help, but your competence in problem solving as well.

CLUE-LESS: A GAME OF INTERDEPENDENCE (AGES TEN AND UP)

I invented a game called Clue-Less to help you experience a scaffolded relationship with your children while they practice means-end thinking. This is a cooperative game, where both players win or both players lose. To begin, you will need to make three copies of a maze like the one below. You can also buy books of mazes at nearly any bookstore.

To prepare the maze, write a problem that the child is having (or might have) in the space indicated, as well as possible obstacles to getting the problem accomplished. Leave the space for the solution empty until the maze is completed. In the first round, your child has to navigate through the maze with a pencil, avoiding blind alleys and obstacles—but he must do it *blindfolded!* You may talk to your child constantly to guide him through the maze ("Go left a little . . . that's right . . . now go straight about a half an inch . . . now right . . . "). Your child gets twenty points for completing the maze, less one point for each time he or she crosses a line or touches an obstacle.

Use a second copy of the maze for the second round. Your child is again blindfolded; however, now you can only make ten comments to help him complete the maze. Again, he can earn twenty possible points for this round, and one point is

THE CLUE-LESS GAME

Problem _____

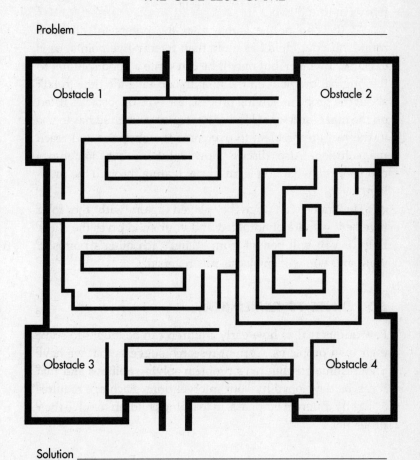

Solution _____

taken away each time he crosses a line or touches an obstacle. In addition, one point is taken away for each comment you must make beyond the original ten comments designated for this round.

In the final round, your child can earn forty points, but

you can only make five comments. Use the same scoring system as in round two.

At the end of the game, total the points for all three rounds. If your child has more than twenty-five points, he is declared a winner, but only if he can write a good solution to the original problem on the final maze. Take the time to talk about the problem-solving process, the type of obstacles listed on the maze, and what kind of strategies your child has to use in the real-life problem to overcome the obstacles and reach the solution. Also discuss how solutions can sometimes change from what you learn by navigating through the problem.

The game can then be played again with the roles reversed; you are blindfolded and your child gives the clues. Both of you will benefit from seeing each other's points of view, and you will enjoy this role reversal.

EQ POINTS TO REMEMBER

Few adults realize how early children can be taught to solve their own problems. Current research suggests that we have underestimated children's problem-solving abilities and that it can be developed by your interventions. Each age requires a slightly different emphasis in teaching children to solve their problems:

- By the time your children enter school, they can begin learning how to generate multiple solutions to a problem.

- By eight or nine, they have the capacity to weigh the pros and cons of different alternatives and choose the best solution.

- Focusing on solutions rather than on problems will make it much easier for children to learn to overcome obstacles.

- Older children and adolescents need a supportive relationship with you to help them make the transition into solving more complex problems. Act like the scaffold supporting a new structure, providing a framework for your children's problem solving, but not interfering.

PART 5

The Social Skills

Of all the EQ skills your child will develop, the ability to get along with others will contribute most to his sense of success and life satisfaction. To operate effectively in a social world, your child needs to learn to recognize, interpret, and respond appropriately to social situations. He needs to judge how to reconcile his needs and expectations with those of others.

SOCIALIZATION

As with all EQ skills, the socialization process begins with a combination of your child's inherited temperament and your reaction to it. When a baby is just six weeks old, she will stare at her parents' faces for a long time and then break into a broad smile. If you smile back, she smiles even more. By three months, your infant can use her head position and gaze as a way to communicate with you. She communicates with expressions that are contented, sober, or frightened. If she is uninterested, she will turn her head away from the subject. If she wants you to stop doing something, she will lower her head. When she is over-stimulated, she will lower her head and her body will go limp.

But even infants differ in their social reactivity and vary considerably in their responsiveness, adaptability, and persistence. Naturally, we are in turn influenced by the behavior of our infants, giving more time and attention to those who are more sociable. This is particularly true at day-care centers where "easier" infants are carried and played with more. Infants with less social temperaments can certainly be as happy and successful as other babies, but it takes more patience and awareness on the part of adults. As we shall see, this holds true for children at every age.

Interest in other children also begins at a very young age. When riding in their strollers, babies will strain to watch other babies pass by. When shown a video of other babies, they will stare quietly in amazement and, if they can, crawl over and touch the screen.

Often, adults don't realize how early in their development children become socially aware and sensitive to social nuances. Brandeis University professor Zick Rubin, author of Children's Friendships, reports on the tact and concern for a friend's feelings shown by a four-year-old as he walked and talked with a friend:

David: I'm a missile robot who can shoot missiles out of my fingers. I can shoot them out of everywhere—even out of my legs. I'm a missile robot.

Jimmy: (tauntingly) No, you're a fart robot.

David: (protesting) No, I'm a missile robot.
Jimmy: No, you're a fart robot.
David: (hurt, almost in tears): No, Jimmy!
Jimmy: (recognizing that David is upset) And I'm a
          poo-poo robot.
David: (in good spirits again) I'm a pee-pee robot.

Looking beyond the bathroom humor of these two boys, you can see a surprisingly subtle interchange. Jimmy realizes that his teasing has upset his friend, and so he makes fun of himself to balance the social interaction. David immediately recognizes this gesture of friendship and does the same, turning a potential conflict into a shared joke. This type of social sensitivity appears more regularly as children experience an increasing number of successful interactions with their peers. As Rubin notes, "[Preschool] children . . . acquire social skills not so much from adults as from their interaction with one another. They are likely to discover through trial and error which strategies work and which do not, and later to reflect consciously on what they have learned."

Naturally, much of the psychological literature is concerned with children who have difficulty with social skills, either due to their innate temperament or to specific psychological deficits that affect their social as well as their academic learning. An estimated 50 percent of children referred for special education services in school are also identified as having poor social skills leading to peer rejection. In many cases, the social problems of the child become more significant than the original school difficulties. Hundreds of studies show that peer rejection in childhood becomes a contributing factor to poor academic performance, emotional problems, and a heightened risk for delinquency in adolescence.

Fortunately, social skills, like other EQ skills, can be taught: by example, by specific interventions and activities, and by making sure that your child has achieved specific age-appropriate milestones.

▪ 12 ▪

Conversational Skills: More Than Just Talk

Many children who have problems getting along with others lack age-appropriate conversational skills. They have problems conveying their needs to others, and seem to have difficulty understanding the needs and desires of others.

Communication problems present a common chicken-and-egg dilemma for many children diagnosed with learning and behavioral problems. For example, in his work with children who have attention deficit disorders (ADD), psychologist David Guevremont notes that while these children are known to be very talkative, they have difficulty initiating verbal interactions and are less likely to be responsive to the communication of other children. Because of their poor conversational skills and other social skill deficits, 50 to 60 percent of ADD children experience some form of social rejection from their peer group, making them more likely to display negative, aggressive, and self-centered behavior, leading to more social difficulties.

Guevremont notes that poor conversational skills are particularly evident when children are trying to make new friends. These children desire to join in the activities of the others, but they choose the wrong social tactics. Studies suggest that popular children tend to approach unfamiliar peers gradually, hovering on the periphery as though they were collecting information before actually doing anything. Popular children are then more likely to verbally initiate contact with questions or comments about what they see. They may say, for example, "That looks like a fun game!" or "How did you learn to do that?" But children with poor social skills are more likely to initiate contact with disruptive, obnoxious, or self-centered behaviors. They may say, "I already know how to play that!" or "I can do that better than you. Let me try."

Fortunately, Guevremont and others have found that conversational skills can be identified and taught. These skills include:

Teaching Children Conversational Skills

Skill	What to Do
Expressing one's needs and desires clearly.	Make statements that describe how you feel, why you feel that way, and what you want.
Sharing personal information about oneself.	Talk about things that interest you and things that are important to you.
Modulating one's responses to the cues and words of others.	Pay attention to what the other person is saying and how she is saying it. Conversations are like seesaws: It takes two people to make them work.

Questioning others about themselves.

Be curious. Find out as much as you can about the person you are talking to.

Offering help and suggestions.

Be aware of what people want. They will usually say something like, "I don't know what to do."

Offering invitations.

If you enjoy a person's company, let him know it by inviting him to participate in activities that you both enjoy.

Providing positive feedback.

Comment on something that you like about what the other person has said ("That's a good idea!").

Staying with the conversation.

Avoid doing other activities. Don't change the subject or go off on a tangent.

Showing that you are a good listener.

Ask questions about what is being said. Ask for clarification or more details.

Showing that you understand the feelings of another person.

Mirror the other person's feelings by saying, "I guess you were really mad when you found out someone had taken your bike."

Expressing interest in another person.	Smile. Nod to show interest. Make frequent eye contact. Ask relevant questions.
Expressing acceptance.	Listen to someone else's ideas. Try to do things the way the other person suggests.
Expressing affection and approval.	Hug, hold hands, pat a person on the back or shoulders. Tell children that you like something about them or something that they are doing.
Expressing empathy.	Describe how you think other people are feeling and show that you care ("You look upset. Do you want to talk about something?").
Offering help and suggestions when they seem appropriate.	Suggest different ways that something could be done. Offer to help out even though you have nothing to gain.

WHAT YOU CAN DO TO TEACH CHILDREN BETTER CONVERSATIONAL SKILLS

The primary way that children learn social communication skills is through conversations with their family. The more you model the skills listed above, the more likely your child will use them in situations with his peers. A major obstacle for many parents is finding time to talk with their children. Some parents do this regularly at bedtime, others make sure that at least several dinners a week are unhurried and followed by meaningful conversation. Long walks or car rides can provide good opportunities for one-on-one communication. Meaningful conversations are characterized by realistic self-disclosure, which includes sharing both thoughts and feelings, faults and failures, problems and solutions, goals and dreams.

For children who seem to have difficulty getting along with others and/or have poor conversational skills, more structured activities may be necessary. Guevremont has found that conversational skills, much like other language skills, can be taught and enhanced with practice. In his social skills training program he uses a gamelike activity he calls "TV Talk Show" to teach basic communication skills. In this game, one child serves as the "host" and the other plays the "guest." It is the host's job to make the guest feel welcome, while learning about the guest's interests, feelings, thoughts, and opinions. Each interview is videotaped for three minutes, and then both children can be scored on specific skills such as those listed below:

The TV Talk Show Interview Form

(Put a check each time the "host" does one of the following. Use one sheet for each interview.)

Asks questions   _____

Shares information about himself/herself   _____

Gives suggestions or help   _____

Gives positive feedback (such as a compliment)   _____

Shares personal information   _____

Provides positive feedback   _____

Shows interest _____

Expresses acceptance and approval of what the
other person is saying _____

Offers appropriate suggestions _____

Eventually, children are asked to hold conversations more
naturally. They are given possible topics to discuss (favorite
toys, games, TV shows, etc.). Then they are asked to generate
their own topics and maintain the conversation for several
minutes.

If your child has a great deal of difficulty having conversations with other children, you may wish to initially play TV
Talk Show with her yourself, using the form in the table as a
guide for the interview and then scoring it. Ideally, videotape
yourself and your child playing the game (if you do not have
a video camera available, an audiotape will do). Obviously,
you should take care to be a good model for your child,
emphasizing your interest in her, drawing her out in conversation, and reciprocating with your own thoughts. If possible,
this game should then be played with another child, so that
your youngster can have the opportunity to develop conversational skills with others her own age.

EQ POINTS TO REMEMBER

- Social skills can be taught.
- Conversational skills help children gain social entry with
  individuals as well as groups.
- Conversation skills include sharing personal information,
  asking questions of others, and expressing interest and
  acceptance.

· 13 ·

The Pleasures
and Significance
of Humor

Psychologist Paul McGhee has suggested that humor may play a particularly important role in how children develop social competence. McGhee explains that children who are "skilled at humor" may be more successful in their social interactions throughout their childhood, noting that "it is difficult to not like someone that makes you laugh." Research has supported the common perception that children who are perceived as funny are more popular, while children who are seen as lacking a sense of humor are described as less likable by their peers. Other researchers have found that even four- and five-year-olds, judged to have a high level of social competence, more frequently initiated humorous interactions with other children. They also laughed more at the humor of others. In another study, eight- to thirteen-year-olds who saw themselves as shy also perceived themselves as being unfunny. And in another study of college students, the quality of being "entertaining" was identified as one of the three basic dimensions of friendship.

HOW HUMOR DEVELOPS IN CHILDREN

Like many other EQ skills, the capacity for humor begins in the first weeks of life. By the age of six weeks, you can put a handkerchief over your face, quickly remove it, and get a smile from an infant in a rudimentary game of peekaboo.

Since infants can appreciate only physical comedy, we all become transformed into Charlie Chaplin, seeking to gain the indescribable joy of watching our baby chortle and giggle. We instinctively learn how to encourage the contagious laughter of our children by giving them an anticipated surprise (peekaboo), by showing them the principle of "cause and effect" (the baby bops your nose and you make a funny face), and by giving them physical stimulation through a tickle or through movement (bouncing the baby on your knee or tossing her gently in the air).

According to Paul McGhee, true humor (more than a physical or perceptual reaction) begins in the second year of life as your child begins to understand the symbolic nature of words and objects. The basis of humor at this age is physical incongruity. To a toddler, putting a shoe on his head instead of a hat is nothing short of hilarious, as is the cartoon cat who tries to chase a mouse into a hole only to get his face flattened like a pancake.

By the age of three, preschoolers find that verbal statements alone can be funny. At first, your child thinks that simply misnaming something is terribly funny. She calls a "foot" a "hand," a "cat" a "dog," and a "mommy" a "daddy." As in most forms of humor, repetition just makes the joke funnier, and the two-and-a-half-year-old may quite literally knock herself over with laughter. Just a few months later, making up nonsensical names is a cause for amusement:

Father:	Come on Tammy, eat your cereal.
Tammy:	(age three) You're a cereal head.
Father:	Yes, I know, now eat your cereal.
Tammy:	(giggling) You're a spoon head.
Father:	Okay, Tammy. Very funny. Now let's eat your cereal so we can get to preschool.
Tammy:	(laughing so hard that she knocks over the bowl of cereal) You're a cereal-spoon-head-poo-poo-head.
Father:	(exasperated, but amused) Okay, Tammy. Whatever you say. I'll give you a banana in the car. Let's go. . . .

Rhyming and nonsense words are also funny to the toddler. When my daughter Jessica was two, she liked to call her friend Rachel on the phone to have a "nonsense" conversation. The conversation always involved just a few "silly" words:

Jessica:	(giggling) Gink-gunk.
Rachel :	(giggling) Gink-gonk.
Jessica:	(laughing) Bink-bonk.
Rachel:	(laughing really hard) Bink-bink.
Jessica:	(laughing so hard she drops the phone) Bink . . .

The context of the humor is always important, but even more so at this stage when children are just beginning to experiment with words. For example, the "gink-gunk" joke that Jessica enjoyed so much was only funny when told to and by Rachel. It was not funny to her if I or anyone else said it. In this stage, children begin to see the patterns in humor and naturally look for them in a familiar place. Children who watch *Sesame Street* perceive that Big Bird's bumbling is different from Grover's snide humor. Both are different from the goofiness of Bert and Ernie. They love the cadence and rhyme of Dr. Seuss's books, but also associate it with his whimsical and colorful drawings. If Dr. Seuss's words are read from a plain sheet of paper, children are not as impressed.

By the age of three, children enter a fourth stage of humor. They laugh at not only physical and verbal incongruities, but at conceptual incongruities, as well. For example, if another three-year-old puts a bottle in his mouth, this is not particularly amusing, but if Daddy puts a bottle in his mouth and acts like a baby, it's a riot. However, if a strange adult did exactly what Daddy did in an attempt to entertain a child, the child might get very anxious and even burst into tears. There is a fine line for young children delineating when something is funny from when it's not, even when it is perceived as a threat. This is why young children are often so ambivalent about clowns. The antics of a clown are out of context for a young child the first time he sees one in person. Clowns on TV or in the movies are in a different context than the ones who pinch your cheek or stick their bulbous noses in your face at the circus or a birthday party. It is only when a child has learned to put a clown in this "live" context that he perceives it as funny rather than frightening.

The next stage of humor emerges between the ages of five and seven, as children begin to develop greater linguistic ability and understand that words can have more than one meaning. At the age of five or six, children begin to tell riddles with double meaning, like the time-honored knock-knock jokes:

"Knock-knock."
"Who's there?"
"Orange."
"Orange who?"
"Orange you glad I'm telling you this joke?"

It's always fun to hear young children entering this phase, as they struggle to master the content as well as the form of the riddle. Several years ago, I interviewed a group of children to see how humor developed at different ages. The children between six and twelve all had jokes to tell me and the other kids, but it was Alexis, a smiling and bubbly five-year-old, who really made me laugh. Clearly thrilled to be in the company of older and wiser children, she had her hand in the air for fifteen minutes before it was her turn to tell a riddle.

"What did the moron say to the caterpillar?" she offered when it was finally her turn, beaming in the sheer joy of the moment. "I don't know," I responded, marveling at how her infectious grin seemed to light up the room. "Did you eat my candy?" she answered excitedly.

"What does that mean?" a nine-year-old asked, muttering the punch line to himself. "That doesn't make any sense. That's not funny," he said to Alexis without bothering to disguise his disdain. "Yes, it is, too!" Alexis responded, still beaming. "Did you eat my candy?" she repeated the punch line for emphasis.

"She's too young to know that's a stupid joke," explained an eleven-year-old to the rest of the group. Still beaming, Alexis simply repeated the punch line again, as if to say, "I'll just keep saying it whether you think it's stupid or not, because *I* think it's funny."

Alexis's riddle revealed that she understood the form of this type of linguistic humor, but she had a problem with the content. Undoubtedly, she was repeating a riddle that she had heard, but one or two of the words were simply wrong. Not quite ready to grasp the concept that it is the incongruity of a word's meaning that makes a riddle funny, Alexis simply assumed that it was your problem if you didn't get it. Researchers studying how children learn humor call Alexis's joke a "pre-riddle."

Elementary-school children show an ever-increasing fascination with the ready-made joke as opposed to the spontaneous, and often crude, jokes that they had previously found humorous. Many children pride themselves on having a storehouse of jokes and riddles, and it is common to see a whole class compete to see who knows more riddles in a certain category ("moron," "knock-knock," "why did the chicken cross the road?" jokes, and so on).

Jokes and riddles in these so-called "latency" years are ways for children to express interest in the basic drives of sexuality and aggression. Many youngsters begin their informal sex education by asking questions about sexual jokes they don't understand. Although it is unfortunate, children also express their hostility and aggression using jokes. Hostile jokes range from those making fun of a particular ethnic, racial, or regional group to the more grisly jokes that seem to surface within days of a real tragedy.

By the middle-school years, ages ten through fourteen, children have reached a level of cognitive sophistication that allows them to see incongruities on a symbolic level. It is at this age that puns and double meanings add a greater sophistication to the form, although not necessarily the content of joke telling. An eleven-year-old asked his teacher, "What is the difference between a cooking pot and a toilet?" "I don't know," the teacher replied. "Well, then I sure won't come to dinner at your house!" answered the child.

In the middle-school years, children may use humor as a weapon against adults as well as other children. The popularity of Beavis and Butt-head, the sadistic and sexually frustrated cartoon couch potatoes, is only one example of how young adolescents use humor as a way to distance themselves from adult values and mores. The class clown who at age seven or eight made farting noises with his armpits or fell to the floor in a mock faint at the sight of small cut is now more often than not a frequent visitor to the principal's office. His antics have become extremely disruptive to the class and disrespectful to the teacher, a thin disguise for his disdain for adult authority. And yet, as unpleasant as this type of humor is to adults, it is a natural part of growing up and testing the limits of authority. By eleventh grade, adolescents who use humor in school are more likely to combine it with positive classroom behavior. Their humor is frequently perceived as a leadership skill.

WHAT YOU CAN DO TO HELP YOUR CHILDREN USE HUMOR AS A SOCIAL SKILL

As with other EQ skills, different children have different natural aptitudes for being humorous. Some kids are simply funnier than others. And yet all children can enjoy humor equally and use it as a way to gain social acceptance as well as deal with inevitable psychological conflicts and anxiety. You can encourage humor in your child and your family as a way to add pleasure to every day, enjoy the company of others, and learn to deal with specific psychological problems and conflicts.

USING HUMOR AS A WAY TO MINIMIZE PAIN AND DISCOMFORT

Humor allows your children a variety of ways to deal with stress and anxiety. It can help them save face after an embarrassing encounter. It can help them deal with anger or express something that is otherwise difficult to say (that is, to say something without really saying it). For example, a friend of mine has a twelve-year-old who wasn't invited to her school's Valentine Dance. When her mother asked if she was upset, she replied with mock despair, "Oh, terribly, terribly! Now I'll have to return my designer dress and cancel my limousine!"

Encourage your children to tell jokes and find humor even in difficult circumstances. Their jokes communicate their likes and dislikes, and they can use humor to express positive or negative feelings about others. Children often use jokes as a way to maintain social status. It is common to see children whispering jokes to each other so that another child won't hear them. A joke might be passed around a classroom like some precious secret, making the rounds of the dominant

Humor is a highly valued social skill that we often don't appreciate in children. It is also an important way to cope with a variety of personal and interpersonal conflicts.

social clique, but never being told to the children viewed as having low social status. In fact, when children are told "the joke," it is an important sign of social acceptance.

Play Silly

Certainly the easiest and most effective way to encourage humor in your child is simply to play. Children love silly games, water fights, even a food fight now and then.

Joke Time

Have a comedy hour at your house. Specify a certain time when your family shares jokes and riddles. "Joke Time" could be after dinner on Wednesday nights, during breakfast on Monday morning (starting the week with a sense of humor), during regular car trips, or after a family meeting. In planning a time when family members make other family members laugh, remember the important psychological uses of humor: to reduce stress, bring people together, cope with difficult situations, and deal with specific fears, problems, and conflicts.

There are dozens of joke books for kids at your local library or bookstore, and family members can write down or memorize one favorite joke a week. Even better, people can tell a funny story, make up a poem, or draw a humorous picture. Self-created humor is always the best at developing a natural sense of humor. Videotape or record your "Joke Times" if you want a really good laugh five years from now.

Model Humor As a Way to Cope with Stress

Use humor in front of your children when you are stressed. Joke in the middle of an argument. Make faces at your bills.

Use Humor to Teach Values and Tolerance

Humor is frequently used as a way to express aggressiveness, even cruelty. Helping children distinguish between hostile and nonhostile humor can be an opportunity to teach tolerance and respect for others. Children must learn that words can be as hurtful as or even worse than hitting or kicking someone. Jokes that make fun of another person's race, religion, ethnicity, or disabilities certainly shouldn't be encouraged. Instead, use such lapses as opportunities to discuss prejudice and scapegoating. Encourage your children to find ways to recognize anger and aggressiveness for what it is and respect the feelings of others.

Clown Around

Shy and withdrawn children may particularly enjoy learning the art of being a clown. Dressing up in a clown costume and wearing clown makeup creates a new persona for children, encouraging them toward more extroverted behavior. Since clowns are usually silent, shy children don't have to worry about what to say. Perhaps the best way to teach clowning is to dress up like a clown yourself! Work out an act with your child where you juggle, chase each other around, do pratfalls . . . just act silly. This is also a great social activity for kids to do together. See if they can "choreograph" a ten- or fifteen-minute clown performance.

Some children like clowning so much that they will want to do it for others, performing at parties for younger children or even entertaining at hospitals or nursing homes. A wonderful resource for would-be clowns is *Be A Clown! The Complete Guide to Instant Clowning* by Turk Pippin. This book gives kids makeup and costume tips, classic sight gags (like the confetti in the "bucket of water"), and even classic clown routines like the fake fight. Pippin's clown rule #1: "Don't act like a clown, *be* a clown."

EQ POINTS TO REMEMBER

- Humor is an important social skill.
- It is one of the most highly prized character traits in children as well as adults.
- While children have different innate abilities in terms of telling jokes and making others laugh, every child is born with at least an appreciation of humor.
- Humor serves different purposes at different ages, but throughout one's lifetime it can be an aid in getting along with others and coping with a wide variety of problems.

· 14 ·

Making Friends: More Important Than You Might Think

Harry Stack Sullivan, a student of Sigmund Freud, emphasized the importance of the social relationships of children on
the development of their personalities. Sullivan believed that
a child's developing personality was equal to the sum of all of
his interpersonal relationships, beginning, of course, with his
relationship with his parents, but also including the profound
influence of his peers.

By the time a child is seven or eight, he begins to move
away from the influence of his parents, and with each passing
year, he looks to his classmates and friends as a source for
affection, approval, and support. While emotional sustenance
is taken for granted in the family, it is an earned reward
among groups of children. The pathway to that reward is
largely through the child's emotional and social skills.
According to Sullivan, friendships among children imprint a
lifetime of habits in relating to others, as well as a sense of
one's own self-esteem nearly equal to that developed by
parental love and nurturance. Conversely, when a child lacks
friends or peer acceptance, particularly in the elementary

school years, he carries with him a sense of incompleteness and unfulfillment, often in spite of significant accomplishments.

At age forty-two, Harvey was a respected and successful orthopedic surgeon. He described his marriage as a "good" one, although he worked seven days a week. But according to his wife, Flo, he spent less than four waking hours with her a week, and she referred to her husband as "The Shadow." Although Harvey loved his three children, now in their teens, he admitted they were a disappointment to him. In spite of giving them every advantage (including his considerable intellectual gifts), they were lackluster students and had little ambition except to party until late each night.

Harvey described himself as having no real friends himself, but noted that he liked some of his colleagues and occasionally had lunch with them. He said that he didn't really miss having friends as an adult, because he had never really had any as a child. As a boy, he was teased mercilessly for being skinny and awkward, but learned to keep his feelings to himself. As an adolescent, he worked hard and never dated. Flo, whom he met in college, was his only girlfriend. Harvey occasionally felt a vague sense of emptiness in his life, but that quickly vanished when he walked into his office past a waiting room full of people.

When Flo announced that she wanted a divorce and some "happiness" in her life, Harvey couldn't blame her. He knew that he hadn't been very successful as a husband, and supposed that being single would give him a little more time to devote to a research project that interested him. He thought this project might even put him in line to head his department at the hospital, and then his life would definitely have more meaning.

Making friends is a skill that is difficult to learn after

childhood. It is a little like swimming, which comes easy to children when they are introduced to the water as toddlers, but when adults learn to swim for the first time, having lacked the opportunity as children, they are typically stiff and unnatural in their movements. While the lack of friends certainly doesn't doom a child to becoming a friendless adult, we must acknowledge that certain EQ skills are influenced by a developmental timetable. When that developmental time period passes, the skill is much harder to learn.

HOW KIDS MAKE FRIENDS

In his book *Children's Friendships*, Zick Rubin describes how children go through four overlapping stages as they learn the art and skill of making friends.

1: In the *egocentric stage*, between ages three and seven, children most often define their friends as others who are simultaneously engaged in a similar activity or simply as kids who are nearby. A "best friend" for a youngster in this stage is often the one who lives in the closest. To put it somewhat unkindly, children at this stage seek friends whom they can use: those who have toys they want to play with or some personal attribute that they may lack. In general, kids in the first stage of friendship are better at initiating social interactions than they are at responding to other children's overtures. In their egocentric frame of mind, they assume that friends think the same way they do and will become upset and even reject a playmate if this proves untrue.

2: In the *need fulfillment stage*, between four and nine years old, children are motivated less by egocentrism and more by interest in the process of relationships. They value friends as individuals, rather than for what they have or where they live. But at this stage, your child is still self-motivated to seek friends because they fill a specific need. Children are drawn to others who share a toy or accept a cookie, but reciprocity is not particularly important. Because friendship becomes a way to meet their needs away from the family, your children may be driven to be with other kids at this age, and may even prefer to be with a youngster whom they don't really like to avoid being alone. Since friends are primarily a function of their present needs, kids typically have difficulty maintaining more than one close friendship at a time. This is a time when you might overhear your daughter saying to a playmate, "You're not my friend. Jodie is."

3: The *reciprocal stage*, occurring between the ages of six and twelve, is characterized by a need for reciprocity and equality. Children are able to consider both points of view in a friendship, and they are concerned and even preoccupied with fairness. They may judge the quality of their friends on a blatant comparison of who does what for whom: an invitation for a sleepover must result in receiving a similar invitation; one birthday gift must have the same value as another; if a child brings an extra dessert to school one day, he will expect one in return the next. Perhaps because of this preoccupation with reciprocity, friendships during this phase tend to be confined to pairs. Groups or cliques during the reciprocal stage are really just a network of same-sex pairs.

4: During the *intimate stage*, between the ages of nine and twelve, children are ready to engage in true intimate friendships. Rather than focusing on overt acts, they are more concerned about the person behind the facade and his or her happiness. Many psychologists consider this stage to be the foundation for all intimate relationships, theorizing that children who are unable to form intimate friendships in preadolescence and early adolescence might never know true intimacy as teenagers or even adults. The passionate sharing of emotions, problems, and conflicts at this stage forms a deep emotional bond that children remember as some of the most significant relationships in a lifetime. In some cases, these friendships actually do last a lifetime.

Zick Rubin writes, "A particularly important criterion of friendship at every age of childhood is the sharing of personal information—'private' facts or feelings that are not known to other people." Sharing personal information, as all therapists know, is one of the key ingredients in developing satisfying relationships, and it seems to have profound psychological benefits. The degree to which one shares personal information, including intimacies and secrets, is probably the most important gauge children use to judge their friendships.

At the age of eleven, Jennifer's parents told her that they were going to separate. Although Jennifer knew many other children whose parents were divorced, this news nevertheless sent her into a kind of shock. She didn't know exactly how to feel, and when asked, she said that she felt "nothing." Like many children when they first hear of their parents' divorce, Jennifer was in a stage of emotional denial, viewing the events in her life as if they were happening in a movie.

The only person Jennifer told about the breakup of her family was her best friend, Julia, whom she knew could keep a secret. She told her "second-best" friend Marcie that her parents were talking about a separation, but she did not tell her that they had actually made a decision. She told another set of classmates whom she liked, but did not consider "best" friends, that something important was going to happen to her, but she wouldn't tell them exactly what it was. Jennifer shared the details of her important secret with the person to whom she felt the closest. She opened herself less to those with whom she had a more distant friendship.

WHAT YOU CAN DO (AND NOT DO) TO HELP YOUR CHILD MAKE AND KEEP FRIENDS

The importance of helping our children establish friendships cannot be overstated, yet we are often confused about what we should or shouldn't do. Once you understand that friends fulfill different needs at different ages, it is easier to determine the role you can play in helping to teach friendship skills.

The Egocentric Stage

For younger children or for those who are withdrawn and tend toward social isolation, it is important to plan activities in which they will be with children who are like them or have similar interests. Initially, it is not as important how children react to one another, but rather that they have the opportunity to do so. Computers and sports are great icebreakers. But even if children just watch cartoons together, this can still be an important shared experience that can build the foundation for later social development.

If you are a single parent, it's wise to resist the urge to spend too much time alone with your children during the weekends and school vacations. By the time they are school age, they are ready to invest more emotional energy with their peers. It is damaging for them to be cast in the role of your companion.

The Need Fulfillment Stage

Once your children begin to enjoy the company of other kids, it's important to reinforce the value of friends. Take your children's friendships seriously by showing interest in their relationships with their friends and encouraging them to talk about their experiences. It's important not to diminish or negate your child's positive feelings about another child, even though you may have misgivings about that youngster. Also, avoid reinforcing your child's negative opinions of other children even if they are being teased or bullied. Resist the temptation to join your child in complaining about his classmates; this serves to reinforce social isolation. Just be a good listener.

It is also important to act as a good role model for your children. How can they develop positive and fulfilling friendships if you don't make time for friends in your own life? Talk frequently to your kids about your friends, what you do with them, and why they are important to you. Include your child in activities with your friends so that they can see how you relate with them and how much your friendships mean to you.

The Reciprocal Stage

By the time children reach the stage of reciprocity, many parents feel they have been relegated to the role of chauffeur, party planner, and bank teller (withdrawals only). You may feel like an irrelevant observer of your children's social life, but in fact your presence and support give them a sense of safety and security as they explore the give-and-take of social interaction. At this stage, your kids may benefit from your knowledge and experience as they learn the joys as well as the sorrows of long-term friendships.

If your child is having difficulty with his friends, you may want to offer examples from your own experience with friends, either present or past. But as in the previous stage, keep your feelings about your child's friends to yourself and avoid giving advice. Allow your youngster to develop patience, endure the hurt that will inevitably come in any close relationship, and make decisions about how to handle negative emotions and experiences for himself. Whether he decides to continue the friendship or give it up and find a new one is truly up to him. The only wrong choice would be for him to turn away from his peers and become socially isolated.

Because it involves the first true interchange of ideas and feelings, children typically have difficulty with this stage of reciprocity. If your child seems unsuccessful in engaging others, even after repeated tries, there are specific friend-making activities that you can help provide.

For example, simply observing friendships in videos, particularly when you point out how each skill is being used, seems to motivate children to seek out friends. If your child is having a hard time making friends, she will also benefit from various role-playing activities with you, using puppets or small figures. You can play out five- or ten-minute dramas, modeling different ways to solve interpersonal problems that your child may bring up. This kind of coaching is particularly effective with children who are able to talk about their previous social successes and problems.

The Intimate Stage

By the time your child reaches the stage of having intimate friendships, your role is now that of guidance. Set age-appropriate limits, impart values, and encourage personal and interpersonal growth. No doubt, as at other transitional stages in your child's life, you will feel a mixture of relief and sadness at your diminishing role in his world. This is also age-appropriate for you!

EQ POINTS TO REMEMBER

- Having a "best friend" is an important developmental task that may influence your child's relationships as an adolescent and an adult.

- While you can't force your child to be with other children, you can model how friends play an important role in your life.

- Make sure your children have age-appropriate opportunities to acquire friend-making skills.

· 15 ·

Functioning in a Group

After a child has learned to make individual friends, the ability to join and participate in a same-sex peer group is the second pillar he needs to build sound social relationships. By age three or four, children like to be around groups of other youngsters. While they still prefer to play with one child at a time, they enjoy doing this in the company of others. Although initially children will play with peers of either gender, by four or five they begin to show a preference for groups of the same sex.

By six or seven, kids begin to appreciate how group membership can enhance their confidence and sense of belonging. Although they may develop a strong sense of loyalty to these groups—"my class," "my baseball team," or "my Girl Scout troop"—the groups are still defined and organized exclusively by adults. Because children typically seek their playmates from within their peer group, a sense of group identity can begin to have as much social significance as the family. Children moving into a new neighborhood at this age normally experience a two- to three-month probationary period in these adult-defined groups before they become full-fledged group members. After that time, they are treated as members of equal status.

When children are seven or eight, they begin to define their peer groups for themselves. These groups most frequently parallel (if not parody) those that they see in the adult world.

Initially, the structure of the group is much more important than its function. Children commonly form secret clubs for the exclusive purpose of defining who can and who can't belong. These clubs are often preoccupied with electing a president, a vice president, and other officers and with setting up a schedule of meetings, rules, and rituals. However, by the time the structure of the group is actually formed (if in fact it ever is), the children typically find no real reason to meet and often move on to other activities.

Between the ages of nine and twelve, children's interest in groups has becomes a preoccupation. They are now almost exclusively of the same sex and, of course, the most common theme of group discussion is the opposite sex. Groups at this age and into adolescence are characterized by strong pressure to conform—a pressure that is often a thin disguise for the most cruel forms of social ostracism.

Take for example the following discussion I overheard at a restaurant in a local mall. I had only casually noticed a group of three ten-year-old girls when I sat down with my bowl of gumbo, assuming they were also there to have lunch and enjoy a bowl of soup on a frigid winter's day. I had no idea that I was within earshot of the membership committee of the "Punk-Out" club, which I learned was formed and named for the express purpose of keeping girls who dressed like "punks" out of the club. Here is a small sample of their voluminous conversation:

Girl 1: Did you see Marty on Friday? Disgusto! Boy is she a pig.

Girl 2:   I know. She's gross. I don't think she washed her hair all week.

Girl 1:   Who does she think she is dressing like that? Does she think that looks cool? She looks like a dirty doper to me.

Girl 3:   (giggling) She probably is! I bet she shoots up with the dopers on South Street or something and then gets so high, she falls asleep in her clothes and comes to school in the same clothes, and then gets high, and then goes through trash cans for stuff to eat, and then comes home and sleeps in her clothes . . .

Girl 2:   Yeah, that's disgusting . . .

Girl 1:   Yeah, and did you see what Sharon wore last week?

And on it went.

I listened to this conversation with a mixture of emotions. I empathized with the girl they were ridiculing. I wondered if she was really a social outcast or whether this was all just talk. Mostly, I felt relief at being a grown-up.

AVOIDING REJECTION FROM A GROUP

Being isolated from one's peer group may be one of the most painful experiences in a lifetime. When adults are asked to rate their childhood as "happy" or "unhappy," peer acceptance or rejection is one of the most frequently cited determinants.

Being rejected from the "popular group" of children can be as painful for today's kids as it was when you were a child, but fortunately there is generally a greater acceptance of diversity today. If children cannot fit into the dominant group of their peers (the "cool" kids), there are still usually several other groups within a school in which they can participate and enjoy a high degree of social status. Thanks in large part to the phenomenal success of Bill Gates and other multimillionaire computer whiz kids, even the onetime "geek" or "nerd" now has a certain social status.

Generally, there are two types of children who experience difficulty in joining peer groups: those who are situationally rejected but become accepted by a peer group within a year and those who are rejected because of some perceived "character difference" and experience prolonged rejection for a year or more.

Children who are situationally rejected are typically perceived as "outsiders," because they have moved from a different school or neighborhood or are temporarily rejected as a result of physical or cultural differences. Over a year's time, these children become assimilated, and their differences may even be seen as strengths. However, children who are rejected for a year or more are perceived as having characterological, unchangeable qualities that make them unacceptable to their peers. Usually, these children fall into either extreme of being too introverted or too extroverted—either highly withdrawn and "painfully shy" or aggressive, argumentative, overly competitive, demanding, and domineering.

Without intervention, children who are rejected for perceived characterological differences usually move further toward the extreme ends of their social group as they get older. The withdrawn girl may not come out of her room for days at a time, may refuse to speak to anyone at school, including her teachers, and by adolescence may be at risk for severe depression and even suicide. The boy perceived as overly aggressive and/or disruptive at eight or nine may be described as antisocial by the time he is ten or eleven. As the aggressive child physically matures, other children and even adults may see him as a threat. He may become isolated and sullen, often preoccupied with violent or vindictive fantasies, or he may find a group of other adolescents who share his predisposition toward antisocial activities.

The child who is socially rejected, for whatever the reason, is two to eight times more likely to drop out of high school before graduating, and is statistically more likely to be arrested for delinquent activities and/or be a habitual user of alcohol or drugs.

WHAT YOU CAN DO IF YOUR CHILD HAS DIFFICULTY JOINING A PEER GROUP

If your child has difficulty in finding a group of friends, whether it is for situational or characterological reasons, you may feel as hurt and as helpless as he does. You may even overidentify with your child's isolation, polarizing the world into "us" and "them."

This attitude of "you and me against the world" may initially feel comforting to both of you. Your child may even respond with a sense of relief and reduced anxiety. But these good feelings are short-lived, because he cannot avoid facing peer rejection again and again if he does not learn to function successfully in a group of age-mates. Even though it may go against your most basic nurturing instincts, it's important not to reinforce his sense of defeat and social failure, but rather empathically work toward helping him acquire the EQ skills he needs to join and function successfully in a peer group. The following are some specific suggestions to support your child if he is experiencing social rejection and isolation.

Act As a Role Model for Your Child by Participating in Your Own Groups

You can never overestimate the influence you have on your children by simply setting an example. If you are not already active in different adult groups, you might consider the positive benefits this may have for you as well as your child. It is important that your children perceive the value of these groups to you. The child who observes his father's excitement over going to softball practice sees how his dad likes to wear his team shirt around the house. If the child attends some of his dad's games, he will obviously be influenced by this important aspect of his father's life. On the other hand, the father who reluctantly becomes a member of the PTA, complains about the frequent meetings, and grouses about how ignorant the other parents are will obviously be giving his child a negative impression of groups, in spite of the fact that he has become a PTA member with the intention of being an involved parent.

Of course, the best way to model the value of groups to your child is to participate in a group together. In Philadelphia, there is a wonderful tradition of neighborhood clubs with the sole purpose of marching together in the annual New Year's Day Mummers Parade. The club members, often including several generations of families, spend the whole year making costumes, practicing music and comedy routines, and having fun together. For thousands of people in Philadelphia, these clubs form a social network that is nearly as important as their families.

In nearly every community, there are church groups, outdoor-activity groups, and hobby-oriented groups in which parents and children can participate together.

Encourage Your Child to Test Different Group Roles Within the Family "Group"

The first group your children experience is your family unit. Although your family is very different from their peer group, it can serve as a vehicle for them to learn group skills without fear of rejection. Family meetings are a time when you act most like a defined group, and they offer opportunities for your kids to practice different group roles. For example, when a family vacation is being planned, your child should certainly be able to voice an opinion and have it considered. Other times, perhaps in planning what to do on a Sunday afternoon, your child could step in and take a leadership role, gathering other people's opinions, taking a vote, and pronouncing the final decision. It is important to have family meetings on a regular basis, ideally once a week, for your children to learn group skills. If family meetings are only called when there is a crisis and emotions are hot, your kids are less likely to benefit from the sense of belonging and participating in a group.

Encourage Children to Join Different Specific Groups Comprised of Children Who Are More Like Them

From the time your children are seven or eight, encourage them to join as many kinds of peer groups as possible. While you may want them to participate in broad-based groups such as Boy Scouts or Girl Scouts, research suggests that children who experience social rejection in school rarely succeed in these groups. Rather, they maintain the same social status on the periphery of the group. Children who have difficulty with amorphous groups of children are more likely to succeed in narrowly-focused groups based on skills, interests, community orientation, and/or social service. These theme-focused groups are more likely to include children with personalities, interests, and social skills similar to your child's. Some common groups that interest children include:

Skill-oriented groups

Athletic teams

Bands and orchestras

Computer clubs

Chess clubs

Drama groups

Dance troupes

Art clubs

Interest-oriented groups

Groups based on hobbies

Nature-oriented groups

Noncompetitive athletic clubs (such as bicycle clubs)

Museum-sponsored classes in the arts or sciences

Religious youth groups

Community Service Groups

Neighborhood "cleanup" groups

Groups affiliated with adult service organizations (such as Lions Clubs of America)

Since most of these groups will meet at your local school, church, or community center, these would be good places to find a list of these groups.

Children's first groups are more concerned with form than content, but they are important in teaching children lifelong skills that are highly valued in the workplace.

Seek Formal Social-Skills Training Groups for Children with Extreme Social Problems

Children who have great difficulty joining a group often lack the specific social skills discussed earlier in this chapter, and by the time they are eight or nine, they may only be able to acquire these skills in structured social-skill training with their peers. Many schools have training programs designed to help children develop greater social sensitivity and awareness of how their behavior affects others. These groups are conducted by trained counselors or teachers, follow a systematic skill-building program lasting at least twenty sessions, and emphasize the application of the skills beyond the group to the broader school setting.

Psychologist David Guevremont emphasizes that social-skills training groups should use diverse real-life situations in the group training and include self-monitoring homework between sessions. A self-monitoring form, such as the one in the following table, asks children to work on very specific skills, recording what happened and rating their success. The forms are then discussed in the formal session.

Social Skills Homework Sheet

Your Name

Date _____ Time_____

The activity _____

The skills you are working on (fill in before the activity and then check off the substeps after the activity)_____

_____

Substeps	**Check when done**
A. _____	_____
B. _____	_____
C. _____	_____
D. _____	_____

Who's involved?

Names   **Ages**

_____   _____

_____   _____

_____   _____

What happened?

_____

_____

Rate the following on a 1 to 5 scale (1 = Very Little, 5 = A Great Deal)

A. _____   I enjoyed myself.

B. _____   I felt part of the group.

C. _____   I used new social skills.

D. _____   I'd like to do this again.

What did you learn that you might do differently?

_____

_____

What will you do for your next assignment?

_____

_____

Guevremont also emphasizes the importance of follow-up sessions after the formal training program has been completed. These sessions will help children talk about new problems that might have arisen as well as continuing difficulties. They will also assure some continued contact with former group members. Scheduling these follow-up sessions at two, four, and eight weeks after the formal ending of the group will also help children anticipate continued progress and be accountable for achieving it.

This type of social-skills training group is only needed if your child remains isolated even after your best efforts to help him make friends. Talk to your school counselor or school psychologist to help locate an appropriate resource.

EQ POINTS TO REMEMBER

- Getting along in a peer group is an important developmental task that may influence your child's relationships as an adolescent and adult.

- While you can't force your child to play with other children, you can model how groups play an important role in your life.

- Make sure your child has age-appropriate, interest-defined opportunities to acquire peer group skills.

· 16 ·

Manners Do Matter

Your children's ability to get along with adults, particularly authority figures, is an important aspect of their social development and a highly valued EQ trait. But American parents, unlike those in most other countries, do not seem to be particularly concerned with teaching their children manners or even respect for adults. This is true in spite of the fact that parents recognize the importance of good manners and are drawn to children who are polite, thoughtful, and exhibit "social graces."

As a nation, we have historically been ambivalent about good manners. On the one hand, our high tolerance for ill-mannered children seems to be a part of our heritage. Weren't our founding forefathers the upstart, unkempt, and ill-tempered British "children" who challenged the aristocratic and dandified King George III? Try to name an American hero or folk hero who was known for his or her proper deportment. Daniel Boone? Calamity Jane? Teddy Roosevelt? Amelia Earhart? We like our heroes with rough edges, unafraid to speak out, honest and ethical, but also brash with just a hint of the rascal. Well-mannered? Even the term seems sissified.

And yet we can't help but respond positively to the child

who greets us politely, sits patiently, and waits his turn to speak, and negatively to the one who ignores our greeting, jumps up and down at the table, and whines when he is not the center of attention. Manners do make a difference—more than most of us are willing to admit.

In a February 1996 poll conducted by *U.S. News & World Report*, nine out of ten Americans said that the lack of social courtesy has become a serious problem in this country and 78 percent said that our manners have seriously deteriorated in the last ten years. Over 80 percent of those polled felt that our lack of manners is a symptom of a much more serious disease, a significant contributor to the increase in violence, an example of our eroding values, and a divisive factor in the nation as a whole.

Even though we know good manners do make a difference, we may do little, if anything, to teach our children even the most rudimentary etiquette. Many in the current generation of children are impolite to their parents, disrespectful to their teachers, and rude to other children as well.

In his article for *U.S. News & World Report*, John Marks profiles Robert E. Lee High School in Montgomery, Alabama, which he presents as a microcosm for the nation as a whole:

> At this racially mixed school in a middle-class neighborhood, getting by means getting mean. Students generally don't open doors or speak to people they don't know. In the hallways, it's shove or be shoved. "If you're standing in the hallway, and someone's coming, if they want to come your way, you better move," explains Cindy Roy, a senior, "because if you don't they're just going to take you down and keep on going."

Unfortunately, the psychological community, also influenced by our cultural ambivalence, has not been able to identify this problem in its sociological context. Even worse, the psychological community may have contributed to it. For the past fifty years, beginning with Benjamin Spock's 1945 classic *Baby and Child Care*, and accelerating in the 1960s and 1970s with the popularization of humanistic psychology, psychologists and educators have advocated a child-centered approach to child-rearing and education, with an emphasis on helping children "feel good about themselves." But we are now learning that the self-esteem movement may have put too much emphasis on the *self*. Children raised in overly child-centered homes have become self-centered teens and adults.

Good manners, per se, does not seem to be an explicit concern of the psychological community. When researching this book, I ran a computer search in the psychological literature using the key words "manners" and "children." The computer's reply: "Nothing found." But noncompliance, the opposite of good manners, is very much a concern. It is one of the primary behavioral problems among children who are referred to counseling. Children classified as having a "disruptive disorder," according to criteria of the American Psychiatric Association, account for nearly 50 percent of clinical referrals. These children are referred for help because of their oppositional, defiant, and antisocial behavior.

I cannot overstate the importance of raising children who are well-behaved—polite, respectful of others, well-spoken—for the sake of their EQ. For decades, study after study of why children succeed in school has shown that those who are liked by their teachers get better grades and have more positive school experiences. Not surprisingly, teachers rate having "well-behaved children" as a key factor in determining a good year of teaching.

WHAT YOU CAN DO TO RAISE CHILDREN WITH BETTER MANNERS

The way to teach your children to behave more politely is to raise the bar on your expectations regarding their manners. When you think that you have raised your expectations high enough, raise them again. Remember that you are swimming against the cultural tide, with Beavis and Butt-head, Howard Stern, and "gangsta" rappers on the top-ten list of cultural icons. Do not tolerate disrespectful, discourteous, or rude behavior under any circumstances. No excuses.

If you are really ready to work on this EQ skill with your child, put yourselves to the test. The table below is a rating scale to determine how others perceive your child's manners. Make copies of it, and ask at least five people to fill it out, including both parents, an aunt or uncle, a friend of the family, a sibling, and, of course, your child. Then average the scores. A perfect score would be fifty. A score under thirty-five should raise a red flag.

The Manners Test

Directions: Enter your child's name in the blank spaces and rate, in the parentheses, the following statements on a 1 to 5 scale, according to the following:

5 = Always
4 = Most of the time
3 = Sometimes
2 = Rarely
1 = Never

Rating

(   ) _____ is punctual.

(   ) _____ is polite.

(   ) _____ has good table manners.

(   ) _____ refrains from talking back.

(   ) _____ does not interrupt others.

(   ) _____ says "please" and "thank you."

(   ) _____ writes thank-you notes after receiving a gift.

(   ) _____ is patient and waits for his/her turn.

(   ) _____ performs gestures of thoughtfulness at every opportunity (for example, holding the door).

(   ) _____ shows general concern and regard for others.

If your child does not score as well as you think she should, take heart that good manners are a value expressed in very specific behaviors, making them relatively easy to modify.

Begin by making a list of specific rules like those that follow. Post it in one or several prominent places.

1. Greet an adult when you see him by saying, "Hello," and inquiring, "How are you?"

216 The Social Skills

2. If introduced to an adult whom you do not know, or whom you rarely see, shake her hand as part of your greeting.

3. Always say "thank you" when someone does something for you, even if it is a little thing. Look at the person and say it clearly, so that he will know you are sincere.

These are just a few. You could probably list dozens of specific rules that might be appropriate for your child, but start with three to five that seem most important to you. New behaviors are always learned best a few at a time.

Once you make good manners a priority in your home, reinforce positive behaviors with praise and approval and discourage negative behaviors with immediate reprimands and consequences. When you feel that the posted rules have been learned well, add another three to five to the list. With some children, you may need to continue the list in this manner, but for many, this might be enough. Kids are keen observers, and for the most part, they want to please their parents. If you make your expectations clear, and if you are consistent in reinforcing (and obviously modeling) these new rules, your child will seek opportunities to show off her new behaviors.

EQ POINTS TO REMEMBER

- There is a national outcry against the loss of civility in our society, and your children are judged every day by the way they treat others. Only you can really make a difference in how well-mannered your children become.

- Good manners are one of the easiest EQ skills to teach, and yet may have a profound effect on your child's later social success.

PART 6

Self-Motivation
and the
Achievement Skills

Self-motivated people have the desire and will to face obstacles and overcome them. To many people, self-motivation is synonymous with hard work, and hard work leads to success and self-satisfaction.

The American glorification of self-motivation and the work ethic was first shaped by the Puritans and other religious groups that came to our shores in the fifteenth and sixteenth centuries. They believed that hard work and self-sacrifice on Earth was the way to a more restful paradise in heaven. Later, America's vast frontier attracted men and women with more earthly ambitions. They saw our land as a means of attaining the wealth and status they were unable to achieve in their country of origin. Even though the motives of these new settlers were very different, again, determination and self-reliance defined their pioneering spirit.

But it was the Industrial Revolution that placed self-motivation on the "top-ten" list of American virtues. Leading the world in inventions and technological ingenuity, Americans began to revere the machines they created. These contraptions of iron and steel, nuts and bolts, and steam and gears did the work of dozens of men, never stopping for a coffee break.

As hard and constantly as machines worked, they still lacked the emotional side of success: the heart, the passion, the courage to overcome obstacles that we associate with great achievement.

OVERCOMING ADVERSITY

The emotional qualities of achievement bring us real satisfaction—even more than the achievement itself. No one embodies our emotional ideal of self-motivation and determination as much as those who have overcome extraordinary difficulties to garner extraordinary levels of accomplishment. There are countless examples of physically disabled persons who have succeeded beyond anyone's expectations, reaching the pinnacle of our social order— celebrity status. There is Jim Abbott, a pitcher for the California Angels who at five years of age threw away his prosthetic right hand, but excelled in high school at basketball, football, and baseball. Or place kicker Tom Dempsey, who, although he was born without a right hand and only half of a right foot, kicked a record-shattering sixty-three-yard field goal for the New Orleans Saints. And, of course, there are the many prominent entertainers like Ray Charles, Stevie

Wonder, and Marlee Matlin, who never allowed disabilities to become liabilities.

Many other famous people have overcome less visible but equally serious learning problems or early school failures. Most people know that Albert Einstein had difficulty with his early school learning, including mathematics, but so did world-famous athletes like Bruce Jenner and Magic Johnson, actors such as Cher and Tom Cruise, scientists like physician Harvey Cushing (who pioneered the basic techniques of brain surgery), and even eminent statesmen such as Winston Churchill and Nelson Rockefeller. Rockefeller was said to have had such difficulty in reading his speeches that he had to completely memorize them before he spoke to an audience.

How did these people and countless others become so self-motivated and succeed beyond anyone's expectations? How can you teach your child these same skills to bring both success and self-satisfaction? We can answer these questions by understanding self-motivation from a developmental perspective.

THE ROOTS OF MOTIVATION

Like most other EQ skills, the basic elements of the motivation to learn and master our environment are part of our genetic heritage. From the first moments of life, a baby is curious about her world and strives to understand it. If you place your forefinger in her palm, she will grasp it. When you sit her up, her eyes will pop open like a doll's, and she will begin to look around. If you lean her body forward across one hand with her feet firmly on the bed, she will exhibit a walking reflex. From her first moments on Earth, she is born with the desire to master her environment—to roll over, sit up, stand, walk, and talk. And she pursues these goals relentlessly.

But something happens to many American children as early as seven or eight, when their schoolwork becomes more taxing. They seem to lose their eagerness to learn and discover. They may become overly concerned about being judged by others as their once natural self-confidence slips away.

Parents and educators have become perplexed about why so many children are complacent about learning at such a young age and seem to be satisfied with so little when the world offers them so much. Even students recognize the lack of self-motivation as an underlying cause of some of the most serious problems in schools today. At a 1996 meeting of the National Association of Student Councils, drugs and alcohol were voted the top-rated problem, but most delegates believed that substance abuse was really just the result of a more general apathy.

For over fifty years, researchers have speculated about the reasons why some people are self-motivated and high achievers and others are not. They offer some concrete answers, which I elucidate in the next three chapters. These answers fall under the general principles of:

1. Teaching your child to expect success.

2. Providing opportunities for your child to master his world.

3. Making education relevant to your child's interests and style of learning.

4. Teaching your child to value persistent effort.

5. Teaching your child the importance of facing and overcoming failure.

· 17 ·

Anticipating Success

[In school] Lincoln for the first time had a chance to
see children from other families and to pit his wits
against theirs. Taller than most of the other students,
he wore a coonskin cap and buckskin pants that were
always too short, so that, a classmate remembered,
"there was bare and naked six or more inches of Abe
Lincoln's shin bone." Unconscious of his peculiar
appearance, he would rapidly gather the other students around him, cracking jokes, telling stories, making plans. Almost from the beginning, he took his
place as a leader. His classmates admired his ability
to tell stories and make rhymes, and they enjoyed his
first efforts at public speaking. In their eyes, he was
clearly exceptional, and he carried away from his
brief schooling the self-confidence of a man who
never met his intellectual equal.

> —*Lincoln*
> David Herbert Donald

Self-motivated children expect to succeed and have no
trouble setting high goals for themselves. Unmotivated children expect only limited success and, according to psycholo-

gist Martin Covington, set their goals at the "the lowest level of achievement that a person can have without experiencing undue discomfort." A child who believes that he is a "C" student and cannot really get a higher grade will consciously or unconsciously gear his efforts toward mediocrity, no matter what his intellectual potential may be.

Children's expectations about their abilities begin at home. In a study designed to find out why American students performed below international averages on mathematics and science tests, as compared to the top-performing students from Japan and Hong Kong, Harold W. Stevenson and Shin-ying Lee interviewed nearly 1,500 students and their mothers in the first and fifth grades. They found that the children from these three cultures had no differences in their innate intellectual abilities; rather, there were significant differences in their parents' interests and expectations. The Japanese and Chinese mothers had higher expectations for their children and stressed the importance of education in their children's day-to-day lives. The children then internalized these expectations into their attitudes about their schooling. While the Asian mothers had higher academic standards for their children, they were also more realistic than the American mothers about their youngsters' academic, cognitive, and personal characteristics. They stressed the importance of hard work to their children more than their American counterparts, who placed a greater emphasis on their children's innate ability.

Most American families have high expectations for their children, but clearly this is not enough. Expectations mean very little if they are not backed up by a parenting style that values learning. Believing that wishes really do come true, we often rely only on praising our young children to build up their self-esteem. ("That's the most incredible picture I've ever seen!") But excessive praise actually has the reverse effect in building self-confidence: When we indiscriminately praise everything our children do, they don't learn to judge their abilities realistically. Consequently, they are more prone to disappointment when placed in a competitive school environment.

When we are serious about wanting our children to succeed, we express ourselves in actions as well as words, and these, in turn, are reflected by the demands of the culture, most notably in the schools. In Japan, for example, children go to school sixty days more a year than in America (one-third more school days) and have an average of four hours of homework per day versus the American average of four hours per week. In America, although we talk about longer school years and higher standards, requirements have generally remained the same. The time we actually spend helping our children may be diminishing.

The following is a checklist of ways you can convey the importance of education to your children. See how many of these activities you already do and how many more you can bring about.

Activities That Convey How Parents Teach the Value of Learning

_____ Have a reading time each evening during which all family members sit together and read silently.

_____ Regularly play board games like Scrabble, Boggle, or Jeopardy, which encourage verbal and reasoning skills.

_____ Encourage children to read the newspaper and discuss current events.

_____ Have nightly discussions on what children have learned in school and think of ways to follow up on these themes.

_____ Schedule regular visits as well as family vacations to include museums, libraries, and places of historical interest.

_____ Make homework a priority (before TV or other forms of entertainment).

_____ Subscribe to children's magazines.

_____ Take your children to visit your place of work or other work settings of interest to them.

_____ Continue your child's learning during the summer through specialty camps, library programs, or supervised projects.

MASTERY: WHAT IT MEANS AND WHAT IT DOESN'T

According to psychologist Martin Seligman, we can best convey our expectations by providing our children with opportunities for mastering their environment. Every time we require our child to look up an answer instead of just giving it to him or find a way to earn money for a new bike rather than telling him to wait for a birthday or holiday, we send him the message that he can learn to rely on his own initiative.

Based largely on his studies of learned helplessness, in which he found that people as well as animals can become unmotivated and even depressed when every action is frustrated, Seligman believes that providing children with mastery experiences such as looking up their own answers or saving for that prized bike strengthens their belief in themselves. They learn that their specific actions can bring predictable outcomes and the road to success is built on their own determination and perseverance.

Many parents wrongly conclude that establishing a sense of mastery is the same as mastering new skills. With this in mind, they may lead their children on a frenetic chase of extracurricular activities—rushing from piano lessons to soccer practice to karate class—often creating a sense of being controlled by the schedule of activities. But paradoxically, this hectic pace can work against children learning achievement skills: The feeling of being controlled by external forces often leads to a lack of motivation.

As a psychological concept, mastery refers to an internal sense of control—the ability to understand, integrate, and respond effectively to one's environment. This sense of being in control is an important factor in self-motivation, and it is one of the distinguishing characteristics of high-achieving individuals.

Giving your children the opportunity to set their own goals is an important way of giving them this kind of control. In a study that tried to improve the grades of underachieving fifth-grade math students, the students were asked to indicate in advance what percentage of test problems they thought they could answer correctly on their weekly quiz. Students were then paid in Monopoly money based on the accuracy of their judgments, making or losing money depending on how close they were to their own expectations, rather than on how they actually performed. Apparently as a result of this perceived control, their achievement scores increased three grade levels during the school year as they suddenly began to see that doing their schoolwork and homework was the surest route to meeting their self-imposed expectations.

PROVIDE OPPORTUNITIES FOR YOUR CHILD TO MASTER HIS WORLD

To help your child develop a sense of mastery and perceived control, which in turn will lead to increased initiative and self-direction, expect your child to do more on her own. Middle-class American parents have an increasing tendency to give their kids more and ask for less, but this does little to teach them self-motivation and a sense of purpose.

Secondly, reconsider how you reward your children (by praise or other means) for things they do freely. At one time, parents were told that constant praise and attention would help our kids develop high self-esteem, but in fact the opposite is true. Whether at school or at home, when children are continually given attention or reinforcement (points, chips, stars, treats) for work they already enjoy doing, they begin to feel that learning is just a way of earning rewards. Although praise and external rewards have their place in motivating children to do things that are difficult for them, reinforcement becomes meaningless when it is excessive. Rely on reinforcement when it is absolutely necessary and no more.

Self-grading is another way to increase your children's sense of control over their school achievement and so improve their motivation. When students are asked to grade their own work along with the teacher, and their "final" grade consists of the average of the student's and the teacher's appraisal, the two grades are usually very close. Simply knowing that their voice counts for something seems to increase their concern about what others think of them.

This principle can also work in your home. Instead of simply checking your child's homework or his success at a chore, ask her to grade herself on a five-point scale, with one being a poor job and five being a job done above expectations. Tell your child that you are also going to rate her performance and then compare your ratings when the task is completed, explaining that she must get a minimum rating of three from you for the task to be acceptable.

You may be very surprised to find that your children are not only quicker to do tasks when they take part in judging their outcome, but they are also much more conscientious about how they do the work.

Still another way of increasing your child's perceived control over his performance is to teach him goal setting and goal management. For example, suppose on Monday, Eric's teacher assigns a book report that is due on Friday. Rather than relying on Eric to set his own work schedule (which usually means the report gets written late on Thursday night) or setting and monitoring his schedule yourself (which does nothing to teach him self-discipline), you could teach him how to set up daily subgoals and monitor them. Being able to break a task into manageable steps is an important time-management tool and a method that helps many people stay self-motivated. Breaking a task into small steps also makes it easier to accomplish difficult tasks.

For example, early in my career as a psychologist, I directed a school for multiple-handicapped children, including those who were deaf, blind, and moderately retarded as a result of a rubella epidemic in the 1960s. Using principles of breaking tasks into smaller and smaller substeps, our vocational workshop staff was able to train these children to perform tasks that no one thought possible, including assembling electronic circuit boards for NASA satellites. We found that many tasks were attainable by substep training. Children who were previously cared for like infants learned how to dress themselves, use appropriate personal hygiene, and even make their beds. Making a bed consisted of teaching our clients over two hundred substeps, but once they learned these steps, they could make their beds with minimal supervision.

The "Step-by-Step Achievement Chart" was designed to help children break assignments into substeps, to apportion the correct amount of time for each step, and to monitor their progress in accomplishing each step. If your children are below the age of ten, they will probably need you to fill out this form for them, but they should still be involved in the process. Using this form for a new or difficult assignment will be an important component of teaching your child work and study habits that can last a lifetime.

Step-by-Step Achievement Chart

Write the assignment below:

_____

_____

Break the assignment or task into logical sequential substeps.

_____

_____

Plan out how long each substep will take and when it will be accomplished.

_____

_____

Have your child check off each substep when it is done.

Substeps	How Long Will Each One Take?	Done
_____	_____	____
_____	_____	____
_____	_____	____
_____	_____	____
_____	_____	____
_____	_____	____
_____	_____	____

MAKE EDUCATION RELEVANT TO YOUR CHILD'S INTERESTS AND STYLE OF LEARNING

Eleven-year-old David was considered a bright but unmotivated student. The fact that one of his parents was a school counselor and the other was a professor of English at a local college made his lack of enthusiasm for school even more apparent. It was not that David was averse to learning; in fact, reading was one of his greatest pleasures. But David wanted to read what caught his interest, and that was usually not what his teacher had assigned. He devoured books on the Civil War, baseball, geology, and any type of science fiction. Most of David's friends were considered to be "C" students whose teachers felt they could do better, an assessment based in part on the children's dazzling knowledge of sports trivia.

David's parents explained to the school guidance counselor how he and his friends would pass their time by naming every player in the National and American baseball leagues, the positions they played, and their lifetime batting averages. Yet not a single one knew the date of the signing of the Magna Carta, the first question on their mid-semester history exam and the subject of three weeks of study.

All children (and adults) learn more readily when they perceive the task as relevant to their lives. Educators, particularly those who teach children from minority backgrounds, have long criticized the standard school curriculum for just this reason, questioning why children will be motivated to stay in school and learn if they cannot relate what they are taught to the day-to-day problems in their lives. A basic premise of emotional intelligence is that the meaningfulness of what is to be learned is a critical factor in whether it is actually taken in.

For example, a sociological study conducted by Geoffrey Saxe of street children living in the urban barrios of Brazil underscores what children are capable of achieving when a task has meaning. Saxe interviewed poverty-stricken children whose very survival depended on being able to sell candy on the streetcorners to earn enough money for the bare essentials of life. He found that although these children had no formal schooling, they created their own intuitively based system of arithmetic that allowed them to carry out complex calculations in order to buy candy at a wholesale price and then resell it at a daily retail price, while taking into account Brazilian inflation, which exceeded 250 percent a year.

While few people advocate abandoning the content of the basic school curriculum simply because it doesn't seem immediately relevant to many children, there is a rising tide of criticism about the way children are taught. Harvard professor Howard Gardner is one of the more prominent critics of schools for still relying on nineteenth-century pedagogical theories on the way children learn. Gardner theorizes that there is not one general intelligence factor, as IQ tests would imply, but at least seven kinds that define how people learn and perform, including verbal, logical-mathematical, spatial, music, kinesthetic, interpersonal, and intrapersonal. Gardner points out that while children might have less innate ability in one type of intelligence, they may have more in another. Regardless of how children learn, most schools really only teach using the first two types, verbal and mathematical.

Gardner's theory of multiple intelligence appears to be particularly relevant to "alternative" programs designed for unmotivated students who would otherwise fail or drop out of the regular school program. In these programs, now being offered throughout the country as part of an educational safety-net, the standard academic curriculum is taught by appealing to all seven intelligences.

The CORE program (Creative Opportunities for Restructuring Education), now part of the Alternative Learning Program at Darien High School in Darien, Connecticut, exemplifies how multiple intelligence theory can be applied through specialized student projects. In studying a unit on World War II, the nine students in Suzanne Doran's program turned their classroom into a 1940s coffeehouse, replete with artwork showing themes related to the war. Led by several musically talented students, the class wrote songs reflecting the mood of the events before and during the war. The project culminated in an afternoon performance, in which the faculty of the school was invited to sip coffee and "experience" the project. They were greeted and waited on by students honing their social skills.

The multiple-intelligence model stresses the importance of hands-on learning and relevance through projects, community involvement, group learning with children of different ages, and visiting mentors. In schools throughout the country, this model and similar programs are being used to keep students in school and maximize their abilities. For the most part, however, these creative models of education are limited to a relatively few number of students—a fraction of those who might benefit from them—and this is unlikely to change. Still, individual teachers and certainly parents can learn from these programs and apply at least some of their principles to aiding underachieving students. The most important benefit of experiential learning programs is that children become self-motivated when the material appeals to their innate intelligences and arouses and satisfies their curiosity. Curiosity, in turn, depends on providing children with sufficiently complex tasks so that the results are not always certain. The tasks should combine elements of playfulness, surprise, and imagination.

BECOMING INVOLVED IN YOUR CHILD'S LEARNING

Only a small percentage of parents become intensely involved in their child's education, but these numbers appear to be growing. The home-schooling movement, for example, consists of parents who do not let their children attend any school, providing 100 percent of their educational needs. This movement is most frequently associated with parents who have strong religious or political beliefs and feel that public schools will undermine the basic principles they want their children to learn. But providing children with all of their educational needs is an extreme position that is impractical for most parents.

If we look at Japanese schools and families as a model for higher levels of student achievement, we can see that American parents typically fall short in the importance they put on their children's education, as well as the time they devote to it. According to Merry White of Boston University, an expert on the Japanese educational system, the way that parents participate in their children's education is really the critical difference between these two cultures. From an economic viewpoint, Japanese and Americans spend about the same amount on the education of their young (about 7 percent of the gross national product), and Japanese classrooms actually have much greater teacher-to-student ratios (40:1 versus about 25:1). It is surprising to many, but Japanese schools offer far less access to technology in the classroom than the average American school, concentrating on a basic curriculum and traditional teaching methods. But the significant difference is that Japanese mothers see the education of their children as their most important responsibility, whereas the typical American parent is more than willing to let the schools do the educating of their children.

While most American families cannot truly emulate the Japanese family, where mothers are single-mindedly devoted to their children and careers for women are frowned upon, even a small shift in the American family's emphasis on education in the home may make a significant difference. If we could spend just an hour a day of active time teaching our children, this would amount to a 20 to 30 percent increase in our youngsters' educational experience. Because of the individual attention that our children would receive, we would expect their learning to accelerate at an even greater rate.

You can begin your involvement by familiarizing yourself with what your child is learning (and not learning) in his classroom. If your child's teacher does not already make you aware of the skills or information taught each week, then you should certainly ask for that information. Teachers follow a standardized curriculum and make up weekly and daily lesson plans. They should be happy to give you a copy if you ask for it. The lesson plans typically have clearly stated objectives for what is to be learned in any particular unit of study and include criteria for how those objectives are to be tested or measured. If your child's teacher cannot provide you with this type of information, you should be aware that it is available through other sources.

American Education Publishing, for example, provides a series of books that covers the basic curriculums for grades one through five. These curriculums follow nationwide standards and are intended to help parents make sure their children don't fall between the cracks of the educational system. There are also dozens of computer programs that can aid you in teaching your child specific classroom content. One of my personal favorites for younger children is Knowledge Adventure's "Jump Start" programs, which provide an entire grade-based learning system covering multiple subjects through entertaining computer games. For example, the program Jump-Start Second Grade provides twenty-two learning modules, covering core second-grade curriculum, including basic grammar, "carry-over" addition, social sciences, and writing. This thirty-five-dollar program monitors your child's performance and adjusts the difficulty level automatically.

The Internet is another rapidly growing source of information for you to learn about how to help in the education of your children. There are dozens of sites to help you become more involved in your child's education and make learning an exciting adventure. For a lengthy list of web sites, start at a site called Internet Educational Resources (www.cts.com/%7enetsales/herc/hercoir.html).*

Through the Internet, your child can have unlimited opportunities to attend classes in cyberspace, communicate with children and adults with similar interests, visit virtual museums, or do research projects by going directly to the source. He can visit web sites such as the White House, the San Diego Zoo, the Smithsonian Institute in Washington, D.C., and thousands of other places around the world.

EQ POINTS TO REMEMBER

- Begin by expecting more from your children. Expecting more of children makes them expect more of themselves.

- Require that they work harder and spend more time doing homework, chores, reading, and learning about their world.

- Give your children opportunities to control aspects of their own learning.

- Teach them how to monitor their time and evaluate the outcome of their efforts.

- If your school-age children do not perform to their abili-

---

*Please note that any electronic mail or World Wide Web address cited in this book is subject to change.

ties, you can work cooperatively with teachers to develop an educational program that breaks learning down into small steps, gives your children a say in setting their own goals and evaluating their own progress, and teaches them through multisensory approaches using art, music, and experiential learning.

- Rather than fault schools for not doing enough, increase the time you spend educating your children.

- Computers, and in particular the Internet, provide unlimited resources and learning opportunities.

· 18 ·

Persistence and Effort

We idealize people who achieve success through hard work, and yet parents as well as many educators are uncertain as to how to instill the EQ skills of persistence, diligence, and ambition in their children. One of the most troubling realizations for parents is when they notice their children have stopped caring about their education, an all-too-common occurrence in our country, where the illiteracy rate keeps rising and 17 percent of children do not complete high school.

Mrs. Campbell dreaded going in for the annual teacher's conference regarding her daughter, Cindy. After all, she already knew that Cindy was an unmotivated student. She seemed not to care in the least about her grades, and her teachers felt she was wasting a fine intellect.

To make matters worse, the teachers implied that the fault somehow lay with the Campbells. But what did the teachers expect them to do? They begged, punished, threatened, and bribed their daughter, all to no avail.

What disturbed Cindy's parents most was how suddenly their daughter became an underachiever. It seemed incredible to them that only a year earli-

er Cindy loved her teacher, always did her homework on time, and was described as a "model" student. Now she was moody, frequently cut classes,
and her grade-point average had dropped from a
solid "B" to a "C–." To the Campbells, as well as to
her teachers, Cindy seemed to be drifting away.
How to get her back was an enigma.

Cindy's story is far from uncommon. Many children at the
age of twelve or thirteen begin to lose interest in school and
simultaneously become less influenced by their parents'
desire for them to achieve. While it is common wisdom that
many teenagers become slaves to their hormones (studying
comes in second when compared with the opposite sex),
developmental psychologists point out that it is actually cognitive changes that may be more responsible for the lack of
motivation in many teens.

Research psychologist Martin Covington describes how
children go through four cognitive stages as they learn the
relationship between effort, ability, and achievement. These
stages significantly influence a child's motivation to learn.

Stage 1: For children in preschool and kindergarten,
effort is synonymous with ability. These youngsters
believe that if they simply try harder they can succeed at
almost anything. You may remember the tower experiment mentioned in Chapter 1, in which four-year-olds
were asked to perform the nearly impossible task of raising a platform with a metal ball on it to the top of a
tower. Yet in spite of their repeated failures, nearly all the
children felt that they would eventually succeed.

Young children do not understand the concept that
each person has innate strengths and weaknesses. They

believe that if a person wants to be the best at running or reading, she simply has to exert more effort. In his book *Making the Grade*, Martin Covington quotes an explanation of one first-grader on the subject of hard work, "Studying hard makes your brain bigger." Covington notes that at this age "most children believe themselves capable of any feat and [they] disregard failure."

Stage 2: Between the ages of six and ten, children begin to see that effort is only one factor in achievement, the other being innate ability, and yet they still focus on the value of effort. Most children in this stage see that there is a one-to-one correspondence between effort and outcome. To be successful, they must work hard.

Stage 3: Between ten and twelve, children further understand the relationship between effort and ability. By now, they are fully aware that a person with less ability can compensate with more effort and a person with greater ability need expend less effort. Most children continue to remain optimistic about their schoolwork, but some children seem to resent the fact that their work is becoming harder and harder and requires more of their time. It is these children who, if unsupervised, will begin to develop the habit of putting off their work or avoiding it altogether.

Stage 4: At about the age of thirteen, or roughly the time that children enter junior high or middle school, their perception of effort as an equal partner in success gives way to the belief that ability alone is the necessary condition for achievement. Lack of ability becomes a sufficient explanation for failure. It is in this stage that underachievement begins to spread like an epidemic, as more and more adolescents take on a pessimistic attitude about their chances of success. Trying hard and not achieving as much as one expects becomes reason enough not to try at all. Too many adolescents then seek the course of least resistance, going through school with minimal effort and being satisfied with mediocrity.

While these developmental stages influence children as they grow, clearly not all children react the same. Many children develop good work habits as well as an unharnessed enthusiasm for learning which do not diminish in adolescence. As with other EQ skills, these attributes are best nurtured when children are young.

WHAT YOU CAN DO TO HELP YOUR CHILD SEE THE VALUE OF PERSISTENT EFFORT

The fact that not all children and adolescents fall prey to the gradual realization that even their greatest efforts will not guarantee success suggests that you can do much to maintain your child's optimistic attitude about the value of learning for its own sake.

Raising children to value effort throughout their lifetime should begin as early as possible. Although most Americans would criticize Japanese parents who hire tutors for their three-year-olds so that they can score high on a preschool admittance test, the fact remains that this early emphasis on the importance of effort has virtually eradicated illiteracy in Japan and made a degree from a Japanese high school comparable to a degree from many American colleges.

William Damon, in his book *Greater Expectations: Overcoming the Culture of Indulgence in Our Homes and Schools,* criticizes those who romanticize childhood as a time when children should be left to develop in an atmosphere free from challenges and unburdened by demands. He writes, "Children need to be engaged not just in activities that seem easy and fun, but also in challenging ones that can help them excel. In order to acquire creative skills, children need extrinsic feedback and reward just as much as they need to do work that is intrinsically interesting. They must learn to sustain their effort even when things get difficult and boring. Children do best in the long run when prepared to cope with the frustration and drudgery that is an inevitable part of creative work."

With this caveat in mind, you can begin today by asking your child to do more: more chores, more homework, more community service. While I personally extol the virtues of using computers in all forms of learning, I also recognize the danger that computers bring in terms of offering children even more instant gratification. It's wise to find a balance between our current cultural imperative to entertain our children seemingly every moment of the day and the need to teach them the necessity and value of persevering in tasks that are not intrinsically rewarding or that are challenging to their patience.

USING TIME MANAGEMENT

One way to create a balance is to teach your children some of the time-management skills used by nearly every adult who must sit at a desk and tackle daily stacks of work. Your child can learn time-management skills even before he can read a clock if you reinforce an awareness of time. When you tell your youngster that she must be in bed by eight, then that is when she must be under the covers. If she learns that she can stall or manipulate you into letting her stay up "just a few more minutes," then you will be giving her the message that

242 Self-Motivation and the Achievement Skills

the external limits of time are not important and she can let her own needs determine the household schedule.

You can introduce children as young as six to the rudiments of time management by using a form like the one in the following table. This form, which you will have to fill out with your younger children, will help them see the importance of prioritizing tasks, estimating the time needed to do a task, working until it is finished, and evaluating its outcome. Remember that time management is a skill that must be taught. You can't expect younger children to understand it the first time or older children to immediately embrace it. But reinforcing these skills over and over again will turn them into lifelong habits. According to our understanding of emotional intelligence and the development of the brain, your child will literally begin to develop neural pathways that will make persistent effort a part of his behavioral repertoire.

Managing Your Time and Your Work

List all the things that you have to do between _____ o'clock and _____ o'clock.

Now prioritize them in order of importance, with the most important task being first and the least important task being last. Then estimate how long you need to complete each task so that it is done correctly. Make sure that you have enough time to do the most important tasks. If there is not enough time, you should allow more time or reschedule the tasks of lesser importance.

When you have completed each task, you should check off the column marked "complete" and write in how long it actually took to complete it. Then rate how well each task was done on a 1 to 3 scale, with 1 = acceptable, 2 = pretty good, and 3 = perfect. Remember that different tasks require different levels of accuracy. It's okay to make your bed in an acceptable way (a rating of 1), but your homework should be perfect (a rating of 3).

TASKS TO DO

Prioritized Tasks	Completed	Amount of Time	Rating
_____	_____	_____	_____
_____	_____	_____	_____
_____	_____	_____	_____
_____	_____	_____	_____
_____	_____	_____	_____
_____	_____	_____	_____
_____	_____	_____	_____

THE VALUE OF HOBBIES

Time-management skills help children learn to achieve by stimulating the neocortex. But you can also reinforce these same skills through activities that engage the limbic system. Teaching through the emotional center of the brain is by definition more pleasurable to your children, but that doesn't mean that it can't be highly effective in changing the way they learn work habits.

Can you think of a time when you were working hard and enjoying it so much that time flew by? When this happens, you don't really regard it as work at all. Many people experience this "zone" when they are doing a hobby (or, as some people say, their work is their hobby). Anna Freud was one of the first people to see the developmental significance of how hobbies teach children work habits. Like other developmental theorists, Anna Freud believed that children should accomplish certain tasks at certain ages in order to progress in their personality development. She explained that hobbies were important developmental tasks for elementary-aged children because they were exactly halfway between play and work, sharing characteristics of both. Like play, hobbies are pleasurable, comparatively free from external pressures, and removed (but not too far) from the child's basic drives. Like work, hobbies require important cognitive and social skills, including planning, delay of gratification, exchanging information with others, and so on.

Observing your child's excitement in searching for information on dinosaurs, carefully constructing a motorized race car, or learning to use a pottery wheel helps you see the potential for her success when she is removed from the competitive pressures of school and academic performance. Hobbies give your children a sense of pride and accomplishment, sometimes for the first time, and by connecting with others who have similar interests, they reinforce the value of knowledge. Perhaps most importantly, hobbies provide a neutral zone of learning in which children can focus on the process of inquiry and enlightenment without the hindrance of being judged.

Many kinds of hobbies can teach the EQ skills that we associate with self-motivation and achievement, but most fall

Hobbies, which are exactly halfway between play and work, are an important way in which children learn persistence. Encourage your children to pursue hobbies that they are interested in for at least a six-month period.

into four major categories: collecting, craft hobbies, science-related hobbies (including computers), and performing hobbies. While many children pursue hobbies that are similar to those of their parents, others select hobbies based on those that have interest to their friends, and still others just wake up one day with a unique interest.

IT'S MAGIC

To understand how hobbies can teach EQ skills, let's take a closer look at one that I frequently recommend for children in counseling (and my own personal favorite)—magic.

Magic can span all four hobby categories, depending on how it is emphasized. Some children enjoy collecting tricks, while others can become interested in making their own tricks (which is not a bad idea, since this hobby can become expensive). Since many tricks are based on mathematical formulas and the science of illusion, this hobby is also a good nonacademic way to introduce these skills. Most of all, magic involves performance, whether your child puts on a show for you, a single friend, or a class talent show. The social aspects of magic provide some of the most important opportunities to learn achievement skills.

Hobbies should provide children with an almost immediate sense of accomplishment. This holds true for magic. When a child masters a trick, he feels that he knows something no one else does, and this adds a new dimension to his self-conception. Magic tricks can range from "self-working tricks" that are easily learned and immediately satisfying to ones that necessitate a great deal of skill and dexterity, requiring considerable memorization and sleight of hand. As with most hobbies, there is just as much pleasure for the novice as for the expert. Still, learning any trick requires sustained effort, practicing it until it seems natural and learning a story (patter) that goes along with each trick.

Magic is a great hobby for impulsive children. It requires that they coordinate their thoughts with their actions and develop a sense of time and timing, which, by definition, these children lack. When performing a trick, the impulsive child learns to get attention in appropriate ways, developing a repartee that simultaneously engages and amuses another person.

From a psychological viewpoint, however, I break with the age-old tradition of magicians who swear never to reveal a secret. Because I use magic to help children who are typically having social problems, I tell them to always reveal the secret at the end of a trick. This avoids putting them in the position of withholding something important from a potential friend. The secret becomes a gift that is shared. Knowing that the secret will eventually be revealed also takes pressure off the child to perform it flawlessly. I tell youngsters to inform their audiences, "I'll show you how it works when I am done." This puts the audience (usually one or more children) in a collaborative rather than an adversarial position. If the trick is performed wrong or the other kids guessed the secret, the magician does not lose face: He was going to reveal it anyway.

YOUR INVOLVEMENT IN YOUR CHILD'S HOBBIES

Using hobbies to teach social and emotional skills will require a slightly different orientation and level of involvement from you, particularly if your child has a short attention span, low motivation, or other problems associated with poor achievement skills. First, make sure that the hobby is at the right level for your child. Most kids will lose interest if the hobby is too difficult and becomes too much like schoolwork. On the other hand, hobbies that have no challenge are unlikely to interest your child for very long.

Secondly, designate a specific time to spend with your child on the hobby. It is impossible to overestimate the importance of the time you spend with your child in teaching EQ skills. If you want him to learn the importance of persistence and other work-related skills, it's wise to model this with your own interest, dependability, and guidance.

For example, if you were helping your young child learn a magic trick, learn it yourself first and then teach it to him, encouraging him to practice both the trick and the presentation. With an older child, you might take a trip to the library to find a book on magic or on magicians, rent and watch a movie on Harry Houdini, help him build a magic table to perform on, or help him explore the world of magic forums and web sites on the Internet (a good place to start is Dodd's Magic Locator at www.netdepot.com/~gargoyle/magic/links.html).

Finally, and most importantly, reinforce your child's patience and persistent effort with praise and encouragement. If he gets bored or frustrated, as will undoubtedly occur on some occasions, suggest that he take a five-minute break, but then go right back to work. It's hard not to project your own levels of stress and exhaustion on your children by suggesting that they "quit for the day" or go on to something more interesting. But kids are born tough and resilient—you may diminish these positive attributes by indulging them when they become frustrated.

Encourage your child to stick with his hobby even if something else attracts his interest or some aspect of it becomes frustrating. To be effective in teaching EQ skills, a hobby should last at least six months, and hopefully much longer. Taking your time to guide your child in selecting a hobby and finding one that will excite both of you is the best way to insure that you can follow through on your commitment to teach the value of persistent effort.

Encouraging your child to have a hobby is only one of many ways to reinforce the importance of persistence. Success in teaching this important EQ skill begins with changing your mind-set—not an easy task in a culture that is preoccupied with immediate gratification and quick fixes. You will have to relate to your child the importance of thoroughness (there is a difference between a straightened room and a really clean room), patience in mastering a difficult task (if the piano teacher tells her to practice scales for twenty minutes, don't let your child stop after five), stamina (demonstrate this with physical exercise—most children could use more of it), and resolve (once a goal is set, insist that it be met).

EQ POINTS TO REMEMBER

- Children's perception of effort and ability changes as they age. Children's optimism about succeeding by means of their efforts may fade in adolescence, as they begin to feel that those with greater ability will always be the ones with more success. You can offset this developmental trend by teaching your children to value persistent effort for its own sake.

- Time-management skills are important aspects of emotional intelligence that will serve your children throughout their lives. It is never to early to teach these skills.

- Hobbies are a unique way to teach the value of effort, because they involve elements of both play and work.

· 19 ·

Facing and
Overcoming Failure

Thomas Edison's maxim that genius is 1 percent inspiration
and 99 percent perspiration is not popular with a generation
brought up on three-minute microwave dinners, ninety-nine-
channel cable access, and dreams of instant lottery riches.
With the possible exception of the children who are raised on
traditional small farms, few kids have the opportunity to see
the cause-and-effect relationship between hard work and success. Children are most likely to idolize celebrities who appear
to have achieved their exalted status due to their appearance
or their natural talent. Even though their hard work and persistence are almost always a part of their success, this is rarely
made apparent in our cultural preoccupation with effortless
celebrity.

Our glorification of celebrities sends two messages to our
children that run counter to their learning the EQ skills of
achievement. Not only do kids learn to devalue the role of
effort, but they also don't understand the importance of failure and learning from one's mistakes.

Your child cannot learn persistence unless he comes to
accept failure. Legend has it that Thomas Edison's search to

find a workable filament for the first electric lightbulb resulted in a thousand mistakes before he succeeded. As Jonas Salk
searched for a vaccination for polio, a disease which prior to
1954 paralyzed and killed thousands of children, he spent 98
percent of his time documenting trials that did not work. Paul
Ehrlich, who discovered a drug that could cure syphilis in the
early part of this century, named his final formula #606, the
prior 605 experiments being failures. But we rarely convey
these stories, and thousands like them, to our children.

Most failures produce a mixture of disturbing emotions,
including anxiety, sadness, and anger, but your child must
learn to tolerate these emotions in order to achieve success. As
Martin Seligman writes in his book *The Optimistic Child*, "In
order for your child to experience mastery, it is necessary for
him to fail, to feel bad, and to try again repeatedly until success occurs. None of these steps can be circumvented. Failure
and feeling bad are necessary building blocks for ultimate
success and feeling good."

THE ROOTS OF UNDERACHIEVEMENT

Unfortunately, many of today's children are not taught to tolerate the negative emotions associated with failure. And if we
are to believe the developmental theory of self-motivation,
they also cannot bear to be perceived as having failed through
some lack of innate ability. Berkeley psychology professor
Martin Covington notes that many children over the age of
thirteen believe that it is more painful to be perceived as
"dumb" than to actually face the social consequences of being
seen as a failure.

Consider, for example, the all too familiar maneuvers that
older children and adolescents use to avoid the embarrassment of being caught unprepared by a teacher's questions:

Once again, thirteen-year-old Billy had not completed his homework. He had spent yesterday afternoon and evening practicing his turnaround jump shot and watching *The Terminator* for the fifth time. He told his parents that he had done his homework in study hall, but neglected to tell them that he hadn't finished it. Now, facing Mrs. Stevens, his seventh-grade history teacher, it was time for a reckoning.

"Who can tell me some of the causes of the Great Depression?" Mrs. Stevens queried her class. Three of the usual eager students raised their hands, but the other twenty-five students kept silent.

To avoid being called on, Billy, without really thinking about it, dropped his pencil on the floor and leaned slowly over to pick it up, hoping to remove himself from Mrs. Stevens's view. But in spite of his slow, deliberate movements in retrieving his pencil, when he finally sat up, Mrs. Stevens was still searching for a volunteer. Quickly, he began a second maneuver, rubbing his eyes vigorously like he had some dust in them. But his teacher was still gazing in his direction. When he could rub his eyes no longer, Billy settled in with the "stare at your paper approach," trying to look like he just found the meaning of life hidden somewhere between a smudge and a doodle.

In the next row, Ellen took a more forward approach—the quizzical look. Cradling her chin in her hands, she gave Mrs. Stevens her best "I'd-really-like-to-give-you-an-answer-but-I'm-still-pondering-the-meaning-of-life" look, assuming that Mrs.

Stevens would perceive her understandable confusion and that calling on her would interrupt her musings.

A third student, Tommy, was well-known to have nerves of steel. Although he hadn't a clue as to what the answer was (he really didn't even listen to the question), he decided to use some "reverse" psychology. He waved his hand wildly in the air, assuming that his teacher would never call on someone who was obviously so eager.

It was Billy whom Mrs. Stevens finally chose, although he was still not ready to admit that he just didn't know the answer. He began with a delaying maneuver, simply restating the question: "You want the causes of the Great Depression?" he asked rhetorically.

"That's correct, Billy," Ms. Stevens replied with a tone of infinite patience.

"That would be the Depression of the 1930s?" Billy asked, showing that he at least knew a few facts.

"Correct again," his teacher said, "the causes of the Great Depression of the 1930s." Mrs. Stevens was familiar with this "cat-and-mouse" game that her students played when they didn't know an answer. Raising her voice just a decibel or two, she asked matter-of-factly, "Billy, do you know the answer to the question or not?"

In response, Billy hung his head and said nothing, reverting finally to the age-old wisdom that it is better to be silent and to possibly be thought of as a fool than to open your mouth and remove all doubt.

Older children have elaborate ploys to avoid being seen as dumb. Parents can teach their children that effort is more important than ability and that being wrong and even failing is part of achieving success.

Most of us have tried one if not all of these time-honored strategies to avoid having our teachers perceive us as dumb or unprepared. Students copy reports directly from an encyclopedia, fake a stomachache or a fever on the day of a big test, or, in the most serious cases, simply stop working altogether based on the mistaken logic that they can't fail if they don't even try. But with far too many children, this becomes a self-defeating pattern of underachievement.

Procrastination is another thin disguise for the fear of failure. There are as many ways to procrastinate as there are activities for children to become engaged in. Dedicated procrastinators can even find ways to do nothing while they seem to be working very hard. Didn't you ever spend more time making the cover for a book report than actually writing it? Or writing and rewriting the first sentence of an essay without having figured out what you really want to say?

Avoiding work in order to sidestep failure is a characteristic of the most hard-core underachiever. According to Covington, "Chronic underachievers avoid any test of their ability by refusing to work, thereby maintaining an inflated opinion of themselves. In order to justify this deceptive cover, underachievers often make a virtue out of not trying. They may take a perverse pride in their unwillingness to achieve by downgrading the importance of the work they refuse to do, or by attacking others who do try as hypocritical, foolish, or stupid. Underachievers may convince themselves that failure is a mark of nonconformity and evidence of their individuality."

In extreme circumstances, children will intentionally handicap themselves in order to avoid school failure. They may develop anxieties and even phobias that take the focus off their fear of not being able to meet the expectations of their parents, teachers, and peers. In adolescence, alcohol and drug abuse is the most common way to mask the fear of failure. It is not a coincidence that at a time when children are most concerned about the perception of their peers, they begin to drink alcohol or take drugs.

This self-handicapping is one of the most unfortunate ways that children use to avoid failure, since it virtually assures a downward cycle of disaffection from adult expectations and irresponsible behavior.

USING COOPERATIVE GAMES TO HELP YOUR CHILD LEARN TO FACE AND OVERCOME FAILURE

The American educational system, indeed the American culture itself, makes it difficult for many children to face "losing." Competition is as American as apple pie, and while we admire the traits of generosity, charity, and kindness, it is the people who win whom we really admire. From infancy, we convey the message to our children that life is a contest with winners and losers, dividing people into those who are "the best" and everyone else who is "not the best." We coo to our babies, "Who is the *prettiest* little girl in the world?" We gush over the scribbling of our toddlers, "How wonderful! That's the *greatest* picture I've ever seen." We put the "A" spelling papers on the refrigerator, the trophies on the mantel, the certificates, ribbons, and newspaper clippings in the family scrapbook.

In spite of our preoccupation with competition, according to many educators there is no such thing as "healthy" competition. They quote studies that suggest the introduction of competitive incentives in any form decreases school achievement. The logic is simple: When students are busy avoiding failure, they do not get truly involved in the task. When winning is the goal, learning is not.

Nor is there evidence that competition builds character. Terry Orlick, a pioneer in the cooperative games movement, believes that competition encourages children to cheat, lie, become saboteurs, and band together to keep others from winning.

Teaching your children to value cooperative effort and

group achievement is an important way to offset our cultural tendency to see the world in terms of winners and losers. Although infants and toddlers are known for egocentrism and possessiveness, between the ages of eighteen and thirty months kids go through a transformation in their ability to engage in prosocial behaviors, becoming noticeably more cooperative, helpful, and willing to share.

Many studies have also found that cooperative and prosocial behaviors are among the most important characteristics in the social acceptance of young children. Observing preschool children on the playground at the beginning, middle, and end of the school year, researcher Gary Ladd and his associates found that those who exhibited more cooperative behaviors increased their social status, while noncooperative children were less well-liked and were chosen less frequently as playmates.

Cooperative games are the primary way educators teach this important social skill. Indeed, studies have suggested that cooperative skills learned in a game situation will generalize to other peer activities. In a study of how cooperative games can be used to modify aggressive behaviors in young children, April Bay-Hintz and her colleagues at the University of Nevada at Reno write that nonaggressive collaboration with others is "one of the most fundamental goals of development and provides a basis for success in friendships, marriage and careers." They note that teaching children cooperative games and activities has led to increases in peer acceptance, sharing, acceptance of differences among other children, and more positive peer relationships.

Teaching your children cooperative games helps them establish the foundation for dealing more successfully with the realities of achievement in a highly competitive world by helping them see that achievement is part of a group process.

In addition, cooperative games and activities teach children afraid to fail the importance of sustained effort. There is no such thing as individual failure in a true cooperative activity: Either everyone wins or everyone loses. The following are some examples of different cooperative games that are fun to play. Once you try them, you will find that children like them as well as, if not more than, traditional competitive games.

The Cooperative Robot

This is a fun game for three people. I like to prescribe it to families in which there is a lot of sibling rivalry or children are going through a particularly "uncooperative" stage. The youngest player starts in the middle and holds hands with the other two players at his side. Now all three players must function as one. The player in the middle is the "brain," and the players on the side must coordinate their hands to do what the brain wants. Try these activities:

1. Make a peanut butter and jelly sandwich and feed it to all three heads. Make sure you've got some milk to go with it!
2. Using a mirror, draw a picture of what you look like joined together and cut the picture out.
3. Do a simple chore like sweeping the kitchen or making a bed.

Cooperative Volleyball

This game can be played with any size group, but three to five players is best. Begin by blowing up a large balloon. The players have to keep the balloon in the air for as long as possible, but no one can hit it again until everyone has hit it once. The team should try to keep breaking its own record!

Get a Little Closer

This game is an adaptation of one played by Indian children of Guatemala. You will need a small box and ten tennis balls or Superballs. All the balls should be the same size, but one should be of a different color or marked with a crayon, designated the "Closer" ball. Set up a starting line about five feet from the target. The first player throws the Closer ball from behind the line and tries to get it as close to the target as possible. The other players take turns rolling the other balls from behind the line so that they nudge the Closer ball until it is touching the box. Play continues until the Closer ball is touching the side of the target box.

Cooperative Air Hockey

This game for two players was inspired by Jim Deacove, another pioneer in the cooperative games movement and a prolific game inventor. You will need eight pencils, a cup, two straws, and a small wad of paper.

Begin by making a "double square" with the pencils, as in the figure on the next page. Each player takes a straw and, working cooperatively, the players must try to blow the wad of paper between the inner and outer squares two times. Because an air stream is unidirectional, it is extremely difficult to navigate the wad of paper without help from the other player. After going around twice, the players must blow the wad of paper into the cup. To add to the excitement of this game, require that the goal be scored in two minutes or less or add more pencils and make the maze more complicated.

COOPERATIVE AIR HOCKEY

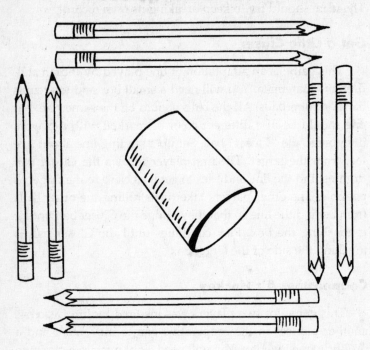

Once children understand the principle behind cooperative games (everyone wins by cooperating or everyone loses), it is almost impossible to play them wrong. And since they are fun, they are self-rewarding. Children will want to play them again and again.

People are never too old to learn to play cooperative games or the value of cooperative effort, nor are they ever too old to learn to face failures, value persistence, or adopt the other qualities that we associate with self-motivation and achievement. Still, we should remember that the younger children learn EQ skills, the better, and that all EQ skills are interrelated. If you are concerned about your child's motivation and success in school, start with just one change in your parenting style and make sure that you are steadfast in your resolve to make that change permanent. Remember the most important rule of motivation for children and parents alike: Success breeds success.

EQ POINTS TO REMEMBER

- Studies suggest that when children reach the age of twelve or thirteen, they are particularly vulnerable to motivational problems. While younger children see the value of effort in achieving their educational goals, teens frequently become preoccupied with ability, or their lack of it, and do anything possible to avoid being perceived as a failure.

- Offset this developmental change by teaching your children to value effort rather than just outcome.

- Teach that success is often built on failure.

- Help your child find gratification in cooperative achievement rather than only individual accomplishments.

PART 7

The Power of Emotions

In their compelling book *When Elephants Weep*, Jeffrey Masson and Susan McCarthy describe countless examples of how animals express the emotions that were once thought to be the defining difference between man and beast.

Congo, a chimpanzee raised by humans, hated it when he was moved to a new zoo enclosure, but took his anger out on the other apes. He would solicit lighted cigarettes from zoo visitors and use these to chase the other animals around the cage trying to burn them. When Maria and Misha, two huskies, were separated, Maria watched daily for Misha's return, but finally, realizing that Misha was not coming back, became listless, irritable, and depressed.

Wela, a bottle-nosed porpoise, once bit her trainer's hand by accident and, hideously embarrassed, went to the bottom of her tank and sulked until her trainer coaxed her out.

Masson and McCarthy note how different species seem to display more of one emotion than another: parrots are irritable and often hold a grudge for no reason; geese, swans, and ducks are famous for their devotion to their mates; elephants seem to be particularly affected by the death of one of their own, showing intense interest in elephant bones, but not the bones of other animals, and possibly even recognize the after-death scent of a loved one.

Through studying other species, as well as the evolutionary development of human emotions, we know that emotions serve specific purposes in a child's development into a happy and successful adult. But we also know that a child's emotional development can go terribly awry, causing him to suffer from a wide variety of personal and social problems.

Most theorists agree that there is a set of basic emotions—including love, hate, fear, grief, and guilt—and that all other emotions are derived from these basic building blocks, much like the way primary colors are used to form a nearly endless array of hues.

As humans, we are capable of hundreds of shades of emotions, and yet it is not our emotions themselves that distinguish us from other animals. Rather, it is our ability to recognize and think about them that places us at the top of the evolutionary ladder. In Part VII, we will examine the EQ skills you can teach your child that will not only harness his or her emotions to cope with the changing requirements of a technological society, but will actually help him use his new understanding of emotions to have a more fulfilling, successful, and even healthier life.

· 20 ·

Emotional Awareness and Communication

Traditional psychotherapy promotes emotional awareness as the primary vehicle for life change. Patients in counseling talk about what makes them angry or sad or guilty, and they work to transform the situations that have caused these feelings. Patients also talk about what gives them joy, pleasure, and pride, and look to find ways to increase these feelings. Talking about one's feelings is the most direct way to understand and control them.

The cortex, or thinking brain, allows us to have feelings about our feelings, to express these feelings to others, and to observe and learn from how they react to them. Teaching children to understand and communicate their emotions will affect many aspects of their development and life success. Likewise, failing to teach children to understand and communicate their emotions could make them unnecessarily vulnerable to the conflicts of others.

Take, for example, Martin, a six-year-old whose parents were going through a particularly vicious divorce. Martin's father insisted that Martin fly to visit him in Boston every weekend, while his mother maintained custody during the week in Richmond, Virginia. Martin barely said a word during the two-and-a-half-hour trip, and insisted on going to bed as soon as he reached either of his two homes. After two months of this arrangement, Martin started complaining of stomachaches, and his teacher said that he rarely talked to anyone when at school.

At the custody hearing, Martin's lawyer asked him, "How do you feel about visiting your father every weekend?"

"I don't know," was Martin's reply.

"Well, are you happy to see your father when you get to Boston?" his lawyer inquired, keeping his own emotions in check and trying not to lead Martin toward one answer or another.

"I don't know," Martin responded again, in a barely audible monotone.

"What about your mother? Are you happy living with her during the week?" the lawyer queried, realizing that he was only going to get one answer from Martin during these proceedings.

"I don't know," Martin said again, and nothing about his demeanor suggested that he did.

Your child's ability to put his emotions into words is a vital part of meeting his basic needs. When your two-year-old becomes angry because you are talking to a friend in the grocery store and he wants to go home and get something to eat, he might have a tantrum, because that seems the quickest way to have his needs met. But your five-year-old will be able to recognize that he is hungry and bored and express this in words. Most likely, you'll meet his needs by offering a snack from the cart. Your ten-year-old should be able to identify a dozen or more of his emotional states. When asked about his reaction to an upcoming trip or to attending his grandmother's funeral, he can draw on a memory bank of emotional experiences and anticipate how he will react to these events.

The words that describe his emotions—happy, excited, sad, worried, anxious—are also connected to the feelings themselves. When he responds that he is anxious about attending the funeral and seeing his grandmother in a coffin, there is a lightning-fast connection from his speech centers to his emotional brain, triggering the subtle physiological responses that we associate with anxiety—a slight quickening of the pulse, a small rise in blood pressure, a tensing of the body.

By the time your teenager turns sixteen and the thinking part of his brain is fully developed, he should be capable of talking about subtle shades of emotions. He can describe feelings in metaphors and images, explaining that he is as "happy as a lark" or "feeling like he is sitting in a dark corner of the basement, and no one knows he is there." He is also able to articulate his physical associations to different emotions, using phrases like a "a sinking feeling in the pit of my stomach" or "all tied up in knots." Physiological descriptions of our emotional states have become part of our common vocabulary, and they are particularly effective at conveying the degree to which we experience an emotion. When we hear a physiological description of a feeling and perceive the nonverbal cues related to that feeling in the speaker's face or posture (he is blushing, pale, stiff, and so on), we often subtly mirror the physiological response ourselves.

THE NATURE OF EMOTIONAL COMMUNICATION

As we have seen, a toddler who has not yet developed language skills will have difficulty putting her feelings into words and may throw a tantrum. A five-year-old has acquired the necessary language, and so has the capacity to use words. Our children's capacity for emotional awareness and their ability to talk about their feelings take place in their neocortex, and so naturally they follow cognitive development.

But like many other EQ skills, our youngsters' developmental readiness to understand and communicate feelings and their ability to do so are two different matters. Although their capacity to talk about emotions is hardwired into their brains (in a sort of developmental preprogramming), whether they are actually able to use this ability depends largely on the culture in which they are raised, and in particular the way that you interact with them and they interact with one another.

In families in which feelings are openly expressed and discussed, children develop the vocabulary to think about and communicate their emotions. In families in which feelings are suppressed and emotional communication is avoided, children are more likely to be emotionally mute. While psychotherapy has demonstrated that people can learn the "language" of emotions at any age, as with other languages, the most articulate speakers are the ones who learn while they are young.

Learning to identify and convey emotions is an important part of communication and, as we shall see, a vital aspect of emotional control. But appreciating the emotions of others is an equally important EQ skill, particularly in developing intimate and fulfilling relationships.

Therapists and counselors have found that it may be more important to be a good emotional listener than to be an articulate speaker when it comes to emotional communication. A "good listener" is both patient and attuned to the emotional needs of the speaker, who interprets this attention as an important form of emotional nurturance. While marriage counselors have long extolled the benefits of active emotional listening in intimate relationships, researchers are now finding that this EQ skill is just as important in the workplace. For example, supervisors describe managers trained in active listening skills as more supportive.

Throughout adolescence and through every stage of adulthood, the person who is perceived as emotionally literate is the one who is most valued as a companion, coworker, and recipient of one's love and trust.

WHAT YOU CAN DO TO RAISE CHILDREN WHO EXPRESS THEIR FEELINGS

One of the simplest and most useful things you can do in promoting emotional literacy is increase your child's emotional vocabulary. Make a "dictionary of feelings" for your children by asking them to name all the feelings that they can think of. Write them down in alphabetical order in a blank book, one feeling to a page. A good way to generate a list of feelings is to look through news magazines that show candid photographs of people (rather than photographs that are posed) and ask your youngster to describe what he thinks each person is feeling. Then, write a different emotion at the top of each page of the dictionary, asking your child to give an example of a time that he or she had that feeling. If your child finds this exercise difficult, illustrate from your own life experience. Younger children will also enjoy drawing pictures of each emotion. Older children might prefer taking a photograph of themselves or someone else to use as a visual reminder of each emotion.

In nearly twenty years as a therapist helping children and their families, I have often prescribed games to encourage children and parents to develop a language of emotions. In one poignant case, I was working with a mother and her two children, ages nine and eleven, to help them with their sense of loss over the sudden death of the children's father. Both children were sullen and uncommunicative, showing more and more signs of depression as the months passed by. Jane's numerous attempts to get her children to talk about their feelings seemed to always end in frustration. "And besides," she explained, "I work two jobs to support us now, and I don't know when I am supposed to have time to sit down and talk to them!"

Usually, when I prescribe a game, my first concern is when and where it will be played. If a parent tells me she barely has time to do the basic household chores, much less have time for herself, I know it is unrealistic to ask her to make time for yet another activity, even if it is in the best interest of her children.

Thinking about when and where this family might play an EQ game to help them more easily express their feelings led me to the idea for an oddly named activity I called Feelings License Tags. I knew that the family spent at least forty-five minutes a day commuting to and from school and other activities, and I remembered how most children like to pass the time on long trips spotting the letters or the state name on the license plates of cars as they passed by.

At their next counseling session, I asked Jane and her kids if they had ever played this kind of activity, and if they would be interested in learning a new car game. "The object of the game," I explained, "is to spot a license with two letters of a feelings word and then tell of a time when you had that feeling. For example, a license tag with the letters 'A' and 'M' could be used to form the word 'mad.'" I said that this was a cooperative game, and that the whole family would get a point each time a license tag was spotted and a feeling was talked about. If they scored twenty points between Monday and Friday, they would win a meal at a fast-food restaurant, and I handed them three coupons that I kept as incentives for just this type of occasion.

At the next session, I noticed a significant improvement in the family's spirits. They had played the game, achieved a score of thirty-five, and had enjoyed their meal (particularly the fact that I had paid for it). I asked them to play a second week, with a different incentive (this time Jane took her children to the movies), and the next time I saw them I again noticed a more relaxed mood in the family. In particular, the children had become more chatty.

When I spoke to Jane in private, she told me how, as a result of playing this game, her children had begun to talk about many feelings and had revealed their sadness and anger at the loss of their father on several occasions. This family was now well on their way to using emotional communication to help them go on with their lives, so I suggested that we take a break from therapy for a month or so. I would check in with them each week by phone.

During the second call, I knew that the game about communicating feelings had served its purpose when Jane explained to me, "You know, Dr. Shapiro, we played Feelings License Tag this week, but we didn't get enough points for some reason, and we all really wanted to go out and see a movie together. So I had to drive around for an extra hour on Friday night just to look for tags so that we could talk about our feelings."

HOW TO HELP YOUR KIDS BECOME GOOD LISTENERS

Just as we can teach our children to become better at expressing their emotions through games, so we can help them become good emotional listeners. In a normal conversation, children are naturally concerned about expressing their opinions about what is being said, seeking opportunities to express their agreement and disagreement. But in "active listening," they become entirely focused on the other person without interjecting their opinions or feelings into the conversation. You can teach active listening skills, which are very much like the listening skills used by professional counselors, to children as young as ten. This EQ skill has been an important part of the training in many school-based conflict resolution programs, as well as in various forms of family counseling. Playing the Active Listening Game, you can teach this skill to your child yourself.

The Active Listening Game

Begin by making two lists of at least six concerns with your child (age ten and over) or adolescent, one for you and one for him. This list could contain anything that might bother you or your child, but it is usually best to start with relatively mild problems or conflicts. Then take four index cards and write the following active listening skills:

1. Restate what the other person has said ("So what you're telling me is . . . ").
2. Clarify what the other person has said ("Can you tell me more about . . . ").
3. Show interest in what the other person is saying (by gesture, voice tone, eye contact, and so on).
4. Label or describe what the other person seems to be feeling ("It seems to me that you are angry about . . . ").

To play the game, each of you in turn selects a concern or problem to talk about for three minutes. It could be a problem you are having with someone else or a difficult decision that you have to make. While one of you is speaking, the other demonstrates the four active listening skills, using the four cards as reminders. At the end of each "round," the speaker gives the listener a point for using each skill and an additional two points if the listener has remained nonjudgmental. Then the speaker and the listener switch roles and play the next round.

The game continues for six rounds, each consisting of a different topic of concern from the lists. At the end of the game, the points of both players are combined, and if the total is over thirty (out of a possible thirty-six), both of you are declared the winners and can give yourselves a suitable reward.

EQ POINTS TO REMEMBER

- Encourage children to verbalize their feelings as a way to deal with their conflicts and concerns and get their needs met.

- Teach children active listening skills to help them develop emotionally rewarding relationships now and as they grow.

· 21 ·

Communication Beyond Words

While it is important to teach your children to talk about their feelings and listen carefully to the expressed feelings of others, research has found that words actually account for only a small part of emotional communication. In a series of studies, psychologist Albert Mehrabian showed that in face-to-face interactions, 55 percent of the emotional meaning of a message is expressed in nonverbal cues such as facial expression, posture, and gesture, and another 38 percent is transmitted through voice tone. That leaves only 7 percent of emotional meaning that is actually expressed in the words that we speak.

THE IMPORTANCE OF NONVERBAL CUES

In their book *Helping the Child Who Doesn't Fit In*, psychologists Stephen Nowicki and Marshall Duke note that problems in nonverbal communication will often inhibit a child's social interactions much more than what he or she actually says in words. They write:

Mistakes in verbal communication will lead others to regard the child who makes the mistake as uneducated and/or unintelligent. On the other hand, mistakes in nonverbal communication will usually get a child labeled as weird or strange. When a person makes a mistake in verbal communication, we make judgments about his or her intellectual abilities. In contrast, when a person commits an error in nonverbal communication, we are more prone to make judgments about his or her mental stability. It is one thing to be around someone we consider uneducated; it is quite another to be near someone we perceive as unstable. Such people threaten our feelings of safety and security. . . .

Unlike verbal behavior, which starts and stops, nonverbal behavior is continuous. Children (as well as adults) are always communicating through their body language and facial expressions, whether or not they are aware of it.

Although the rules for nonverbal communication are not typically made explicit to American children, we do have some very specific implied rules. It becomes blatantly apparent when they are broken. Nowicki and Duke point to the example of elevator etiquette. Imagine riding in an elevator with a nine-year-old child who faces the back of the elevator rather than the door, who stares at you unrelentingly, or who stands very close to you, even though there is sufficient room in the elevator. Immediately, you would get the sense that there is something "unusual" about this child, although you might be hard-pressed to say exactly what it is.

Our awareness of the rules for nonverbal behavior appears to reside in the emotional parts of our brain, normally just out of reach of our cognitive understanding, and yet available for analysis when we recognize the importance of this type of communication. Understanding the power of non-verbal communication can aid your child in developing leadership skills, becoming assertive, and empathizing with the needs and problems of others.

AREAS OF DIFFICULTY IN NONVERBAL COMMUNICATION

Nowicki and Duke list six areas of nonverbal communication in which children typically have difficulty, often causing them to be perceived as "different" and experience varying degrees of social rejection:

1: *Speech pattern and rhythm that is "out of sync" with another child.* Imagine a child from New York City talking to another child from Baton Rouge, Louisiana. Each child will perceive the other as talking strangely, and they may even find each other difficult to understand.

2: *Interpersonal space.* Standing too close or too far away from another child or touching another child inappropriately makes them feel uncomfortable.

3: *Gesture and posture.* Gesturing is an important part of how children communicate the emotional content of their words. A slouched or too casual posture often communicates disrespect or disinterest, even though this may not be the child's true feelings.

4: *Eye contact.* During a conversation, the average individual spends 30 to 60 percent of the time looking at the other person's face. Differences on either side of this norm can be read as being inappropriate.

Understanding the nonverbal language of emotions is an important aspect of helping children with their problems. Approaching an angry child from the front with a stern posture will be perceived as a threat and is almost sure to lead to a confrontation. Approaching an angry child from the side and avoiding direct eye contact is a much more appropriate way to help him calm down.

5: *The sound of speech.* All aspects of sound that communicate emotion either in speech (voice tone, intensity, and loudness) or in nonspeech (whistling, humming, noises, and so on) sounds are important. Nearly one-third of a child's emotional meaning is carried through this so-called paralanguage. Nowicki and Duke note that a habit even as minor as the constant clearing of one's throat can lead to social rejection.

6:   *Objectics.* Children, like adults, use objects such as clothes, jewelry, and hairstyles to convey social meaning. While some children become preoccupied with their appearance as a way to communicate their social status or group identity, others seem oblivious to the messages that their appearance conveys. Children and particularly adolescents who are unaware of how their appearance affects others may be more vulnerable to social rejection.

Nowicki and Duke make a compelling argument for parents to be aware of the way that children communicate nonverbally if their child is experiencing social rejection, particularly if their child has a learning disability or other psychological problem that might contribute to peer rejection. In fact, all children will benefit from learning about nonverbal emotional communication.

TEACHING YOUR CHILD NONVERBAL COMMUNICATION SKILLS

The following games were inspired by the dozens of activities suggested by Nowicki and Duke to teach specific nonverbal communication skills.

The "Sound-Off" Game (ages seven to twelve)

To play this game, videotape an age-appropriate drama from TV and show it to your child with the volume turned off. Ask him to describe how each person on the video is feeling. Stop the tape whenever he wants and give him a point if he can describe how a facial expression, gesture, or posture reveals how the actor might be feeling. Then rewind the tape and play it with the sound on so that you can check his answers. Have him accumulate fifteen points in fifteen minutes.

Feelings Charades (ages six through teens)

With a group of three or more, make a deck of about twenty feelings cards by writing different emotions on index cards. Have the youngest member of the group go first, picking a card and then acting out the feeling without words in three minutes or less. The person who guesses the feeling correctly keeps the card and takes the next turn. The person with the most cards at the end of the game is the winner.

If there is a wide age range in the group or disparity in the skill of the players, simply take turns acting out the charades so that each person gets a chance to practice learning how feelings can be communicated without words. As children increase their skills at this game, add new and more subtle feelings to the deck.

Guess the Feeling (ages five to ten)

Read a simple sentence into a tape recorder five times, but each time you read it, change your tone of voice to reflect a new feeling. For example, say the sentence, "I left my bags in the car," like you are happy, sad, mad, afraid, and worried. Give your child one point each time she identifies the emotion correctly. Then have your child read a new sentence five times, trying to convey different feelings through her voice tone. Again, give her a point for each successful effort.

Picture Yourself with Feelings (ages five to twelve)

In this activity, children learn to explore their own feelings and how they express them through their face and body by making a dictionary of how emotions are expressed nonverbally. An instant camera will be necessary. You'll also need sheets of loose-leaf paper and a binder.

Begin by asking your child to make a face that expresses a particular feeling. If he has difficulty doing this, ask him to think of something that makes him feel that specific emotion, such as, "You get mad when Tommy teases you, don't you? How do you think you look when he teases you?" Some children will still have difficulty with this. They may think they look mad, but it doesn't show. If this happens, ask your child to look at herself in the mirror and literally shape her face with your fingers or through your suggestions (tell her to lower her eyelids, scrunch up her nose, and so on). Now take the mirror away and snap a picture. Place the picture in the binder and ask her to write down all the times she has had that particular feeling.

Now repeat the process by taking a picture of your child showing a posture that expresses this feeling. Again, you may have to literally move her body to help her understand how postures change with different emotions. You may want to include other children in the pictures to show more subtle feelings like affection, jealousy, or pride.

Make a section in the binder for each feeling. Use it periodically as a diary to help children record their feelings, noting when and why they occur and what they can do about problematic feelings.

EQ POINTS TO REMEMBER

- Help your child develop the ability to understand the nuances of emotional communication by teaching him to read the nonverbal language of emotions.

- Emotional communication includes being aware of the nonverbal behavior of others (gesture, body language, facial expressions, and so on), as well as your children's own nonverbal communication. Something as simple as making a child aware of his posture when he sits at his desk can make his teachers think better of him.

- Emotional communication is also conveyed by the way people speak. Some children need more help than others in understanding how emotions are conveyed in voice tone, speed of speech, and so on.

▪ 22 ▪

Emotional Control

In the early part of the century, Sigmund Freud theorized that learning emotional control was the benchmark of personality development that defined civilized man. Freud believed that the personality of a developing child is shaped by two powerful forces, one seeking pleasure, the other trying to avoid pain and discomfort. These primary life instincts, represented by a theoretical structure he called the id, are controlled by a moral center, the superego, which in effect is the internalization of parental authority. When a child's id impulses tell him to go take some candy from the cabinet, his superego reminds him that taking things without permission is wrong. If he takes the candy anyway, his superego will respond by punishing him with guilt over his actions, which could be manifested in untold nefarious ways, including nightmares, psychosomatic illnesses, and panic attacks. But the child still wants the candy!

Freud postulated that to negotiate between basic impulses and the threat of punishment, a child develops an ego, as middleman or emotional manager. The ego becomes the developing child's voice of reason, an adaptive force that allows him to get what he wants in a socially appropriate way that offends neither the outside world nor his inner world of rules and sanctions. To get his candy, the child can wait until dinner and ask for the candy for dessert, perform an unexpected chore and hope that his reward might be a treat, or simply ask for what he wants and reason with his parents that a piece of candy might make his day go a little better. Freud believed that the more a child can consciously be aware of and weigh his various options, the more likely he is to be successful in achieving his goals through compromise.

Therapists and counselors who help children develop emotional control still treat them based on these same assumptions—namely, that to help a child tame his unconscious passions, you must help him develop ego control mechanisms, including insight, planning, delay of gratification, and an awareness of others. From our view of emotional intelligence and neuroanatomy, these techniques still seem to be appropriate for teaching emotional control, but we have also developed a much more sophisticated understanding of how our emotions develop and why these techniques work.

THE NEUROSCIENCE OF EMOTIONAL CONTROL

Neuroscientists now believe that our emotions are conveyed and controlled by a lightning-fast communication system in the brain that is dominated by the thalamus, the amygdala, and the frontal lobes of the cortex, with support from a variety of other brain structures and glands that send information in the form of biochemicals to the rest of the body. Judith Hooper and Dick Teresi, in their book *The 3-Pound Universe*, compare the thalamus to the flight control center at O'Hare Airport. They write, "No signal from the eyes, ears, or other sensory organs can reach the cortex without passing through it." Sensory input, whether it is from a harsh voice or an attractive suitor, is routed by the thalamus to different areas of our higher brain center, the cortex, where we make some meaning out of it. The frontal lobes of the cortex appear to be particularly important in emotional control, and many scientists believe that this is the site of self-awareness.

But not all of the information goes from the thalamus directly to the thinking part of the brain. A part of it also goes to the amygdala, the resident manager of the emotional brain. The amygdala reads and reacts to various sensory input much more rapidly (and less precisely) than the cortex, and can trigger an emotional response long before the thinking brain has figured out what to do.

In intense emotional situations, such as when a child is confronted by the fierce bark of an angry dog or the stress of an exam, the amygdala activates a nerve running to the adrenal gland, which secretes the hormones epinephrine and norepinephrine to put the body on alert. These hormones in turn activate the vagus nerve, which sends signals back to the amygdala.

The amygdala is capable of emotional learning and emotional memory, which may be entirely apart from the conscious learning and memory that takes place in the cortex. Neuroscientists such as Joseph LeDoux believe that the brain's emotional memory, which is distinct from the more familiar cognitive memory, may be why the traumas of childhood can affect us as adults, even though we can't consciously remember them. Emotional memories, such as feeling abandoned when our cries were not answered quickly enough, are stored in the amygdala without the benefit of words or even conscious images, and yet they can still play an important role in how we feel and act.

Understanding the neuroanatomical aspects of emotions makes us realize that there are really two systems by which children learn emotional control. While Freud's theory reflected his intuitive understanding of how the thinking part of the brain handles emotions, he did not see the significance of the emotional brain, which is capable of bypassing the thinking part altogether. Thus, when stimulating what Freud called a child's ego-strengths, we are really activating cortical (thinking) functions of the brain, but neglecting the complex system of the emotional brain, which plays a much more significant factor in handling strong emotions.

What all this implies for teaching children emotional control is that talking to children to help them develop insight into their feelings—whether in a family meeting, the principal's office, or in a therapy session—is clearly not enough. Talking triggers the control centers in the thinking part of the brain, but has relatively little impact on emotional control. Intuitively, every parent knows this is true. Have you ever tried to talk a child out of his fear of getting a shot at the doctor? Have you ever tried to tell an adolescent that it's not a big deal that she has broken out in a discoloring rash just before a date, and that beauty is, after all, only skin-deep? Or for that matter, have you ever tried to tell an adult who is deathly afraid of flying that he is safer on a plane than in his car? In these examples and countless others, we know that when emotions rage, reasoning fails.

To help children with emotional control, we must fight fire with fire, providing emotion-based solutions to emotional problems. We must teach the emotional brain as well as the thinking brain.

HOW TO TEACH YOUR CHILD EMOTIONAL CONTROL

Without question, the most common emotional problem facing children today has to do with anger control. Children characterized as angry, aggressive, or oppositional account for an estimated 40 to 50 percent of all clinical referrals. We could speculate for pages as to why children seem to have more problems controlling their anger than ever before, but the real question is what we can do about helping them tame their angry monsters. The answer lies in emotional reeducation. Here's how it worked in my office during a hot game of Stay Calm, a variation on Pick Up Sticks.

> Billy concentrated with all his might, his hand slightly trembling as he reached for the red stick just below the green one. If he could just move the red stick a quarter of an inch without moving the yellow one, then he could have it out.
>
> Then Peter blew in Billy's ear. He made a noise like a duck and started calling Billy names like "fart-face," "butt-head," and "stink-breath."
>
> Billy ignored his brother, breathing deeply and slowly, keeping his muscles limber and eyes focused on his task. He knew that to win this game, he would have to ignore his sibling's antics. Concentrate, he told himself, pick up one stick and then the other. Don't pay attention to anything but what is in front of you. And he picked up the red stick without moving any of the others.

Billy and Peter were playing the Stay Calm game in my office to help them deal with teasing. The usual way to play Pick Up Sticks requires each player to remove one stick at a time from a pile without moving any of the others. It is a simple game that requires concentration and fine motor coordination. But in this EQ game, designed to teach emotional control, while Billy tried to pick up the sticks, Peter was allowed to tease him in any way that he liked, as long as he didn't actually touch him. Each player got one point for each stick he picked up and two points if he showed no reaction whatsoever to the teasing.

Games like Stay Calm go a long way toward teaching emotional control. Emotional education, or what some educators are calling emotional literacy, must be directed to the emotional and the thinking part of the brain. It is not enough to have children talk about what they should do when they are teased, they must actually practice controlling their temper while they are being teased.

As we have seen earlier, our nonverbal emotional communication is more significant than the words we speak. We must train our children to recognize the early physical signs of their emotional reactions in order to learn self-control. When your child gets angry, his face flushes, his body tenses, and he goes into a state of hyperalertness, evident in his body posture, facial expression, and gestures. Successful training in anger control teaches your children to be aware of their body changes and to respond by calming themselves—by breathing deeply or distracting themselves (for example, by counting backward). You can accomplish this training in role-playing situations like the Stay Calm game, in which your children are exposed to situations that might make them angry, but in which they practice self-calming techniques instead.

Videotaping these scenes is a particularly effective way to encourage emotional control. We have long known that children imitate the negative behaviors they see on television or in the movies, but there is also evidence to suggest that they unconsciously imitate positive images as well. After your children successfully respond to provocations with self-control, they then watch their reactions on TV. When they see themselves ignoring verbal taunts and responding with a relaxed posture rather than with a fight response, they get a positive

visual image of how they look when they are successfully controlling their emotions. When they view such a videotape
repeatedly, particularly with you or other important people
present to reinforce their emotional control, this EQ exercise
can be extremely effective.

You can also teach the emotional brain self-control by providing a wide variety of experiences that evoke positive emotional reactions. Physical challenge programs, where adolescents are encouraged to do a variety of high-risk activities
(while being safely harnessed in), have gained popularity for
helping aggressive and delinquent youths build trust and
group support by providing physical challenges that stimulate positive emotional responses. During a day in this program, older children and teenagers might be asked to climb to
the top of a twenty-foot pole, balancing on one foot when they
get there, or swing on a rope from one high treetop to another.
While they perform these death-defying stunts, they are harnessed in safety gear. Trained supportive counselors talk them
through the physical challenge. This kind of experience could
be called a "positive trauma," as the teenager's emotional
brain is imprinted with a sense of trusting others and group
cooperation while his or her most basic emotions of survival
are aroused.

Other, more direct techniques teach children and adolescents to control their emotions by using new cognitive skills.
For example, in many schools around the country children are
being taught conflict resolution skills, including negotiating
and peer mediation, to deal with a rising tide of aggression
between students and teachers and students and other students. As a result of programs like the one designed by the
New York City Board of Education—implemented in over one
hundred schools—teachers have seen a significant decrease in

acts of aggression and violence. Similar programs are being taught to families as a way to decrease sibling fighting and parent-child conflicts.

Teaching children to negotiate instead of argue or fight involves five steps:

1. Children should sit face-to-face and agree to work together to solve a conflict. They should also agree to respect the other person's opinion and refrain from name-calling or put-downs.

2. Each person should state his point of view (what he wants and why), and then state the other person's point of view. Successful negotiation cannot take place unless it is agreed that everyone has a right to his or her own point of view.

3. The most essential aspect of negotiating is to create win-win solutions. Both children should agree on at least three possible solutions that are compromises, but which allow each child to have something that is important.

4. The two children then evaluate each option. At this point, they are now on the same side, seeking an outcome that will satisfy them both.

5. Finally, the children should create an agreement or plan of action to put the best solution into effect. This agreement should detail who, what, when, where, and how the solution will be implemented.

Since children and teenagers may have difficulty in accomplishing this kind of negotiation on their own, conflict resolution programs often train students as peer mediators. Peer mediators are usually much more effective than adults at

It is surprisingly easy to teach children skills like negotiation and peer mediation. These EQ skills are effective for controlling problems in aggression both at home and in school.

encouraging kids to follow the rules and come to an agreement. Children as young as nine or ten can be trained to act as effective mediators. Surprisingly, many programs have found that youngsters who had previously shown poor control and frequently got into trouble could be trained to become extremely effective mediators. By assuming this new role, their own behavior dramatically improved.

EQ POINTS TO REMEMBER

- Emotional control, particularly controlling anger and aggressiveness, are the most common emotional problems faced by today's children.

- From an evolutionary point of view, our ability to get angry quickly and fight fiercely has insured our survival as a species, but in a time when 105,000 children in the United States bring guns to school every day, getting angry and expressing it has become a dangerous emotional alternative.

- Fortunately, there are many ways to stimulate the thinking part of the brain to help children inhibit and control their anger.

- Conflict resolution techniques teach skills like negotiating and mediating, and should be a part of every child's education.

· 23 ·

Emotional Healing of the Mind and Body

Perhaps the most significant breakthroughs in the area of emotional intelligence have come from a new understanding of the healing power of our emotional brain. These techniques are far different from the "talking therapies" that try to help children and teenagers develop insight into their problems. They view the more severe emotional problems of children from a biochemical standpoint.

For example, Megan Gunmar, a developmental psychobiologist at the University of Minnesota, believes that along with the more obvious physical reactions to trauma, including a rise in blood pressure and heart rate, the body releases an excessive amount of the hormone cortisol, which normally helps the body respond to danger. Too much cortisol can lead to temporary and possibly permanent damage to a part of the emotional brain called the hippocampus, causing memory lapses, anxiety, and an inability to control emotional outbursts, aggression, and impulsivity.

Of even more concern is evidence that children exposed to continual trauma, such as abuse or neglect, may have permanent damage in the part of the brain in which problem solving takes place and language develops. Psychiatrist Bruce Perry of the Baylor College of Medicine found that a group of neglected children had cortical areas that averaged 20 percent smaller than those of children in a control group. A smaller cortical area leads to a lower IQ and EQ.

INTERVENTIONS THAT HEAL THE MIND

Recently developed techniques suggest that the brain chemistry triggered by trauma may be changed through relatively simple interventions. Traditionally, the treatment for a young traumatized child consisted of play therapy, in which the child was allowed to play with a variety of toys while the therapist patiently observed and reflected on her choice of objects and the way in which they were used. It was assumed that in their play, children would reenact aspects of the trauma, allowing them to gain control over the painful emotional memories as the cognitive brain put words and meaning to the disturbing impressions of the emotional brain and the child gained some psychological distance from the original trauma. Children over the age of ten or eleven, who may be too old to express themselves through play, benefited from a more direct relationship with the therapist, who provided a nurturing atmosphere in which older children and adolescents could slowly learn to trust again.

But while these methods have proven to be successful for many children and adolescents, this type of play therapy is available to only a handful of children and adolescents. Only about 20 percent of the children who might benefit from this type of therapy can get the help they need. Play therapy is typically performed by therapists and counselors with years of training, and the therapy itself can take from six months to several years.

In the last few years, cognitive and behavioral techniques,

including many of the "thinking" EQ skills described in Part III of this book, have been used to help children who have experienced various kinds of trauma. These techniques seem to help lessen some of the emotional impact of the trauma, and they simultaneously give children the opportunity to organize their feelings in a way that the thinking part of their brains can control.

Therapeutic games have been particularly successful in stimulating the thinking part of the brain to deal with emotional trauma. For example, Dr. Toni Cavanaugh Johnson, a psychologist who specializes in treating abused children, developed a card game called "Let's Talk About Touching" to be played by psychotherapists and other mental health professionals with child victims of sexual abuse. Using the format of simple card games like Go Fish or Concentration, children answer direct questions about their current feelings and the actual trauma, learning ways to cope and make sure that these events will not reoccur. Such a frank and direct approach surprises and even shocks many adults, but children seem drawn to these and other games. Talking about the trauma openly and without shame can desensitize the child to the emotional trauma. It stimulates changes in the thinking brain so that it can better organize and defuse traumatic emotional memories.

The game format lends itself to emotional healing because of the repetition inherent in this kind of play. Even counselors are surprised that traumatized children often ask to play these games over and over again, providing the essential rehearsal for developing new neural pathways from the thinking to the emotional brain. Therapeutic games of this type are currently being used in war-torn countries like Bosnia, Kuwait, and South Africa to help children more readily deal with the violence of the past and uncertainties of the future.

WHAT YOU CAN DO TO HELP YOUR CHILD COPE WITH A TRAUMA

While it is common sense that all children who experience serious trauma be sent for immediate professional help, often it's hard to know what constitutes a "serious" trauma for a child. Some children are traumatized by single events such as witnessing violence; losing their home to a hurricane, flood, fire, or earthquake; the death of a family member; or a hospital stay. Others live in war-torn countries, exposed to daily bombings and deprivation, and yet seem relatively resilient. Few professionals, however, would disagree that children who are sexually or physically abused should always be treated by a mental health professional for trauma.

If your child has been exposed to a traumatic event, it is wise to assess the extent of emotional damage that has occurred and stimulate his natural defense mechanisms. The first can be accomplished by using a quick symptoms checklist like the one below. If even one symptom persists for more than a month after the trauma, seek a professional consultation.

Symptoms Checklist for Children Exposed to a Trauma

_____   The child expresses fears or anxieties that did not exist before the trauma, for no apparent reason.

_____   The child withdraws from other people and shows marked signs of distrust.

_____   The child shows anger and aggressiveness to a degree that was not present before the trauma.

_____ The child shows unusual or odd behaviors, including tics, stuttering, or peculiar mannerisms.

_____ The child shows constant signs of depression, including sadness, lethargy, irritability, and overactivity (sometimes depressed children exhibit the opposite behaviors of what we see in depressed adults).

_____ The child expresses statements of guilt or self-blame.

_____ The child has excessive physical complaints, including persistent stomachaches, headaches, and reports of unexplained pain.

_____ The child has sudden disinterest in school and schoolwork.

_____ The child has pronounced changes in his or her sleeping or eating habits.

_____ The child becomes self-destructive and/or accident prone.

_____ The child acts "babyish" and expresses a desire to be treated as a baby.

The new ways to treat traumatized children by stimulating the thinking part of the brain suggest that we can reduce the long-term effects of trauma by intervening immediately after the event has occurred and for at least several weeks thereafter. The following are some techniques that you can easily implement:

- Have your child talk about what happened. You may feel that you should leave him alone after a trauma, particularly if he does not seem to be upset, but the calm that is sometimes observed in children who have experienced a trauma is really a kind of shock. Behind their placid exterior, they may be on emotional alert. Getting children to describe the experience and put labels on their feelings may initially make them more upset, but in the long run it will help them cope and lessen the chance of developing trauma-related symptoms.

- Have your child repeat positive statements that reinforce his belief that he has survived the trauma and can cope with the aftermath, such as:

  I am all right and undamaged by _____ (the trauma).

  I can go on with my life in spite of _____ (the trauma).

  I can get support from people who care about me if I need it.

- Help your child become aware of signs of distress in his body by doing a daily "body scan." Let him mentally review his body from the head down, being aware of tension in his neck, shoulders, arms, trunk, and legs.

- Encourage your child to practice daily relaxation techniques (described on pages 302–303). This is particularly important if he reports stress, tension, and discomfort, but it is also important in developing the biochemicals related to emotional healing. A daily prescription of fifteen to twenty minutes of relaxation exercises, supervised by a nurturing adult, may be the single best way to alleviate future problems.

PSYCHONEUROIMMUNOLOGY: AN EMOTIONAL APPROACH THAT CAN HELP HEAL YOUR CHILD'S BODY, TODAY AND IN THE FUTURE

No aspect of emotional intelligence is more exciting than the current flurry of research that shows how we can train our minds to prevent and overcome disease. Dozens of studies as well as hundreds of anecdotal cases have shown that emotional and social skills can be important factors in fighting even life-threatening diseases like cancer and heart disease. If this research proves to be even partially true, it would be unconscionable not to teach children the EQ skills that could someday prolong their lives.

This new field of research on the healing power of emotions is called psychoneuroimmunology, or PNI. This term refers to the study of the connection between the mind and the emotions—the central nervous system, the autonomic nervous system, and the immune system. The basic premise of this research is that the mind can produce chemicals that protect the body from disease, and can, in some cases, even reverse the disease process.

To understand the implications of this new science, we begin by relinquishing our concepts of "mind" and "body" and think of them as one neurological system. The nervous system consists not only of the brain, but the spinal cord, nerves, and ganglia. This system can be further subdivided into the central, peripheral, and autonomic nervous systems. We have known about this "hardwired" system since the early days of modern medicine, but it has only been a little more than a decade since we have understood that there is also a second "soft-wired" system, or what neuroscientist Dr. Candace Pert, a pioneer in this field, calls a "psychosomatic communication network," which plays an important part in emotional intelligence.

This chemical system, consisting of neuropeptides (strings of amino acid) and their receptors, are theoretically the bio-chemical correlates of emotions. According to Dr. Pert, these neuropeptides and receptors are found in the parts of the brain associated with emotion and sent out by the brain to tell the body how to respond.

Pert notes that each neuropeptide is like a brick used in building a house "that can be used in the basement of a house or in the attic of a house—it serves different functions in different locations, but it's the same brick." A single neuropeptide coordinates every aspect of this body to fulfill this one need, as in the case of angiotensin, the aspect of the animal's functioning that screams, "I want water, I want to save water, I don't want any water to be lost."

The discovery of this system of emotional biochemicals, consisting of neuropeptides and their receptor sites, has some fascinating implications for preventive health and even healing. Although the exact mechanisms of how these biological messengers of emotion might work are still just speculative, the implications might cause a revolution in our Western understanding of health.

What is surprising neuroscientists is that many of the EQ skills I have talked about not only have observable immediate effects in making a child happier and more successful, but also have subtle biological effects with significant long-range implications. Take, for example, the EQ skill of humor and its importance in a child's social success. Scientists are now finding that humor also plays an important part in the immune system, and perhaps should be part of every child's prescription for staying well.

While it is not surprising to find that humor is a natural

stress reducer—relaxing the muscles, lowering our awareness of pain, and decreasing blood pressure—the biochemical changes we experience when we laugh are nothing short of astounding. In laboratory experiments in which scientists told subjects jokes and showed them funny videos, one study found that the hormones associated with stress were reduced and key aspects of the immune system were enhanced. In fact, the immune system's responses to humor, some of which were still measurable a day later, were particularly impressive. There were increases in:

- Natural killer cells that attack viruses and tumors.
- T cells that organize the body's immune system.
- The antibody immunoglobulin A, which fights respiratory infection.
- Gamma interferon, a hormone that turns on the immune system, fights viruses, and regulates cell growth.
- B cells, which produce antibodies against harmful microorganisms.

As a result of these findings, the hallowed halls of medicine may soon begin to echo giggles, guffaws, and peals of laughter. Morton Plant Hospital in Clearwater, Florida, has a clown school on site, and its graduates patrol the halls looking for a laugh. At Fox Chase Cancer Center in Philadelphia, a volunteer pushes a humor cart featuring a six-foot clown on the front passing out comedy tapes, squirt guns, and whoopee cushions. Many pediatric units around the country host frequent visits from clowns and other comedians, recognizing that laughter and mirth can be serious medicine. As Dr. Lee Berk, a noted researcher on humor and health, notes: "This is not alternative medicine. This is real medicine."

EQ SKILLS YOU CAN TEACH YOUR CHILDREN TO ENHANCE THEIR PHYSICAL HEALTH

Understanding the integration of mind and body helps us see why teaching children virtually any EQ skill will help them physically and why anything that helps a child stay healthier will help them emotionally. For example, teaching a child the psychological skill of self-calming is an important way to address a wide variety of emotional problems from tantrums to test anxiety to fear of dogs. Every adult concerned with helping children deal with difficult emotions should include some form of relaxation training in their efforts.

Relaxation Techniques

Relaxation or self-calming techniques are some of the most important psychological skills your child can learn. Besides being an antidote to specific stressful situations, progressive relaxation can make children, adolescents, and adults feel refreshed, more relaxed, even invigorated. These positive "feelings" are not just in the mind, but in the body as well. In his classic book *The Relaxation Response,* which helped bring the benefits of meditation from the ashram into the executive boardroom, Harvard professor Dr. Herbert Benson explained that relaxation has the immediate effects of reducing our need for oxygen, increasing our alpha brain waves (associated with creativity), decreasing our blood lactate (a substance produced by the metabolism of skeletal muscles and associated with anxiety), and decreasing the rate of our heartbeat.

Dr. Dean Ornish, a more recent advocate of the benefits of relaxation techniques, considers it one of the five essential components of his now famous "Life Choice Program." Dr. Ornish has shown that even severe coronary heart disease can be reversed by attending to the psychological as well as the physical needs of the patient (the other components are a very low fat diet, moderate exercise, smoking cessation, and emotional support).

During relaxation training, your child will sit quietly in a comfortable chair and slowly relax each muscle of her body, usually starting at the center of her body and moving outward (chest muscles, then stomach muscles, back muscles, arms, legs, hands, feet, and so on). While she is relaxing each muscle group, instruct her to breathe deeply and slowly and visualize herself in a familiar calm and tranquil place, such as lying in a field of grass staring at the clouds. Use all the

Many therapists believe that self-calming is the single most important EQ skill that can be taught to children. It not only helps in emotional control, but may also stimulate the immune system to protect children from physical illness.

senses. Describing the cool breeze, the smell of the grass, and the feel of the dew on her skin helps distract her from her daily concerns and brings her body to a restful state.

After several weeks of training in relaxation, children over the age of ten should be able to use this skill when they first feel their bodies begin to respond to stress or an unwanted emotional state.

Reducing the Effects of Stress

The stressors associated with modern life seem to take more and more of an emotional toll, and yet, in general, we do not teach our children the importance of dealing with this stress. As Michael Norden writes in his book *Beyond Prozac*: "Unfortunately, now that we require more tolerance of stress, our brains are less able to cope. Evidence shows that our modern lifestyles and artificial environments take a costly toll. The way we sleep, the way we eat, even the air we breathe draw on the same account, weakening the specific neurochemical 'stress shield' that Prozac is designed to bolster—the vital neurochemical known as serotonin. In a certain sense, our lifestyles have made us 'Prozac deficient,' or more accurately, serotonin deficient."

Norden goes on to extol the benefits of serotonin, which, like other neurotransmitters, does different things at different sites throughout the body, depending on the receptor site. Scientists have identified at least twelve distinct receptor sites that respond to serotonin. These sites are associated with diverse positive effects, from regulating such important body functions as temperature and blood pressure to controlling psychological impulses and inhibiting anxiety.

While Dr. Norden believes that many emotional problems are caused by a serotonin deficiency, he is quick to explain that this does not imply that everyone should be on Prozac. He notes, rather, that there are many natural ways to increase the body's production of serotonin, including:

- Increased exercise (ninety minutes of vigorous exercise can triple the amount of serotonin in the brain).

- A low-calorie, low-fat diet with no more than five hours passing between meals (except during sleep).

- Exposure to light during the dark winter months.

- Appropriate amounts of sleep (sleep deprivation can cause a 20 percent decrease in brain serotonin).

Is your child's lifestyle one that will increase his ability to produce the biochemicals necessary for emotional well-being, social success, and even physical health?

Common sense tells us that a healthy body leads to a healthy mind, and yet modern life has taken us far beyond the dictates of reason. With the typical American child watching far too much TV, getting too little exercise, and having a diet too high in calories and fat, should we really be surprised that we are facing a crisis in our children's mental health? Paradoxically, even as we look to the future for the scientific research that will help you raise a child with a high EQ, we know that many of the maxims of the past were in fact correct after all, as in Ben Franklin's maxim "Early to bed, and early to rise, makes a man wealthy, healthy, and wise." But can we take lessons we have learned about the past and apply them to the future of children in the next millennium? Or will we continue to let our march toward progress take an emotional toll on our children?

In the next chapter, we will see how technology can help you teach your child many different EQ skills, even while you pay attention to creating a more sensible lifestyle in which to raise them.

EQ POINTS TO REMEMBER

- The healing power of our brains is largely untapped.
- New research shows that children can be taught various forms of mental and physical healing by stimulating specific biochemicals produced in the brain.
- Creating a lifestyle for your children that will strengthen their bodies' immune system will help them now and for decades to come.

PART 8

Computers and EQ: A Surprisingly Good Combination

We are in the middle of a true revolution in the way that we raise our children, and we are only beginning to understand how this might affect them by the time they reach adulthood. As Peter Drucker writes in his book *Post Capitalist Society*, "[E]very few hundred years in Western history there occurs a sharp transformation. Within a few short decades, society rearranges itself, its worldview, its basic values, its social and political structure, its arts and its key institutions. . . . And the people born then cannot ever imagine the world in which their own parents were born."

It is hard to believe, but only a decade ago, social scientists bemoaned the introduction and immediate popularity of electronic games like Nintendo, fearing that the addictive qualities of this new form of entertainment would rob children of the simple joys of throwing a ball or building a fort in the snow. At that time, only a few visionaries could see how this same technology could be used to teach math and reading skills, to put an entire encyclopedia on a disk as thin as a penny, or that rather than isolate children from each other, this new digital media could bring them together.

Although the psychological community is still somewhat resistant to using computers as an adjunct to treatment, much less prescribing computer-related activities for children at home, it is difficult to ignore the potential for computers in advancing children's emotional and social development. With technology progressing at such a rapid pace, the only real limits are our imagination.

When it comes to technology, many parents are often way ahead of many teachers and child therapists, who resist what they believe is a cold and hard medium. With a computer in nearly one out of every two homes, and with an increasing number of public libraries offering a computer center with an Internet connection, the majority of American children will soon have access to a dazzling array of technological advances. The significance of these advances on the well-being of children cannot be overestimated. President Clinton's 1996 reelection campaign included access to the Internet as one of the country's three most important educational objectives for children (the other two being universal literacy for eight-year-olds and the opportunity for a college education for every eighteen-year-old).

In this section, I will highlight some of the ways that computers can be used to teach many of the EQ skills already discussed in this book, and how they can do it more quickly, effectively, and with less expense than anyone might have thought possible.

COMPUTERS TO THE RESCUE

Norman Schwarzkopf and Stephen Spielberg are names that we don't usually associate with advances in children's mental health or medicine. But, in fact, the world-famous movie producer and military commander recently joined forces to demonstrate how ingeniously computers can be used to help seriously ill children fight loneliness and isolation and even muster the forces of EQ to battle life-threatening illnesses.

The story began when General Schwarzkopf was distressed by a young girl's loneliness and isolation when he visited her on a bone marrow transplant ward at a Jacksonville, Florida, hospital. It seemed to him that the psychological stress caused by her hospitalization could only adversely affect this child's chances of survival. Approaching Spielberg with his concerns, the two founded Starbright World, a computer network that links hospital pediatric units through modems and allows severely ill children across the country to interact with each other as if they were across the hall.

Even a child recovering from chemotherapy or surgery can visit strange and magical worlds from his bedside with just the click of a computer mouse. In the *Starbright World* program, children can visit three separate areas: a cave world with secret hiding places, a sky world where kids can fly, and a tropical world replete with the sounds of exotic birds and waterfalls. Children are represented in these worlds by animated characters called avatars, whom they can control. As they journey through the worlds, children encounter the characters of other youngsters from different hospitals in the form of avatars. When they click on another character, they can play a game with that child or carry on a conversation.

The program is now in effect at six hospitals around the country, and not surprisingly it has been an instant hit, reducing pain, stress, and anxiety for children who can finally talk to someone else who really understands what they are going through. At Mt. Sinai Hospital in New York City, researchers are also investigating whether this program will reduce the length of the hospital stay for children with cancer, assuming that as ill youngsters become actively engaged in a cybersocial life, they will need less pain medication, which in turn will result in a better appetite and more energy to heal.

What is nearly as interesting as this story of innovation is the realization of how quickly and inexpensively technology is being developed for broad consumer use. The same technology underlying the *Starbright World* program, conceived in 1994 and costing thousands of dollars to install, is now available to anyone with a multimedia computer, a high-speed modem, and access to the Internet.

HOW THE COMPUTER CAN INCREASE YOUR CHILD'S EMOTIONAL INTELLIGENCE

Unlike any other educational or psychological tool, nearly all children are drawn to computers. With the new generation of multimedia software and the Internet's seemingly unlimited capacity, computers fulfill all the major requirements for learning EQ skills. They:

- Stimulate the emotional as well as the thinking parts of the brain.

- Provide the repetition needed for developing new neural pathways.

- Make learning interactive, so that the teaching seamlessly adjusts to the child's preferred learning style.

- Provide built-in reinforcement.

To the surprise of many, computers have not served to isolate children, but rather to teach them a wide variety of social skills.

Computer programs stimulate the emotional part of the brain by combining animation, voices, music, video images, color, and a myriad of surprises. By comparison, traditional books seem as flat and as archaic as cave drawings. Take, for example, a recently published program called *Pajama Sam in "No Need to Hide When It's Dark Outside,"* designed to entertain children while helping them with the common fear of darkness. The program opens with full animation, music, and speech, not very different from a cartoon show on television. Sam is reading a comic book about his favorite superhero, Pajama Man. When his mother tells him it is time to go to bed, Sam must face his fear of the darkness. Sam explains that "darkness" is hiding in the magical world behind his closet, and he decides to don his superhero outfit to go after it. From this point on, the child using the program must help Sam find various objects to help him on his journey, decide which direction to go, and face problems presented to him by talking trees and strange creatures. This kind of program presents an ideal environment for simultaneously stimulating the emotional brain and the thinking brain. As the animated cartoon brings the child into the dark and mildly scary world behind Sam's closet, he must continually use his problem-solving and self-calming skills to proceed with the story and help Sam with his quest.

The best computer programs to teach EQ skills involve games that motivate your child to play them again and again. We know that to develop new neural pathways in the brain, an activity must be repeated innumerable times, and computers are the ideal medium for repetition. Unlike humans, they never tire of reading a story, explaining a fact, or playing a game. None of us can have the patience and endurance of a computer, nor can we be as entertaining, day and night, with just the click of a mouse.

Early reports even suggest that the computer may be the first worthy opponent for the seemingly invincible power of television. One survey found that children with new computers in their homes watch 20 percent less TV than before the computer arrived. Recently, a parent told me that her learning disabled son, who hated going to school, now insists on spending two hours a day in the local library playing educational games and corresponding with pen pals on the Internet. He even helps out in the school's computer center, aiding other children (and teachers) in honing their computer skills.

Unlike television, which even at its best involves strictly passive learning, computers require your children to interact, think, problem solve, and behave in ways that they might not want to. For example, a program called *The Lie* tells the story of Susie, who fibs to her mother when Mom asks whether Susie has a weekend homework assignment. Susie lies and says "no." But as the story progresses, Susie's little green-monster lie grows and grows, causing more and more mischief.

When the monster messes up Susie's room, before your child can go on to the next page he must put away the toys and books that the monster has thrown around by clicking on each item and dragging it to its appropriate place. If your child puts the wrong item in the wrong place, Susie corrects him with phrases like, "No, silly, that goes in the closet!" When he drags an article of clothing to the closet, the computer hangs it up for him.

When I played this story game for the first time, I was anxious to see how the story would turn out. I was impatient to find out how Susie would deal with the ever-increasing trouble caused by her lie. To be honest, I really didn't feel like cleaning up Susie's room, but I had to do it to proceed with the story. I mustered my patience and put away each item, although I wasn't in a cleaning-up mood just then. Indeed, I was surprised to find myself thinking very much like a child, wondering aloud about the rules of cleaning up ("Why does this toy go on the bookshelf instead of the toy chest? Can't this computer see that's a better place? Maybe the toy chest is too full. I'll put it on the shelf."). Mustering my own patience, I learned the lesson of the story: Lying makes more trouble than it's worth.

UNEXPECTED BENEFITS

Perhaps the most surprising way that computers enhance the learning of EQ skills is how they bring people together. Detractors of technology have envisioned a world of children locked in their rooms staring bug-eyed at a computer screen, shunning any human contact that might remove them from the magnetic draw of their keyboard and mouse. But that does not seem to be happening. As we have seen in Chapters 14 and 15, children are naturally social when given the developmentally appropriate opportunities. They love to share their experiences, both with other children and adults, and when computers are located in a den or living room, they are often the hub of family activity.

Many parents are finding that computers actually increase the time that they spend with their kids in educational activities. It is particularly significant that fathers appear to be the most likely parent to bring a computer into the home and explore its many uses with their children. This is an important shift in family roles since, even with all the changes in sex roles that have occurred over the last twenty-five years, fathers still spend only a fraction of the time that mothers typically do in promoting their child's education. Computers may begin to even out this trend and provide kids (particularly boys) with the opportunity to benefit from a male role model in learning EQ skills.

Another unanticipated social benefit of giving children access to computers is that they promote social experiences through on-line services and the Internet. We will explore how electronic communication will impact the lives of our children later in this section, but first we will examine how widely available computer software, costing less than most video games, can be adapted to teach a variety of EQ skills.

· 24 ·

Software That Can Increase Emotional Intelligence

A 1996 survey done by *Family PC* magazine found that there were about 3,000 computer programs designed for children, with about a third of them intended for educational purposes. In the next few years, with the increasing number of computers being used in homes and in schools, we can expect these numbers to double and triple on an annual basis. Software will become more sophisticated in combining elements of education and entertainment. Although the number of programs designed to teach EQ skills is still small, there are many ways that you can adapt popular software to teach the skills that make up your child's emotional intelligence.

The largest group of EQ-friendly software helps children express themselves creatively. These programs allow children as young as four and up through adolescence to create and print their own books and comic books, make plays and animated cartoons, and communicate their thoughts and feelings without restriction.

STORYTELLING SOFTWARE

Storytelling, writing, and art have long been tools used by mental health professionals to help children learn many of the EQ skills covered in this book, including realistic thinking, problem solving, and emotional expression. In counseling sessions, children draw pictures and write stories that reflect their problems or concerns and discover that in expressing themselves, they can find new ways to think and cope. Through multimedia computer programs, these activities have become so engaging to youngsters that they will often choose them over arcade-style games. You, along with your children's teachers (and mental health professionals), can easily offer supportive guidance to make these activities emotionally meaningful.

As you will remember from Chapter 6, positive modeling stories are an effective way to help your children develop realistic thinking and coping skills, which in turn will aid them in dealing with a wide range of problems from the divorce or the loss of a parent to dealing with a bully to handling their own illness. The principle behind a positive modeling story is to show your children age-appropriate and realistic ways to think about a problem and then choose a responsible course of action.

For example, Sally moved to a new neighborhood at age six and found herself ostracized by the other children in her class. Sally came home from school every day complaining that no one would sit with her at lunch or talk to her at recess.

From our developmental understanding of how children make friends, we know that social rejection as a result of being new to a school is common, and may last up to six months. We also know from our developmental perspective that children at this age are most likely to succeed socially by making a single friend who is similar to them or lives close by.

This knowledge then formed the basis for Sally's parents to write a story on the computer with her about a little girl who, like her, is lonely and friendless. In composing the story, Sally's parents encouraged her to think of ways that the protagonist (called Sarah) could find a new friend. Once it was written, Sally printed out her story in the form of a book, which her parents read to her every night. The book reassured Sally that there were specific things she could do to make her future less lonely (such as inviting a classmate to a movie, joining a dance class, practicing ways to join other children in their play, and so on).

Sally and her parents used a program called *My Own Story* to create her book (there are more than a dozen other programs currently available that they could have used). *My Own Story* allows children to click on different scenes, people, and objects, and then move and resize them to make professional-looking illustrations for each page. When each picture was completed in Sally's book, her parents typed the story, based on their discussion with Sally, at the bottom of the page. When they were all satisfied with the results of one page, Sally clicked to the next page and created a new picture to continue the story.

When the book was finished, they printed out a professional-looking book that could have been created by a professional writer and artist. Other programs, like the popular *Kidswork*, will actually read aloud the stories that children write. Once the story is typed in, one need only click the sound button and the computer will read the story in a male or a female voice, in English or in Spanish.

Older children would probably prefer programs like *Comic Maker*, which allows kids eight and older to create their own superhero-style comic books, selecting from dozens of heroes and villains, as well as a multitude of background scenes. Once the scenes are selected, your children can format their comic book with speech, thought balloons, and comic cells so that it looks very much like the magazines that they buy. The only difference is that their comic book is about superheroes who solve problems similar to the ones that they are struggling with in their day-to-day lives. The villains might represent the bullies, the fears, or the physical pains of an illness, and the heroes will use the superpowers of EQ to save the day.

SOFTWARE THAT HELPS CHILDREN LEARN NEW WAYS TO THINK

Advances in multimedia programs in the last few years have taken storytelling to a new and exciting level, allowing older children and teenagers to create animated cartoons and plays in which characters move, speak, and interact. These programs offer a fascinating new way to teach EQ skills, particularly the cognitive skills of the cerebral cortex, which require more repetition than noncomputer techniques can usually provide.

For example, in Chapter 3 I described how the Penn Prevention Program in Philadelphia helps children at risk of depression change their internal dialogue (the way that they talk to themselves), learning to think with more realistic optimism. Programs of this type typically use puppets for younger children and role-playing and written exercises for older children.

But many kids tire of these techniques, and without continued practice, they cease to work. And that's where computers can help. Programs like *Hollywood* for children ages eight to twelve and *Hollywood High* for teenagers allow children to learn new ways to think by creating animated cartoons. Children can type in thoughts or statements for a variety of characters, who then say exactly what is typed. As they create cartoons, writing in dialogue that reflects the new thinking, problem-solving, and coping skills they have learned, they can also select a character's mood (which changes his or her facial expression), posture, gestures, and voice. As we have seen in Chapter 21, learning about these nonverbal cues is a critical aspect of raising a child's EQ.

SOFTWARE THAT TEACHES VALUES

Since their inception, one of the greatest concerns about video and computer games has been their violent content, and few would argue that this concern is without merit. Although there are now many alternatives, violent games remain popular with children, and the realism of the violence depicted continues to increase. For example, in the highly popular game *Doom*, the victims of the players' weaponry are shown screaming, decapitated and delimbed, lying in pools of blood.

Do these games cause children to be more violent and aggressive? Probably not. Do they desensitize children to the feelings of others and the real violence that exists in the world? Undoubtedly. If we are to acknowledge the potential of computers in helping children learn EQ skills, we must also recognize their potential for harm. Most computer programs are now marked with the age range for which they are intended. Games that are violent contain warnings on the package. It's wise to be aware of the games that your children are playing and to actively discourage them from playing those with highly violent content.

Fortunately, there are an increasing number of nonviolent games that mimic the challenges of the popular arcade games, but avoid violent content and even teach cooperation. For example, *Alien Arcade*, designed for the four- to six-year-old set, has the same basic play as some of the early point, shoot, and dodge arcade games, but instead of blasting spaceships, your child throws bananas at Quasar Klutzes to get them off her ship and removes fungus eggs that might gum up the ship's works. In another game, children turn Stink Snakes into Happy Faces.

There are also an increasing number of animated story-books that teach values to young children. Like *The Lie*, these storybooks will read themselves to children who are not yet readers and challenge them to interact with the story in a way that traditional books could never do. Some additional titles include: *The Berenstain Bears Get in a Fight*—a story of sibling rivalry; *Why Do We Have To?*—a story about the importance of rules; and *The Safety Scavenger Hunt*—where children go through a house and find unsafe items in each room, making the house safe to play in. These storybooks provide continuous opportunities for children to make values decisions and see the consequences of those decisions as the stories progress. Parents are advised to play the games with their children to reinforce the values being taught.

VIRTUAL REALITY PROGRAMS

Another kind of software that holds enticing promise for teaching emotional intelligence creates a virtual world for children to acquire and practice EQ skills. For several years, psychologists around the country have been using computers to create a three-dimensional world that is so close to reality, it feels like you are "virtually there." People with phobias like a fear of riding over a bridge or a fear of flying have been the primary users of these programs. Putting on special glasses that are hooked up to a computer, therapists give their patients a sense that they are crossing the Golden Gate Bridge or boarding a 747 airplane, and patients are gradually desensitized to their anxieties and fears.

Although they are not quite as realistic, a new generation of computer programs also give children and adolescents a sense of "being there." Despite the fact that these programs have been developed for entertainment rather than psychological techniques, their value in teaching EQ skills is obvious. For example, *Graham Wilson's Haunted House* might be used to desensitize a fearful child, the same way the more sophisticated treatments work for adults. This program takes children through a truly spooky haunted house, replete with ghosts, eerie music, and flashing lights. As players try to find thirteen keys hidden around the haunted house, they could be chased by an assortment of monsters trying to cast spells on them. Players have a variety of ways to escape or fight back, encouraging children to face and overcome their fears.

Another program called *Who Do You Think You Are?* uses video clips of real people to teach EQ skills. This program, which would be appropriate for adolescents and young adults, teaches the user how to understand his own personality based on the Berkeley Scale, which measures five personality dimensions. One part of the program, called "First Impressions," shows the adolescent video segments of twelve individuals talking about themselves. The computer user then rates the person in the video according to the five dimensions of the personality scale, basing his judgments on voice tone, gesture, phrases, and so on. A tutorial even teaches the player how to look for various indicators of a person's character, replaying specific aspects of the video to demonstrate a point.

Unlike any other medium, the computer then allows the user to practice his observational skills over and over again, with just the click of a mouse.

EQ POINTS TO REMEMBER

- Computer programs can teach a variety of EQ skills by simultaneously stimulating the emotional and thinking parts of the brain.

- Computer programs are particularly effective at teaching EQ skills to children, because they hold children's interest while providing the repetition needed for teaching many types of emotional skills.

- Although there are only a few computer programs that are designed to teach EQ skills, there are an increasing number of programs that stimulate creativity and realistic thinking. There are also many programs that teach values and can even give children a "virtual experience" to help them cope with their problems.

▪ 25 ▪

Emotional Intelligence
in Cyberspace

Imagine that your children could visit a huge amusement park, any time of the day. A twenty-dollar pass would give them unlimited access for a month. And as they enjoy themselves, they learn. Riding the cable cars, they pass signs that explain how the human heart works (an Internet web site found at http://sin.fi.edu/biosci/heart.html lets children listen to a heartbeat, follow blood through the vessels, and even watch open-heart surgery) or why those pesky roaches are so hard to get rid of (the "yuckiest" site on the Internet is all about roaches and can be found at http://www.nj.com/yucky). Strolling by the arcade, they could visit the White House (at http://www.whitehouse.gov/ kids can tour the executive mansion and send E-mail messages to world leaders). If they were looking for some company while they sipped a soda, they could go to a global village, where everyone is ten to fifteen years old (a real-time chat site used by children all over the world can be found at http://www.kidlink.org/IRC). Now imagine an amusement park a thousand times bigger, more interesting, and more educational than any you have ever enjoyed, and you are approaching the excitement of the Internet.

The potential for developing EQ skills on the Internet is almost beyond our imagination. The Internet motivates children to learn, brings them together in cooperative projects, and gives them the opportunity to make friends from around the country and the world, breaking down stereotypes and prejudices. It makes learning a multisensory, interactive experience with endless possibilities. Judging from the speed that it is being developed and accepted, the Internet—and in particular its visual component, the World Wide Web—may be one of the most important new influences in your child's development.

Until recently, relatively few parents and educators saw how much the Internet could affect their child's education, providing them access to entire libraries, newspapers, magazines developed just for kids, or "virtual" museums. Even fewer people saw how the Internet might stimulate emotional intelligence: teaching social skills and motivating underachievers to learn, giving children a sense of mastery and real power.

What we didn't realize was how quickly a "text only" medium, which was primarily used by scientists and the military, could come alive with colorful graphics, animation, voices, and video images. Nor did we see how quickly this technology would become available. By the turn of the century, there will be Internet connections in nearly every school and library, and between 40 and 50 percent of all homes. In the first decade of the twenty-first century, our children will most likely be carrying small notebook computers in their backpacks that have instant access to the Internet or similar services. The teaching methods that schools now use will become obsolete. The future is coming, and it looks good for children. Today's parents, educators, and mental health professionals must lead the way.

GOING ON-LINE

Connecting to the Internet becomes easier with each passing month. If you buy a computer today, it will likely be "Internet ready," coming with a high-speed modem and preinstalled software that can have you connected to the Net in less than half an hour. If you already have a computer, you will need a high-speed modem to connect to a telephone line and an on-line service to connect to the Net. You can reach the Net by going through a popular service like Prodigy, American Online, and CompuServe. There are also an increasing number of services that will connect you directly to the Internet and World Wide Web. Most services charge a fixed monthly fee of $20 or less—probably less than you would spend taking the family to a movie and dinner at a fast-food restaurant.

While explaining how to get hooked up to the Net is beyond the scope of this book, take my word for it, it's child's play. In fact, if you are put off by the technological jargon and overwhelmed by the Internet's possibilities, you may want to pick up a book written for kids and read it yourself, such as *Cybersurfer*, by Nyla Ahmad.

CONNECTING WITH OTHERS

When my daughter went to summer camp at age nine, I probably wrote to her three or four times in the six weeks that she was away. I meant to write her more, but I work hard during the summers, and the time just seemed to slip away. She probably wrote to me about the same amount. Now she is nineteen and away at college, and we correspond almost every day. The difference? Electronic mail.

When I come into the office each morning, I turn on my computer and check my E-mail. There is always a short note from Jessica. I write back a paragraph or two, responding to her questions, making jokes, telling her about my work or travels. Then I click on the button that says "Reply," and the message is sent 300 miles away in an instant. Jessica checks her E-mail and replies to me after her classes are over and before she begins her evening assignments.

Similar rituals are being repeated all over the country with children of all ages. A father from Oregon E-mails his ten-year-old daughter in Minnesota, who lives with her mother. A businesswoman in Manhattan requires her two children in New Jersey to E-mail her when they arrive home from school. They greet her, tell her about their day in a sentence or two, and tell her what their homework assignments are. She E-mails back what time she and her husband will be home and what they will be having for dinner.

Electronic mail, once thought of as a cold if not frigid method of communication, is the most common way that people use the Internet and on-line services. Not only do parents and children use this medium to stay in touch, but teachers use E-mail to send parents progress notes, counselors and psychologists use it to give advice, and, perhaps most importantly, children use it to correspond with other children with similar interests.

The most popular use of on-line services with older children and teenagers is what are called "chat rooms," a type of live or "real-time" electronic mail. Thousands of chat rooms exist for children and teens, who come to a specific chat site out of common interests or just to socialize. In a chat room, two to twenty-five children or teens type messages back and forth to each other. The computer displays a message on each person's screen when a new person enters or leaves the "room." These are open conversations, since everyone reads what everyone else is saying, although private conversations can also be held if both parties agree.

For many children, and particularly for teens, chat rooms are an ideal way to socialize and meet many of the age-appropriate social challenges that I described in Chapters 14 and 15. Many teenagers are drawn to chat rooms because of an unanticipated benefit of communicating in cyberspace—anonymity. When you are communicating through an on-line service or the Internet, it doesn't matter whether you are tall or short, fat or thin, white, black, or purple. In a society in which physical appearance is so important in how we judge others, this electronic cloak of invisibility makes it easier for many children and teens to express themselves. In a chat room, it is only your words and thoughts that count.

In a *USA Today* article on how children are using the Internet, Lindsey, a seventeen-year-old, explains, "It's like an alternate world in some ways. It's the same as having a big group of friends, but you don't see what anyone looks like. It's like the ideal that everyone speaks of when they say that you shouldn't judge people based on race, age, [or] sex." Other teens describe how they were ostracized at school because of their dress or looks, but in cyberspace, superficial characteristics have no relevance. As Wayne, a fifteen-year-old from Winnipeg, Manitoba, explains, cyberspace can be a refuge for teens who are shy and feel rejected: "Before I was on-line, I must say I was a lost child. I've grown so much, because I was able to talk openly to people. No one on-line thinks about your age or eye color or skin color or anything. They see you from the inside."

The opportunity for children to talk to other children about common problems or concerns, like the ill children participating in Schwarzkopf and Spielberg's *Starbright World* program, has brought a new meaning to the concept of self-help groups. There are on-line chat rooms for children with learning disabilities, children with attention deficit disorders, adopted children, and many more. In these groups, which are most easily found through the various forums on the major on-line services, children and teenagers meet under the quiet supervision of an adult systems operator and exchange ideas, experiences, and support. There are many groups like this on the Internet, such as the Ability OnLine Network, run by Dr. Arlette Levfebre, which connects sick and disabled children from around the country and the world (http://www.ablelink.org).

According to psychologist Sherry Turkle of the Massachusetts Institute of Technology, the explosive popularity of electronic communication is understandable when we realize that the teenage years are "a time to try new things, experiment with identity and ideas, [and] have passionate friendships. If you had to imagine a medium that was tailor-made for addressing some of those needs and demands, you almost couldn't do better."

Younger children are more likely to be attracted to Internet sites that involve more than just talk. There are hundreds if not thousands of sites in which they can meet other children from around the world for fun and games, as well as educational projects and even community service. The Computer Clubhouse @ the Computer Museum (http://www.net.org/clubhouse/index.html) is a place where kids hang out and develop their own projects, including family trees and an on-line art gallery. Earth Force (gopher://gopher.earthforce.org:7007/) is an organization of children who want to work together to save the environment.

Opportunities are almost unlimited for children to educate themselves on the Internet. From our understanding of EQ, this medium seems uniquely suited to the ways that kids like to learn. When they "surf" the World Wide Web, they automatically take control of their learning. They typically start out at a web site where they can find links to popular children's sites and also do searches for sites of particular interest. For example, Yahooligans! (http://www.yahooligans.com), the kids version of the popular adult page Yahoo!, links children to games, education, science, sports, news, and clubs, as well as "new and cool sites."

When children follow their natural interests, the issue of educational relevancy becomes irrelevant. With the freedom to explore, they pursue their natural curiosity and imagination, and what they find increasingly rivals the excitement of the most exciting software. Over the next several years, nearly every popular web site for children will engage them through music, animation, and interactive 3D worlds.

DANGERS ON THE INFORMATION HIGHWAY

The Internet will inevitably open up a new world for teaching children cognitive as well as emotional and social skills, but we must still be aware of the major potholes on the information superhighway. Fortunately, solutions have been quickly forthcoming to address parents' most serious concerns.

Our first concern has naturally been for our children's safety. Newspapers have been quick to report on kids who have been lured away from home by a cyber pen pal, or who have been solicited for or exposed to pornography. To address this concern, various software programs such as *CyberPatrol* have been developed that allow parents to block access to specific sites and prevent them from searches based on specific words. Increasingly, web browsers, such as Microsoft's Internet Explorer, are becoming available with built-in rating and blocking systems.

While safety and privacy will probably always be an issue, for the most part the Internet is probably a lot safer than your neighborhood mall, and many of the same precautions should be taken depending on your child's age.

A second concern is that computers may offer too much of a good thing. Groups are already being formed by adult "computer addicts," and some worry that children will hang up their baseball gloves and abandon their bicycles to become slaves to the terminal. But again, technology has so far been successful at solving problems nearly as fast it creates them. Many programs like *CyberPatrol* feature time clocks that allow parents to limit access to the computer through a code that only they know. When the time allotted for computer use is over, the program just quits.

But nothing can really take the place of parental supervision. Experts advise that you sit down at the computer with your children and find the appropriate sites for them to visit. In his book *Childproof Internet: A Parent's Guide to Safe and Secure Online Access*, Matt Carlson suggests creating an agreement with your children that determines how much time they can spend on the computer for work, how much for play, what information they can put into the computer (for example, children should not divulge their names and addresses without your knowledge), and, if appropriate, how much money you're willing to spend on on-line services (some sites have fees).

Also, because this is truly a new way for people to interact, teach your children etiquette for using on-line services (for example, using all capital letters when writing to someone is considered to be shouting). Show your kids how to handle unpleasant situations, discuss what real dangers exist online, and cover other rules of conduct.

It is my belief, however, that the greatest danger involving children and the Internet is for those who do not have access to it. The single most important problem that the computer revolution could cause is that disadvantaged and at-risk children will be even further disenfranchised from society. If technology is only available to middle- and upper-class families, then the gap in our society will widen in terms of knowledge, job skills, and even basic literacy. Children's advocacy groups like The Children's Partnership argue that this can only be avoided through joint ventures between the public and private sectors, which commit revenues to put computers in poorer schools, libraries, and neighborhood centers.

THE FUTURE OF RAISING CHILDREN WITH A HIGH EQ

Someone recently described my approach to teaching children emotional intelligence as looking backward and forward at the same time. Increasingly, social scientists have looked at the changes that have occurred in child-rearing during the last thirty years and concluded that, in spite of our best intentions, our children seem to be worse off. While we give our children much more, we spend significantly less time really interacting with them. As we have tried to increase our children's self-esteem through praise and attention, we have become too permissive in our discipline and expect too little. In trying to create a Disney-like world of childhood innocence, we have not realized that stress and discomfort are as much a part of our human experience as love and nurturance. When we seek to eliminate every obstacle, we deprive our children of the chance to learn important coping skills to meet the challenges and inevitable disappointments of growing up.

We cannot turn the clock back, nor should we. While there are lessons to be learned from the past, they pale in the light of the future that awaits our children in the next century. The technological revolution that is taking place will shape our children's lives in ways that we can barely imagine, any more than people in the nineteenth century could envision how the automobile, the phone, the television, or the discovery of antibiotics would affect our every waking moment. There is one thing, though, we can be certain of. The future will be amazing, and the opportunities for raising emotionally intelligent children in new and exciting ways will be endless. If we learn lessons from the past and embrace the changes that are sure to come in the future, we will be raising children to succeed in the twenty-first century.

EQ POINTS TO REMEMBER

- The Internet and on-line services have opened new ways for children to learn and communicate. Rather than isolating children from other people, advances in technology seem to be bringing people together, breaking down barriers of place and prejudice.

- Although there are some safeguards that parents should heed as their children spend more time in cyberspace, the benefits of this new medium far outweigh the problems.

- The most serious danger is to children who might be left behind by not having access to computers and the new technologies.

■ REFERENCES ■

BOOKS AND PERIODICALS

Ahmad, Nyla (1996). *Cyber Surfer*. Toronto, Ontario: Owl Books.

American Education Publishing (1993). *Comprehensive Curriculum of Basic Skills*. Columbus, Ohio: American Education Publishing.

Barkley, Russell A., Ph.D. (1995). *Taking Charge of ADHD*. New York: Guilford Press.

Beck, Arron (1979). *The Cognitive Theory of Depression*. New York: Guilford Press.

Bennett, William J. (1993). *The Book of Virtues*. New York: Simon and Schuster.

Benson, Herbert (1975). *The Relaxation Response*. New York: Avon.

Bloch Douglas (1993). *Positive Self-Talk for Children: Teaching Self-Esteem through Affirmations*. New York: Bantam Books.

Carlson, Matt (1996). *Childproof Internet*. New York: MIS Press.

Children's Defense Fund (1996). *The State of America's Children Yearbook, 1996*. Washington, D.C.: Children's Defense Fund.

Conari Press Editors (1994). *Kids' Random Acts of Kindness*. Berkeley, California: Conari Press.

Covington, Martin V. (1992*). Making the Grade*. New York: Cambridge University Press.

Damon, William (1995). *Greater Expectations*. New York: Free Press Paperbacks.

_____ (1988). *The Moral Child*. New York: The Free Press.

Delisle, Jim (1991). *Kid Stories*. Minneapolis, Minnesota: Free Spirit Publishing, Inc.

DeShazer, Stephen (1985). *Keys to Solutions in Brief Therapy*. New York: W. W. Norton.

Donald, David Herbert (1995). *Lincoln*. New York: Touchstone Books.

Donavin, Denise Perry (1992). *Best of the Best for Children*. New York: Random House.

Drucker, Peter (1993). *Post Capitalist Society*. New York: HarperBusiness.

Eisenberg, Nancy (1992). *The Caring Child*. Cambridge, Massachusetts: Harvard University Press.

Ekman, Mary Ann. "How Can Parents Cope with Kids' Lies?" in Ekman, Paul, *Why Kids Lie* (1989). New York: Penguin Books.

Ekman, Paul (1989). *Why Kids Lie*. New York: Penguin Books.

Elias, Marilyn. "Caring Parents Produce Healthier Adults," *USA Today*. March 7, 1996.

Elias, Maurice J., and John F. Clabby (1992). *Building Social Problem-Solving Skills*. San Francisco: Jossey-Bass Publishers.

Ellis, Elizabeth M. (1995). *Raising a Responsible Child*. New York: Birch Lane Press.

Farnham, Alan, Anne Faircloth, and Tim Carvel. "Are You Smart Enough to Keep Your Job?" *Fortune*, January 15, 1996.

Finkelstein, Barbara, Anne E. Imamura, and Joseph J. Tobin (1991). *Transcending Stereotypes*. Yarmouth, Maine: Intercultural Press.

Friend, Tim. "Teens and Drugs: Today's Youth Just Don't See the Dangers," *USA Today*. August 21, 1996.

Gardner, Howard (1993). *Multiple Intelligences*. New York: Basic Books.

———— (1993). *The Unschooled Mind: How Children Think & How Schools Should Teach*. New York: Basic Books.

Gardner, Richard A. (1970). *The Boys and Girls Book About Divorce*. New York: Bantam Books.

Gibbs, Nancy. "The EQ Factor," *Time*. October 2, 1995.

Goldstein, Arnold P. (1988). *The Prepare Curriculum*. Champaign, Illinois: Research Press.

Goleman, Daniel. "In Virtual Reality Phobias Cease to Exist: Lifelike Electronic Images Allow People to Face What They Fear Most," *San Francisco Chronicle*. September 2, 1995.

———— (1995). *Emotional Intelligence*. New York: Bantam Books.

Guerney, L., and B. Guerney (1985). "The Relationship Enhancement of Family Therapists," in L'Abate, L. and M. Milan (eds.), *Handbook of Social Skills Training and Research*. New York: Wiley, pp. 306–524.

————, and Ann D. Welsh (1993). "Two by Two: A Filial Case Study," in Terry Kottman and Charles Schaefer (eds.), *Play Therapy in Action*. Northvale, New Jersey: Jason Arronson, pp. 561–88.

Guevremont, David. (1995) "Social Skills and Peer Relationship Training," in Barley, Russell A. (ed.), *Attention Deficit Hyperactivity Disorder: A Handbook for Treatment*. New York: Guilford Press.

Hart, Archibald D. (1992). *Stress and Your Child*. Dallas: Word Publishing.

Hart, Louise (1993). *The Winning Family: Increasing Self-Esteem in Your Children and Yourself*. California: Celestial Arts.

Hartley, Robert (1986). "Imagine You're Clever," *Journal of Child Psychology and Psychiatry and Allied Disciplines*, pp. 383–98.

Hellmich, Nanci. "A World to Share: A Computer Playspace to Ease Suffering," *USA Today*. November 8, 1995.

Henry, Tamara. "On-Line Use Is Pupils' Gain," *USA Today*. October 17, 1996.

Herbert, Wray, and Missy Daniel. "The Moral Child," *U.S. News & World Report*. June 3, 1996.

Hoffman, M. (1982). "Development of Prosocial Motivation: Empathy and Guilt," in Eisenberg, N. (ed.), *The Development of Prosocial Behavior*. New York: Academic Press.

Hooper, Judith, and Dick Teresi (1992). *The Three Pound Universe*. New York: Jeremy P. Tarcher/Putnam Books.

Hunt, Morton (1993). *The Story of Psychology*. New York: Doubleday.

Johnson, Toni Cavanaugh. *Let's Talk About Touching: A Psychotherapeutic Game for Children Who Have Been Sexually Abused*. Available from the author: 1101 Fremont Ave., Suite 101, South Pasadena, CA 91030 (Sale restricted to mental health professionals only).

Jones, Rachel. "Sharp Rise Reported in Teenagers' Drug Use," *Philadelphia Inquirer*. August 21, 1996.

Joseph, Joanne M. (1994). *The Resilient Child*. New York: Plenum Press.

Kagan, Jerome (1995). *Galen's Prophecy: Temperament in Human Nature*. New York: Basic Books.

——— (1989). *Unstable Ideas: Temperament, Cognition, and Self*. Cambridge, Massachusetts: Harvard University Press.

Kohlberg, L. (1964). "Development of Moral Character and Moral Ideology," in Hoffman, M. L., and L. W. Hoffman, (eds.), *Review of Child Development*, v. 1. New York: Russel Sage Foundation.

Kostelnik, Marjorie J., Laura C. Stein, Alice Phipps Whiren, and Anne K. Soderman (1993). *Guiding Children's Social Development*. New York: Delmar Publishers.

Krantz, Les, and Jim McCormick (1996). *The Peoplepedia*. New York: Henry Holt and Company.

Kurshan, N. (1987). *Raising Your Child to Be a Mensch*. New York: Ivy Books.

Lazarus, Wendy, and Laurie Lipper (1996). *America's Children and the Information Superhighway*. Santa Monica, CA: The Children's Partnership.

LeDoux, Joseph (1996). *The Emotional Brain*. New York: Simon and Schuster.

Lewis, Barbara A. (1991). *The Kid's Guide to Social Action*. Minneapolis, Minnesota: Free Spirit Publishing.

_____ (1992). *Kids with Courage*. Minneapolis, Minnesota: Free Spirit Publishing.

_____ (1995). *The Kid's Guide to Service Projects*. Minneapolis, Minnesota: Free Spirit Publishing.

Lewis, Shari. (1982). *One-Minute Bedtime Stories*. New York: Doubleday.

March, John (Undated, self-published). *How I Ran OCD Off My Land*. Available from author: Program in Child and Adolescent Anxiety Disorders, Department of Psychiatry, DUMC Box 3527, Durham, North Carolina.

Marks, John. "The Uncivil Wars," *U.S. News & World Report*. April 22, 1966.

Masson, Jeffrey Moussaieff, and Susan McCarthy (1995). *When Elephants Weep*. New York: Delacorte Press.

McGhee, Paul (1996). *Health, Healing & The Amuse System: Humor as Survival Training*. New York: Kendall-Hunt.

_____ (1994). *How to Develop Your Sense of Humor: An 8-Step Training Program for Learning to Use Humor to Cope with Stress*. New York: Kendall-Hunt.

McGrath, Patricia A. (1990). *Pain in Children*. New York: Guilford Press.

Mehabian, Albert (1987). *Silent Messages*. Belmont, California: Wadsworth.

Miller, Donald, and Guy Swanson (1960). *Inner Conflict and Defense*. New York: Holt, Rinehart, and Winston.

Miller, Leslie. "New World to Navigate: New Worries for Adults," *USA Today*. August 17, 1996.

Miranker, Cathy, and Alison Elliott (1995). *Computer Museum Guide to the Best Software for Kids*. New York: HarperCollins.

Moyers, Bill (1995). *Healing and the Mind*. New York: Doubleday.

Murphy, Shane, Ph.D. (1996). *The Achievement Zone*. New York: G. P. Putnam's Sons.

National Mental Health Association (1995). *Getting Started*. Alexandria, Virginia: National Mental Health Association.

Norden, Michael (1995). *Beyond Prozac*. New York: ReganBooks.

Nowicki, Stephen Jr., Ph.D., and Marshall P. Duke, Ph.D. (1992). *Helping the Child Who Doesn't Fit In*. Georgia: Peachtree Publishers.

Ordovensky, Pat. "Students Use Gifts to Help Others," *USA Today*. May 17, 1996.

Oldenberg, Dan. "Experts Stymied by Lack of Moral Values Among Young," *Los Angeles Times*. March 30, 1988.

Olness, Karen (1993). Interview with Bill Moyers in *Healing and the Mind*. New York: Doubleday, pp. 71–83.

Orlick, Terry (1982). *The Second Cooperative Sports and Games Book*. New York: Pantheon Books.

Ornish, Dean (1995). Interview with Bill Moyers in *Healing and The Mind*. New York: Doubleday, pp. 87–113.

Pert, Candice (1995). Interview with Bill Moyers in *Healing and The Mind*. New York: Doubleday, pp. 177–93.

Pippin, Turk (1989). *Be a Clown! The Complete Guide to Instant Clowning*. New York: Workman Publishing.

Radke-Yarrow, Marian, and Carolyn Zahn-Waxler (1984). "Roots, Motives and Patterns in Children's Prosocial Behavior," in Stabu, Ervin et al. (eds.), *Development and Maintenance of Prosocial Behavior*. New York: Plenum.

Robinson, Ambrose, and Freda Robinson (1996). *How to Raise an MVP*. Detroit, Michigan: Zondervan.

Rubin, Zick (1980). *Children's Friendships*. Cambridge, Massachusetts: Harvard University Press.

Russek, Linda, and Gary Schwartz. "The Harvard Mastery of Stress Study 35-Year-Old Follow-Up: Prognostic Significance of Patterns of Psycholophysiological Arousal and Adaptation," *Psychosomatic Medicine*, v. 52, no. 3 (May-June 1990), pp. 271–85.

Salovey, Peter, and John Mayer (1989). "Emotional Intelligence," *Imagination, Cognition and Personality.* v. 9, no. 3, pp. 185–211.

Schwartz, Jeffrey M., M.D. (1996). *Brain Lock.* New York: ReganBooks.

Seligman, Martin E., Ph.D. (1995). *The Optimistic Child.* Boston: Houghton Mifflin Company.

Shapiro, Francine (1995). *Eye Movement Desensitization and Reprocessing.* New York: Guilford Press.

Shure, Myrna B., Ph.D. (1994). *Raising a Thinking Child.* New York: Henry Holt and Company.

Spock, Benjamin, Ph.D., and Michael B. Rothenberg, M.D. (1945). *Dr. Spock's Baby and Child Care.* New York: Pocket Books.

Stevenson, Harold, and Shin-ying Lee (1995). *Child Development and Education in Japan.* New York: W. H. Freeman.

Strayhorn, Joseph M. (1988). *The Competent Child.* New York: Guilford Press.

Thornton, Stephanie (1995). *Children Solving Problems.* Cambridge, Massachusetts: Harvard University Press.

Van der Meer, Ron, and Ad Dudink (1996). *The Brain Pack.* Philadelphia: Running Press.

Vygotsky, L. (1978). *The Mind in Society: The Development of Higher Psychological Processes.* Cambridge, Massachusetts: Harvard University Press.

Wallerstein, Judith (1996). *Second Chances: Men, Women and Children a Decade After Divorce.* New York: Ticknor & Fields.

White, Merry (1988). *The Japanese Educational Challenge: A Commitment to Children.* New York: Free Press.

White, Michael, and David Epston (1990). *Narrative Means to Therapeutic Ends.* New York: W. W. Norton and Company.

Wilen, Joan, and Lydia Wilen (1996). *Folk Remedies That Work.* New York: HarperCollins.

Wood, D., J. Bruner, and G. Ross (1976). "The Role of Tutoring in Problem-Solving," *Journal of Child Psychology and Psychiatry,* v. 17, pp. 89–100.

Zajonc R. B., S. T. Murphy, and M. Inglehart (1989). "Feeling and Facial Efferent: Implications of the Vascular Theory of Emotions," *Psychological Review, 96,* 395–416.

COMPUTER SOFTWARE

Pajama Sam in "No Need to Hide When It's Dark Outside." Humongous Entertainment, 13110 N.E. 177th Place, Suite 180, Woodinville, Washington 98072–9965; 800–499–8386.

Hollywood. Theatrix Interactive. 1250 45th Street, Suite 150, Emeryville, California 94608; 510–658–2800.

Berenstain Bears Get in a Fight. Living Books, P.O. Box 6144, Novato, California 94948.

Who Do You Think You Are? The Berkeley Personality Profile, Harper Interactive. HarperCollins Publishers, 10 East 53rd Street, New York, New York 10022.

Kids Works 2. Davidson & Associates, Inc. P.O. Box 2961, Torrance, California 90509; 800–545–7677.

Sheila Rae the Brave. Living Books. P.O. Box 6144, Novato, California 94948.

The Lie. Davidson & Associates, Inc. P.O. Box 2961, Torrance, California 90509; 800–545–7677.

Graham Wilson's Haunted House. Microsoft Home, Bryon Press Multimedia Company, 175 Fifth Avenue, Suite 2122, New York, New York 10010.

My Own Story. MECC, 6160 Summit Drive, North, Minneapolis, Minnesota 55430–4003.

Why Do We Have To? StarPress Multimedia, 303 Sacramento Street, Second Floor, San Francisco, California 94111; 415–274–8383.

Safety Scavenger Hunt. StarPress Multimedia, 303 Sacramento Street, Second Floor, San Francisco, California 94111; 415–274–8383.

INDEX

Achievement chart, 228–29

Affirmative caring, 27–30

Affirmative discipline, 30–34

American Library Association, 64

American Psychiatric Association, 213

Amygdala, and emotions, 15, 16, 18, 73, 284

Antisocial behavior, shame as punishment for, 73–74

Apologies, and guilt, 78–79

Attention deficit disorders (ADD), 173

Axline, Virginia, 71

Barkley, Russell, 29–30

Baxter, Lew, 111

Bay-Hintz, April, 257

Beck, Aaron, 100

Behavioral point system, in discipline, 34

Bennet, William, 64

Berk, Lee, 300

Blame, and criticism, 102

Bloch, Douglas, 120–21

Books

for community service activities, 58

for learning styles, 234–35

for teaching honesty, 64

Brain chemistry

cognitive behavior modification and changes in, 110, 111–12

emotions and, 12–19, 283–85

imagery and, 125

impacts of child-rearing on, 18–19

interpersonal problems and, 153–54

repetition in self-talk and, 121

teaching emotional skills and changing, xii–xiii

time management and, 242

Brainstorming, 154–56

Braithwaite, John, 76

Brunner, Jerome, 162

Caring

affirmative, and parents, 27–30

children and, *see* Empathy and caring

Checklist

children's privacy, 68

parent's EQ, 37–44

parent's problem solving, 141

teaching the value of learning, 223–24

Child-rearing; *see also* Parenting

brain chemistry and impacts of, 18–19

"good enough parent" and, 25

implications of EQ for, 6

shaming in, 73–74, 75–76

social patterns and changes in, 11–12

341